Dancing
IN THE
DARK

REFLECTIONS ON LIFE
STORIES OF HOPE AND INSPIRATION

Blessings!
Richard Exley

RICHARD EXLEY

PRAISE FOR *DANCING IN THE DARK*

Richard Exley's writing is moving, practical, vivid, filled with the Word, often raw, and in a style he might refer to as "Blue Collar." His stories evoked memories of my past and I found myself tearing up on more than one occasion. Although he often speaks of the frailties and troubles of man, he always gives us hope through the Word and the grace of Jesus. I intended to read only a few selections from *Dancing in the Dark,* but once I got started, I couldn't put it down.

—Frank Davis
"Life's A Marathon!"
Pastor, Author, and Attorney

Dancing in the Dark, is Richard Exley at his best. He packs more soul stirring truth in a single story than many writers do in an entire book.

—Karen Hardin
President, PriorityPR Group & Literary Agency

No one can share a story of hope, inspiration and the powerful message of God's love as well as Richard Exley. What you hold in your hand is more than a book to be read. It is a companion to walk with you through life. **Dancing in the Dark** is a collection of poignant and heartwarming stories of real people and their struggles and their victories. As I read this book, I found myself a part of every story. Our friend, Richard Exley has given all of us a wonderful gift. Keep this companion close and your life will be richer.

—Dr. Chuck Stecker, Author, International Speaker
President, *A Chosen Generation*

Dancing In the Dark is a great gift to us all. Richard Exley's sage musings and crisp writing style bring coherence to life's confusions and Rock solid encouragement for a brighter future. Do your soul a favor and read this insightful book – slowly.

—David Shibley
Founder / World Representative Global Advance

Richard Exley has done it again! *Dancing in the Dark* is a must read. His heartfelt stories and penetrating insights will encourage you no matter how dark the night.

—Sharon Steinman
Author, *Shattered: Coping With the Pain of Divorce; A Devotional Journal of Hope and Healing*

Dancing in the Dark is about learning to experience God-life to the fullest even in the midst of pain and difficulty. Richard Exley offers much needed hope, grace, and encouragement.

—Max Davis,
Author of *When Jesus Was A Green-Eyed Brunette* and *Dead Dog Like Me*

Dancing in the Dark is filled with transparency, humor, practical experience, and insight to enable you to become all you can be in Christ through the power of the Holy Spirit. Another brilliant example of how God can love us even if we "spill our milk."

—Linda Cargill
Author *Survival 101—
Practical Advise for Minister's Wives*
Oklahoma District Superintendent's wife

Dancing in the Dark is a refreshing collection of stories that are sure to light a fire in your heart as well as move you to tears."

—David P. Ingerson,
International President and CEO of Christians in Action Missions International, author of *The Caleb Years: When God Doesn't Make Sense*

DANCING IN THE DARK

is dedicated to the congregations of

The Assembly of God in Holly, Colorado,

First Assembly of God in Florence, Colorado,

The Church of the Comforter in Craig, Colorado,

Christian Chapel in Tulsa, Oklahoma,

and

Gateway Church in Shreveport, Louisiana.

I am profoundly grateful to each of you. You loved me in spite of my feet of clay. You trusted me to lead you and care for your souls. Your ministry to me was as great, or greater, than my ministry to you. I will always be in your debt for you were the instruments the Lord used to make me into a pastor and a man of God.

CONTENTS

Introduction

I f you're looking for a self-help book or a Bible study, this isn't that book. Don't misunderstand me; *Dancing in the Dark* has some insights that will enrich your life and help you become a better person, as well as some perspectives to enhance your understanding of Scripture, but that is not its primary purpose. *Dancing in the Dark* is designed to cause you to pause and reflect, to think deeply about the life you are living. At least that is what I was doing as I wrote these essays.

Like you, I am a busy person and most of the time I feel like I am suffering from information overload. No matter how much I read, or how hard I try, I can't take it all in. I don't want to stop learning, but I would like to make some sense of all the information I'm force-feeding myself. I can't help asking what good it does to accumulate all of this information if I can't assimilate it. *Dancing in the Dark* is my attempt to make sense of what's happening in my own life and in the world around me. If I've written it well it will speak to you in ways that will help you do the same.

Some of the essays are theological. "Does Jesus Love You When You Spill Your Milk?" examines the unconditional love of God, while "No Easy Answers" and "Does Steel Float?" takes a hard look at suffering and death. "How Does Anyone Stay Married Fifty Years?" examines the love that sustained my parents through sixty-one years of marriage. "Telling Daddy Goodbye" and "Memories of Mother" were birthed as I tried to come to grips with my grief following their passing. The strength of these essays is their common humanity. Although the stories are uniquely mine, if I have written them well you will re-live your own life stories while reading them.

"Bank Failures and Bailouts" examines the economic meltdown during the last weeks of the Bush Presidency, while "Unintended Consequences" looks at the connection between the 1973 *Roe v. Wade* Supreme Court decision and the subsequent proliferation of mass murders in each succeeding decade. "God and Caesar" addresses our responsibilities as citizens of the Kingdom as well as citizens of these United States. These essays invite you to examine current affairs from a fresh perspective.

Other topics include essays on growing old, befriending a homeless couple, finding peace in the midst of trouble, trying to make sense of suffering, and many more. I have not arranged them in any particular order or by topic. This was done by design in an attempt to resemble life, which comes at us randomly.

One final word—I'm a discriminating reader. I value style nearly as much as substance and nothing frustrates me more than a poorly written book. In the margins of several books in my library I have written, "Lots of words but no music." I want *Dancing in the Dark* to sing. Of course, I want it to make you think, but that's not enough. I want you to feel, to laugh or cry, or even throw the book across the room in a fit of temper. I may have failed. I may have just produced a lot words without any music. You will be the judge of that.

Finally, I want to invite you to get a tall latte with an extra shot of espresso. Find a comfortable chair in a quiet place and open *Dancing in the Dark*. Let it speak to the deep places in your life, the places you've been too busy to examine. From time to time, put your finger between the pages and listen to your own life. Who knows, maybe by the time you've finished reading you'll be dancing in the dark.

—Richard Exley
July 2017

Chapter 1

Dancing in the Dark

The thing that makes her situation so remarkable is not the tragedy she has suffered, but the way she has chosen to respond. Instead of succumbing to self-pity or anger, she is seizing every minute and living each one to the very fullest.

"When I was old enough to understand," writes novelist Chaim Potok in *The Chosen*, "[my father] told me that of all people a *tzaddik* (a righteous, wise man) especially must know of pain. A *tzaddik* must know how to suffer for his people, he said. He must take their pain from them and carry it on his own shoulder. He must cry, in his heart he must always cry. Even when he dances and sings, he must cry for the sufferings of his people."[1]

I can hardly be considered a *tzaddik*, but that's been my experience as well. Even as we celebrate the joys of life, there is another part of us that grieves for those who suffer so cruelly. And it is this brokenness, this spiritual sorrow that is our rite of passage. It gives our life an authenticity it would not otherwise have. Thus it was with Jesus, whom the scriptures refer to as a man of sorrows and acquainted with grief (Isaiah 53:3). That doesn't mean he was a melancholy man, but only that he carried

1

humanity's pain in his heart even when he was enjoying a meal with friends, or laughing with children, or celebrating at a wedding. Jesus' experience teaches us that it is not only possible to experience joy and sorrow simultaneously, but that it is mandatory if we are to live as authentic human beings.

> SOME OF THE MOST PROFOUND JOYS I HAVE EVER WITNESSED OR EXPERIENCED HAVE COME IN THE MIDST OF GREAT SUFFERING OR PROFOUND LOSS.

Some of the most profound joys I have ever witnessed or experienced have come in the midst of great suffering or profound loss. Consider this experience related by a remarkable woman who refuses to let life defeat her. In a two-year period she lost her mother in a fatal accident, suffered a painful and unwanted divorce, and saw the last of her four children graduate and leave home. On top of all of that, she was diagnosed with breast cancer. Radical surgery followed and then chemotherapy. Since her husband had divorced her and her children had moved away, there was no one to take care of her, so she took care of herself.

She could have succumbed to self-pity and given up, but she didn't. Instead, she decided to chase her dream. Although she was weak and sick from the chemo, she enrolled at a local college, determined to get her degree if it was the last thing she ever did. As she told a friend, "I had to make a choice, to beat it or let it beat me. I decided to beat it. After all it's only cancer!"

The road hasn't been easy. She had to take all of her classes online between trips to the hospital for treatment. Assignments had to be completed while contending with the side effects of all the medications she was taking. Had she chosen to quit, no one would have blamed her, but she wouldn't give up and now she has a college degree. More importantly, she has refused to let her circumstances determine the quality of her life. No matter how dark it gets she just keeps dancing!

Now she's facing another challenge. Doctors have discovered another spot—near the base of her skull this time, but like she says, "It's just cancer and between me and God we can accomplish anything.

Like I said, she just keeps dancing!

The thing that makes her situation so remarkable is not the tragedy she has suffered—many people suffer unspeakable tragedies—but the way she has chosen to respond. Instead of succumbing to self-pity or anger, she is seizing every minute and living each one to the very fullest. As a consequence she is joyously alive, albeit in the face of great adversity.

Does she grieve? Of course she does. Is she afraid? Sometimes. Especially when she thinks of her three grandchildren growing up without her, but she refuses to live in fear. If she had been given a choice, she would not have chosen divorce or cancer, but in the midst of it she has found strength she never knew she had and an appreciation for life unlike anything she has ever known.

Life on our fallen planet is seldom easy and it is often filled with circumstances that try the strongest faith. Yet, more often than not, it is these dark times that produce the most profound and enriching experiences. From experiences like hers and scores of others, the Lord teaches us to find joy in the most unlikely places and to worship at all times. Some call that experience a sacrifice of praise. I call it dancing in the dark.

---

[1] Chaim Potok, "The Chosen," (New York: Simon & Schuster, 1967).

Chapter 2

Does Jesus Love You When You Spill Your Milk?

God turned His pockets inside out, He bankrupted heaven, when He poured out His love through the gift of His dear Son. He has nothing left to give. If His love doesn't win our hearts, nothing will!

One Sunday morning I was making my way through the educational wing of the Church of the Comforter in Craig, Colorado, pausing at each door to listen for a minute or two as the teachers expounded the Word of God. The last classroom I stopped at was the Nursery class. Being careful not to be seen by the children, I peeked into the classroom. What I saw brought a smile to my face. Brenda (my wife) was sitting on a small chair surrounded by eight or ten two- and three-year-olds. As I listened from the hallway I heard her say, "Children, does Jesus love you when you obey your parents?"

With one voice the children chorused, "Yes, Jesus loves us when we obey our parents!"

Then she asked, "Does Jesus love you when you share with your brothers and sisters?"

Another chorus of joyous "Yeses."

"Children, does Jesus love you when you pick up your toys?"

More "Yeses."

Pausing, she waited until every child's attention was focused on her and then she asked in her most somber voice, "Children, does Jesus love you when you spill your milk?"

In an instant all the joy was sucked out of that room. The children's faces lost their color and the light went out of their eyes. Finally, one little tyke responded in a mournful voice, "No, Jesus doesn't love me when I spill my milk."

WHATEVER GAVE THEM THE IDEA THAT JESUS LOVED THEM ONLY WHEN THEY WERE GOOD?

Standing outside the door to the nursery class my heart hurt. I couldn't help wondering where those tiny tykes had picked up such a tragically flawed theology and at such an early age. Whatever gave them the idea that Jesus loved them only when they were good?

Once more Brenda asked, "Children does Jesus love you when you spill your milk?"

This time no one even bothered to answer. They just sit there looking at the floor, squirming in their misery.

Finally she answered her own question. "Yes, Jesus loves you even when you spill your milk!"

The children looked at her as if she were mad, as if she had lost her mind. So she repeated herself, "Yes, Jesus loves you even when you spill your milk!"

They just sat there dumbfounded, with their months hanging open. Surely they had misunderstood her. Didn't she know that in their world there was only one unpardonable sin—spilling your milk? Didn't she know that every one of them had spilled their milk? Didn't she know that what she was saying was too good to be true?

Once more she said, "Yes, Jesus loves you even when you spill your milk; especially when you spill your milk!"

Suddenly the children were smiling and laughing, giving each other high fives. They had just heard the most incredible news—Jesus loved them no matter what they had done, even if they had spilled their milk!

Of course you realize this essay isn't about spilling your milk. It's about God's unconditional love. Most of us probably understand the unconditional love of God as a theological concept, but how many of us have experienced it as a life changing reality? From my earliest days in Bible College I grasped the theological concept but it didn't become a heart reality until several years later.

During my mid-twenties I went through a difficult period—mostly of my own making—and found myself nearly forced out of the ministry. As a result I ended up selling cars at a Pontiac dealership in Houston, Texas. During that year I also served as a part-time youth pastor with S. Worth Williams, a wise and godly pastor. Every Monday morning Pastor Worth drove fifty miles across Houston to the dealership to care for my soul.

One morning he leaned across my desk and looked me in the eye. "Richard," he said, "I want you to think of the worst thing you have ever done."

Instantly I dropped my eyes. Although I wasn't a bad person by the world's standards, I had done some things that I was deeply ashamed of and I was afraid he might see the shame in my eyes. I considered and discarded a half a dozen sinful episodes before finally settling on one. When I had that dark deed firmly fixed in my mind I numbly nodded.

"Now," he said, "I want you to remember the most Christ-like thing you have ever done; that moment when the love of Jesus shone through you with other-worldly brilliance."

I was sure there had been moments like that in my life, but for the life of me I couldn't think of one. With painful clarity I remembered my misdeeds, my sinfulness, those moments when I sorely disappointed my Lord; but try as I might I couldn't recall a time when I was especially Christ-like. Maybe it's like that for you, too. It seems you can never forget the evil you have done, but it's nearly impossible to remember those moments when you truly pleased the Lord.

"WHEN DID GOD LOVE YOU BEST? IN THE MOMENT OF YOUR SHINING CHRIST-LIKENESS OR IN THE MOMENT OF YOUR SINFULNESS?"

Be that as it may, I finally thought of something and when I nodded at Pastor Worth he asked me the question that was to forever change my life. "Richard, when did God love you best? In the moment of your shining Christ-likeness or in the moment of your sinfulness?"

Suddenly I had an epiphany, a revelation of God's unconditional love, right there in the car dealership of all places! In a voice thick with feeling I managed to say, "God loves me best always!"

Think about it. We are the objects of God's love but we are not the cause of it. Before we could earn His love, before we deserved it, God demonstrated His love for us. Romans 5:8 says, "...God put his love on the line for us by offering his Son in sacrificial death while we were of no use whatever to him" (MSG).

God does not love us because we are so loveable, for if the truth be told we are not all that loveable. In fact, the Apostle

Paul indicts every last one of us when he writes: "There's nobody living right, not even one, nobody who knows the score, nobody alert for God. They've all taken the wrong turn; they've all wandered down blind alleys. No one's living right; I can't find a single one" (Romans 3:11-12 MSG). Think about it. There's none of us deserving of God's love. Not one. Still, God loves us!

Sometimes I'm tempted to think God loves me because I so desperately need to be loved, but that's not the case either. God's love is not based on what we do, either good or bad; or what we need. It is not about us; it's about Him. He loves us because of who He is, because that is the kind of God He is!

"Who among the gods is like you, Lord? Who is like you— majestic in holiness, awesome in glory, working wonders? In your **unfailing love** *you will lead the people you have redeemed. In your strength you will guide them to your holy dwelling"* (Exodus 15:11,13 NIV, emphasis mine).

Since we are not the cause of God's love, there is nothing we can do to make God love us less—no disappointing failure, no willful rebellion, no sinful disobedience, nothing. Speaking through the prophet Jeremiah the Lord says, "I've never quit loving you and never will. Expect love, love, and more love!" (Jeremiah 31:3 MSG).

"Who then can ever keep Christ's love from us? When we have trouble or calamity, when we are hunted down or destroyed, is it because he doesn't love us anymore? And if we are hungry or penniless or in danger or threatened with death, has God deserted us?

"No, for the Scriptures tell us that for his sake we must be ready to face death at every moment of the day—we are like sheep awaiting slaughter; but despite all this,

9

*overwhelming victory is ours through Christ who loved us enough to die for us. **For I am convinced that nothing can ever separate us from his love.** Death can't, and life can't. The angels won't, and all the powers of hell itself cannot keep God's love away. Our fears for today, our worries about tomorrow, or where we are— high above the sky, or in the deepest ocean—**nothing will ever be able to separate us from the love of God** demonstrated by our Lord Jesus Christ when he died for us"* (Romans 8:35-39 TLB, emphasis mine).

If there is nothing that can separate us from the love of God, if there is nothing we can do to make God love us less, then it must also be true that there is nothing we can do to make God love us more. No matter how faithfully we serve, or how fervently we pray, or how much we give, God cannot love us more. Even if we were to die a martyr's death God could not love us one iota more. He cannot love us more because He already loves us completely and totally, with His whole being! "But from everlasting to everlasting the LORD's love is with those who fear him . . ." (Psalm 103:17 NIV).

EVEN IF WE WERE TO DIE A MARTYR'S DEATH GOD COULD NOT LOVE US ONE IOTA MORE. HE CANNOT LOVE US MORE BECAUSE HE ALREADY LOVES US COMPLETELY AND TOTALLY, WITH HIS WHOLE BEING!

Bob Creson, President of Wycliffe Bible Translators USA, shares an amazing testimony related by translator Lee Bramlett. He writes, "Lee was confident that God had left His mark on the Hdi culture somewhere, but though he searched, he could not find it. Where was the footprint of God in the history or daily life of these Cameroonian people? What clue had He planted to let the Hdi know Who He was and how He wanted to relate to them?

10

"Then one night in a dream, God prompted Lee to look again at the Hdi word for love. Lee and his wife, Tammi, had learned that verbs in Hdi consistently end in one of three vowels. For almost every verb, they could find forms ending in i, a, and u. But when it came to the word for love, they could only find i and a. Why no u?

"Lee asked the Hdi translation committee, which included the most influential leaders in the community, 'Could you "dvi" your wife?' 'Yes,' they said. 'That would mean that the wife had been loved but the love was gone.'

"'Could you "dva" your wife?' 'Yes,' they said. 'That kind of love depended on the wife's actions. She would be loved as long as she remained faithful and cared for her husband well.'

"'Could you "dvu" your wife?' Everyone laughed. 'Of course not! If you said that, you would have to keep loving your wife no matter what she did, even if she never got you water, never made you meals. Even if she committed adultery, you would be compelled to just keep on loving her. No, we would never say "dvu." It just doesn't exist.'

"Lee sat quietly for a while, thinking about John 3:16, and then he asked, 'Could God "dvu" people?'

"There was complete silence for three or four minutes; then tears started to trickle down the weathered faces of these elderly men. Finally they responded. 'Do you know what this would mean? This would mean that God kept loving us over and over, millennia after millennia, while all that time we rejected His great love. He is compelled to love us, even though we have sinned more than any people.'

"One simple vowel and the meaning was changed from 'I love you based on what you do and who you are,' to 'I love you, based on Who I am. I love you because of Me and NOT because of you.'

"God had encoded the story of His unconditional love right into their language. For centuries, the little word was there— unused but available, grammatically correct and quite under- standable. When the word was finally spoken, it called into question their entire belief system. If God was like that, and not a mean and scary spirit, did they need the spirits of the ancestors to intercede for them? Did they need sorcery to relate to the spirits? Many decided the answer was no, and the number of Christ-followers quickly grew from a few hundred to several thousand."[2]

That's the power of God's unconditional love! It can do what no other power in heaven or on earth can do. Only His love can win the wayward heart and bring sinful men and women to saving faith. It turned unbelieving Cameroonians into passionate Christ-follow- ers and it can do the same for us.

THERE IS NOTHING WE CAN DO TO MAKE GOD LOVE US LESS—NO DISAP- POINTING FAILURE, NO WILLFUL REBEL- LION, NO SINFUL DISOBEDIENCE, NOTHING.

Let me say it again. There is nothing— absolutely nothing—that can separate us from the love of God. There is nothing we can do to make God love us less—no disap- pointing failure, no willful rebellion, no sinful disobedience, nothing. No matter what we may do He will always love us! But having said that, I must hasten to add that if we continue to sin deliberately after we have experienced His redemptive love we break His heart and we break fellow- ship with Him. The Apostle John makes that clear: "If we claim to have fellowship with him and yet walk in the darkness, we lie and do not live out the truth. But if we walk in the light, as he is in the light, we have fellowship with one another, and the blood of Jesus, his Son, purifies us from all sin" (1 John 1:6-7 NIV).

Anytime I write or preach about God's unconditional love, some people get nervous. Not because the unconditional love of

God is unscriptural, but because they fear there are "carnal" Christians who will abuse it. Their concerns are justified, at least to some degree, because in these last days we are seeing more and more misguided "Christians" who are turning the grace of God into a license for immorality. The Living Bible puts it this way: "some godless teachers have wormed their way in among you, saying that after we become Christians we can do just as we like without fear of God's punishment . . ." (Jude 4 TLB).

Not true!

God loves us unconditionally, but that does not mean He winks at our disobedience or overlooks our sin. Hebrews 10 couldn't make it any clearer: "If we **deliberately keep on sinning** after we have received the knowledge of the truth, no sacrifice for sins is left, but only a fearful expectation of judgment and of raging fire that will consume the enemies of God" (Hebrews 10:26-27 NIV, emphasis mine).

If God's unconditional love, expressed through the sacrificial death of Jesus Christ, cannot cause us to turn from our sins and live with Him in the light, "no sacrifice for sins is left" (Hebrews 10:26 NIV). God turned His pockets inside out, He bankrupted heaven, when He poured out His love through the gift of His dear son. He has nothing left to give. If His love doesn't win our hearts nothing will!

Does Jesus love you when you spill your milk—when you make a sinful mess of your life? Absolutely! He loves you just the way you are—warts and all—but He loves you too much to leave you that way. Embrace His love. Be embraced by it. Let it heal your hurts and forgive your sins. Let it make all things new in your life. That's what it is designed to do. "When someone becomes a Christian, he becomes a brand

HE LOVES YOU JUST THE WAY YOU ARE— WARTS AND ALL— BUT HE LOVES YOU TOO MUCH TO LEAVE YOU THAT WAY.

new person inside. He is not the same anymore. A new life has begun!" (2 Corinthians 5:17 TLB).

---

[2] Letter written by Bob Creson, President, Wycliffe Bible Translators USA

Chapter 3
Blue-Collar Christianity

I spent several afternoons with a wonderful old woman named Pearl, who was dying of stomach cancer. From her I learned the ministry of presence—the power of just being there—and the holy art of living until we die.

In our house, Christianity wasn't a moral code, church membership, or a way of behaving in public. It was a lifestyle—love with its sleeves rolled up! If there was a job to do, we did it. If there was a need, we did our best to meet it. Pleasing God and serving others was our highest goal. Dad called that "Blue-Collar Christianity!"

Once, when I was still in elementary school, we came out of church after prayer meeting on a Wednesday evening and saw a transient family in a beat-up old car parked in front of the church. They looked tired, and a hungry baby whimpered from the broken-down back seat. Even as a child, I could see the hollow look in their eyes and the quiet desperation that had prematurely aged their faces, leaving them flat and empty. Most

> IN OUR HOUSE, CHRISTIANITY WASN'T A MORAL CODE, CHURCH MEMBERSHIP, OR A WAY OF BEHAVING IN PUBLIC. IT WAS A LIFESTYLE—LOVE WITH ITS SLEEVES ROLLED UP!

likely they were good people, just down on their luck, and too proud to ask for help. Still, it was obvious that they were hoping some of the Lord's people would have compassion on them.

Unfortunately, compassion seemed in short supply as several members of our congregation barely glanced their way, before hurrying to their own cars and driving away. Thankfully my father was cut from a different piece of cloth. He practiced what he preached; believing that faith without works is dead (see James 2:14-18). Without a moment's hesitation, he walked over to the driver's side of the car, stuck out his hand, and introduced himself.

"Hello. I'm Dick Exley. Have you folks had supper?"

With a sheepish look the man mumbled, "No sir. We ain't et since yesterday."

"Well then you can follow us home and Irene will fix you something to eat." Almost as an afterthought Dad added, "And if you don't have a place to stay you can spend the night with us."

We didn't have much ourselves, as I recall, but my folks were always more than willing to share what little we had. Soon the kitchen was full of friendly smells as Mother put together a simple meal of homemade bread, fried potatoes, and thick slices of ham. I followed Dad down into the half-finished basement where we collected two quarts of home-canned peaches for dessert. As we ascended the stairs, I distinctly remember the sound of ham sizzling in the skillet. Since that night it's always sounded like love to me—God's love!

Due to the example bequeathed to me by my parents, I entered the ministry with a commitment to "Blue-Collar Christianity." It was a good thing, too, for my first church was a small congregation located in the southeastern Colorado town of Holly, with a population numbering less than one thousand.

16

For the most part, my congregation consisted of down-to-earth people—farmers and ranchers who had weathered drought and dust storms, tornadoes and hail, blizzards and tough times. They weren't impressed by big words and theological concepts. Their Christianity was of a more practical kind. Early on I realized that my effectiveness did not depend on the quality of the sermons I preached, but in the way I lived and how I loved. If I hadn't been a "Blue-Collar Christian," my congregation would not have heard a thing I had to say.

It was my job to clean the church, take care of the yard, shovel the walks in winter, and, in general, maintain the place. Oh yes, I was also expected to preach three times a week, teach a Sunday school class, lead the singing, visit the sick, and bury the dead.

> FROM HER I LEARNED THE MINISTRY OF PRESENCE—THE POWER OF JUST BEING THERE—AND THE HOLY ART OF LIVING UNTIL WE DIE.

Soon I found myself lending a hand where needed. I drove a grain truck at harvest time and helped round up the cattle in the fall. In between, I spent several afternoons with a wonderful old woman named Pearl, who was dying of stomach cancer. I sat with her at the kitchen table in the ranch house, drinking coffee while she told me how she and her husband had homesteaded the place. From her I learned the ministry of presence—the power of just being there—and the holy art of living until we die.

I remember another elderly lady, a longtime member of the church, whose health no longer permitted her to attend services. She lived across the alley, just south of the church, and each week I would go to her home and share the midweek Bible study with her. It was the least I could do, but she always made me feel as if I were doing her a special favor. Today I suppose we would send her a CD of the service, but somehow I don't think it would be the same. Not for me anyway, for without those weekly visits my theology of the Church would be sadly lacking. She taught me that the Church isn't just a weekly worship service, but a holy fellowship where people really care about each other.

At its heart, Christianity is not sermon or song, but kindness—a cup of cold water in His name. Sometimes it means giving comfort in the moment of tragedy or encouragement to a family in crisis. At other times, we help celebrate a fortieth birthday or a fiftieth wedding anniversary. Just doing what we can to let our lights shine. Some people call that charity. I call it "Blue-Collar Christianity." How "Blue-Collar" are you?

Chapter 4
The Bridal Gown

"If I live to be a hundred I don't think I will ever be as happy as I was that day! Though Roger had failed both Jody and me, our heavenly Father—my eternal husband—had provided."

W hat would you do if your husband of nearly twenty-five years told you he wanted a divorce? Suppose he went on to say that he did not love you and, in fact, had never loved you. Imagine him admitting to a three-year affair with one of your friends, whom he intended to marry as soon as his divorce from you became final. Suppose he ordered you and your seventeen-year-old daughter to move out of the house that very day.

That is exactly what happened to Martha. What did she do? She threw herself on the mercies of God. Like David of old, she said, "My soul finds rest in God alone; my salvation comes from him. He alone is my rock and my salvation; he is my fortress, I will never be shaken" (Psalm 62:1 & 2 NIV).

Although her world was falling apart, she experienced a kind of relief, as strange as that sounds. For three years she had known something was going on, but her husband denied it. He said it was her imagination. Her illness was making her paranoid. She was jealous. She didn't trust him. The stress was unbearable, causing her lupus to flare. At times she wondered if she was losing her mind. Now at last she was vindicated. It hadn't been her imagination.

The weeks immediately following their separation were filled with terrible pain and desperate hope. Bit by bit the details of her husband's deceit came out. The scope of his sin was much greater than she had imagined. Still she was ready to forgive him, ready to rebuild their marriage. God could restore their love, of that she was sure. But her husband would have none of it. His words were biting and cruel. It was all her fault. She was responsible for destroying the marriage, such as it was. He could not imagine living with her under any circumstances. Little by little her hope faded, then died. The divorce was granted. Her marriage was over.

> THOUGH GOD IS ALL-POWERFUL, HE WILL NOT VIOLATE OUR HUMAN WILL. IF WE ARE DETERMINED TO DESTROY OURSELVES AND THOSE WHO LOVE US, HE WILL NOT OVERRIDE OUR WILL.

Did God fail her? Was her faith in His sufficiency misplaced? Absolutely not! Though God is all-powerful, He will not violate our human will. If we are determined to destroy ourselves and those who love us, He will not override our will. He will deal with us, be it ever so severely, in an attempt to bring us to our senses, but in the end the choice is ours. God did not fail her, but her husband did. He broke faith with her. He sinned against their marriage. He divorced her.

Now, nearly five years later, Brenda and I are sitting with Martha in the sunlit breakfast nook at her home in Durango, Colorado. As we listen, she recounts the saga of God's faithfulness. "During those dark days immediately following my divorce, the Word of God was my only hope. With only a high school education and limited secretarial skills, my chances of landing a decent job were not good. When you throw in my age—forty-two—and my poor health, things really looked grim. I was suddenly poor; a single parent with little hope for brighter days ahead.

"Not only was I dealing with my own grief, but I was trying to help my children deal with theirs. Night after night I had to listen to Jody cry herself to sleep. She had idolized her father and his actions had left her devastated. It was bad enough that Roger should do this to me, but how could he do it to the children?

"The only way I could go to sleep at night was to listen to the Bible on cassette tape. I literally filled my mind with the Word of God. It became my meat night and day. One of the passages that spoke most clearly to me comes from Isaiah 54."

Picking up her Bible she opens it and begins to read, beginning with verse 4:

"Do not be afraid, you will not suffer shame.
Do not fear disgrace; you will not be humiliated.
You will forget the shame of your youth
and remember no more the reproach of your widowhood.
For your Maker is your husband—
the Lord Almighty is his name—
the Holy One of Israel is your Redeemer;
he is called the God of all the earth.
The Lord will call you back
as if you were a wife deserted
and distressed in spirit—
a wife who married young,
only to be rejected," says your God.

For a brief moment I abandoned you,

    but with deep compassion I will bring you back.

                     (Isaiah 54:4-7 NIV)

Pushing her Bible across the table toward Brenda and me she says, "Look at verse 5: 'For your Maker is your husband—'

"That verse was particularly comforting to me because Jody was planning to be married in just a few weeks and I had no way to pay for the wedding. If God was truly my husband then He would provide. With that promise in mind we planned the wedding as if we had the money in the bank. Nothing elaborate mind you. In fact our plans were rather modest, still they were beyond our means.

"One Saturday morning Jody and I went to a sidewalk sale. While we were browsing through the sale racks, in search of a bargain we could afford, she spied a bridal shop. In an instant she lost all interest in the sidewalk sale. Now she had eyes only for one thing—bridal gowns.

"Turning to me she said excitedly, 'Can we just look mom, can we?'

"I had to bite my tongue to keep from saying, 'Why torment yourself, honey? You know we can't afford a wedding gown.' Instead I smiled at her and said, 'Of course we can.'

"While she was looking at the gowns I was fuming on the inside. Had it not been for Roger's pigheaded selfishness, Jody could have had a bridal gown for her wedding.

"'Mom,' she called from across the shop, holding a dazzling gown up against her, 'may I try it on?'

"I smiled an answer and she disappeared into the dressing room. A few minutes later she stepped out looking absolutely stunning. The gown looked like it had been made for her. The naked desire in her eyes made my heart hurt.

"I walked across the shop to stand beside her as she admired herself in the mirror. Trying to appear nonchalant I reached for the price tag hanging from the sleeve. To my amazement it had been marked down from $700 to $100.

"There must be some mistake, I thought. I've never heard of a bridal gown costing only a hundred dollars. Turning to the clerk I asked, 'Is this price correct?'

"'Yes it is,' she said.

"Nervously I began examining the gown more closely. Unable to spot any obvious flaws I asked, 'Why is it marked down so much? Is there something wrong with it?'

"'It's what we call a model gown,' the clerk explained. 'We've used it in several style shows. We're now closing out that line and have no further use for it.'

"Without a moment's hesitation I said, 'We'll take it,' luxuriating in the look of pure joy that flooded my daughter's face.

"While waiting for the clerk to ring it up, I made my way to a closeout table near the door, where I discovered a matching veil for $10. Although I only had $122 in my checking account it was just enough. With tax the total came to $118.80.

"If I live to be a hundred I don't think I will ever be as happy as I was that day! Our heavenly Father—my eternal husband—had provided."

> "IF I LIVE TO BE A HUNDRED I DON'T THINK I WILL EVER BE AS HAPPY AS I WAS THAT DAY! OUR HEAVENLY FATHER— MY ETERNAL HUSBAND—HAD PROVIDED."

We talked for a long time that morning, marveling at the way God had restored her life. Her health was better than it had been in years. According to the doctor her lupus was in full remission. She was remarried to a wonderful Christian man who was devoted to her. Financially she was more secure than she had ever been in her life.

Still, as I think about all God did for Martha, I keep returning to that bridal gown. It wasn't the most significant thing He did, not by a long shot. In fact it's hardly worth mentioning when compared to either the physical or emotional healing He worked in her life. Maybe its very insignificance is what makes it stand out to me. If God is concerned about a "little thing" like that, then surely He will not rest until He has taken care of the really big things that concern us.

Chapter 5

How Does Anyone Stay Married Fifty Years?

"Grandma, how does anyone stay married for fifty years?"

Her question was raw with the pain caused by her parents' recent divorce and an uneasy silence settled over the room. Pulling her close, my mother said, "Honey, Grandpa and I were able to stay married all these years because we could always talk about everything."

D uring the closing months of WWII, the man who was to become my father began exchanging letters with a beautiful, but timid, eighteen-year-old girl named Irene. They could hardly have been less alike. She was a true innocent, having never traveled more than ten miles from her birthplace in northeastern Colorado, while he was a Navy man, having spent much of the war stationed in Hawaii. In the late summer of 1945 he was transferred to the naval base in Corpus Christi, Texas, and given a two-week furlough. He immediately set out for Sterling, Colorado, determined to find out if that dark-eyed beauty was as pretty as her picture.

Not surprisingly it was "love at first sight" and after a whirlwind courtship they were married on November 7, 1945, in the Assemblies of God church in Sterling, Colorado. Following the ceremony, they adjourned to Aunt Elsie's house for a small reception before heading to the Continental Trailways bus depot, where they boarded a bus bound for Denver, Colorado. It was late afternoon when they arrived in the state capital and an early snow had dusted the foothills west of the city, causing Irene to squeal with delight. After collecting their suitcases, they walked to an inexpensive hotel where they freshened up before setting out for a nearby church to attend prayer meeting.

NO MATTER HOW MUCH THEY LOVED EACH OTHER, THEY KNEW IT WOULD TAKE MORE THAN LOVE TO SUSTAIN THEM WHEN THE HARD TIMES CAME, AS INEVITABLY THEY WOULD.

When I learned this unusual bit of family history I couldn't help asking, "Who goes to prayer meeting on the first night of their honeymoon? What were they thinking for heaven's sake?" Reflecting on it now, I'm convinced that they realized, at least intuitively, that if their marriage was to last a lifetime it had to be built on something stronger than romance. No matter how much they loved each other, they knew it would take more than love to sustain them when the hard times came, as inevitably they would.

As newlyweds they made a decision to build their marriage on a foundation of faith. Like Joshua of old they determined, "as for me and my family, we will serve the LORD" (Joshua 24:15 NLT). As an outward demonstration of that commitment they attended a prayer meeting as their first official act as a married couple. From that day forward Jesus Christ and His Church provided the strength that enabled them to remain true to their marriage vows no matter what difficulties they faced.

After my father died, my mother grieved unspeakably. One afternoon while sitting with me on the porch overlooking Beaver

Lake she broke down weeping. After a while she was able to compose herself and when she did she said, "I can't do this. I can't live without your father."

Thinking of their baby daughter who died in infancy I asked, "How did you make it when Carolyn died?"

Without a moment's hesitation Mom replied, "When Carolyn died I had your father to comfort me. When I needed to talk he listened to me. When my grief was too deep for words he held me. Now I have no one . . ."

Her voice faded and for several minutes we sat wrapped in silence, each of us lost in our own thoughts. Finally, mother spoke again in a voice I had to strain to hear. "When I married your father I was barely nineteen and terribly naïve. I had no idea what to expect. I knew nothing about the ways of a man and woman in marriage, nor did I know how babies were made. When I realized what was expected of a wife I nearly panicked. I've never told anyone this but we didn't consummate our marriage for nearly a month."

> "YOUR FATHER WAS SO PATIENT WITH ME. I THINK THAT'S WHEN I REALIZED THAT HE LOVED ME MORE THAN HE LOVED HIMSELF."

She paused, giving me a moment to absorb that startling bit of information, before continuing, "Your father was so patient with me. I think that's when I realized that he loved me more than he loved himself."

After a few minutes she excused herself saying, "I'm tired now. I think I'll go in the house and take a short nap."

Sitting alone on the porch I found myself reminiscing and my thoughts gravitated toward my parents' fiftieth anniversary celebration. Following the reception the entire family returned to their home where we shared memories and family stories late into the evening. My nine-year-old niece had snuggled up on the couch beside her grandmother and when there was a pause in the conversation she asked, "Grandma, how does anyone stayed married fifty years?"

Her question was raw with the pain caused by her parents' recent divorce and an uneasy silence settled over the room. Pulling her close, my mother said, "Honey, Grandpa and I were able to stay married all these years because we could always talk about everything."

That's another key isn't it? Communication—the ability to talk about everything. By talking things through instead of blaming each other and retreating into silence, you keep the channels of communication open even as you strengthen each other and your marriage.

> BY TALKING THINGS THROUGH INSTEAD OF BLAMING EACH OTHER AND RETREATING INTO SILENCE, YOU KEEP THE CHANNELS OF COMMUNICATION OPEN EVEN AS YOU STRENGTHEN EACH OTHER AND YOUR MARRIAGE.

During their sixty-one years Dad and Mom had some tough things to talk about, the kind of things that would have done a lesser marriage in. Things like a failed business venture and the resulting financial pressure. Shortly after they married, Dad went into the water well drilling business but he could never make a go of it. He was undercapitalized and his ancient equipment was badly worn and kept breaking down. The thing that finally did him in was a job related injury that laid him up for weeks. Without insurance or worker's compensation, it put him out of business. Refusing to declare bankruptcy, Dad and Mom spent the next several years digging out of debt.

In times like that it is easy to blame each other. Under similar circumstances many a wife has been known to berate her husband, to accuse him of poor judgment or blind ambition.

Many a husband has been known to blame his wife for not supporting him. Did my parents have those kinds of destructive conversations? Perhaps, but I doubt it. When a couple hurls accusations like that at each other their relationship is sorely wounded, sometimes fatally. I never saw any indication of those kinds of wounds in my parents' marriage.

Just weeks before their eleventh anniversary, Dad and Mom suffered their most devastating blow. Their fourth child, our long awaited baby sister, was born severely hydrocephalic. At birth, Carolyn's head was larger than the rest of her body. She wasn't expected to live and even if she did, the doctors said she would never be normal.

It seemed each day brought some new disappointment. Soon we realized that Carolyn was both blind and deaf and her head continued to grow more and more disproportionate to the rest of her body. She died in her sleep, at home, early one morning. Our family doctor arrived shortly thereafter to make the official diagnosis, and later the mortician came and took Carolyn's tiny body away.

When a child dies it often sounds the death knell for the marriage. Not so for my parents. Although their grief was unspeakable, it did not drive them apart. Instead they clung to each other, finding strength in their love. Nearly two years later God blessed Mom and Dad with another child, a beautiful little girl, healthy in every way. But their troubles were not over. While pregnant with Sherry, mother lost her hearing and the following summer Dad severely injured his back while working for Baker Oil Tools, Inc. When it became apparent that the damage was permanent, the company gave him the choice of transferring to the home office in Houston, Texas, or being terminated. That may seem like a no-brainer, but complicating things was the fact that Mom was an only child and the sole caregiver for her elderly mother who was crippled with arthritis. How could she move a thousand miles away and leave her?

Dad suggested that Grandma sell her place and come to Texas with us. A suggestion Grandma quickly vetoed saying, "Dick, there's no house big enough for two women."

To Mother she said, "Your place is with your husband. Go to Texas with him. God will take care of me."

So Mom and Dad bid Grandma goodbye and left for Houston on a Sunday afternoon in December, 1959. That tearful parting is forever etched in my memory. I can still see Grandma standing by the gate, leaning on her two crutches as she watched us drive away. Dad's back injury was so painful that we made a bed for him on the back seat of the 1955 Buick so he could lie down. Mother was driving and depending on me to help with the younger children. I was only twelve years old, but I was the oldest so I had to carry my share of the load. I can only imagine the things Mom and Dad talked about late into the night as they prepared to make the biggest move of their lives not knowing what the future held.

There's more. In the years ahead, Mom and Dad would suffer as two of their children endured the trauma of divorce and all that entails. Dad would undergo two open-heart surgeries and suffer from fibrosis of the lungs. Mother's hearing loss—first experienced when she was barely thirty years old—would continue to deteriorate until she could barely hear at all even with the strongest hearing aids. Because of the fibrosis in his lungs, Dad could only speak in a whisper. They had always talked about everything, but now Daddy could hardly speak and Momma could barely hear, so they gave up talking for touching. Anytime Momma was within reach Daddy reached out to touch her hand and if no one was watching he would pat her on her bottom. She was always caressing his cheek or running her fingers through his thinning hair.

For sixty-one years, three months, and one day they remained completely devoted to one another. When it became impossible for my father to leave his bed during the last week of his life, mother remained by his side, taking what little food she ate sitting up in bed beside him. Hour after hour she lay beside him, propping herself up on one elbow so she could look at him. Although we urged her to take a break she refused, saying over and over again, "I promised your father I would never leave him and I'm going to stay right here." And that's where she was when Daddy took his last breath and went to be with the Lord.

Following my father's death mother visited his grave nearly every week. She and my sister had developed a routine of cleaning the tombstone and arranging fresh flowers. The last time they went to the cemetery—just a few days before Mother suffered a fatal aneurysm—they completed their familiar routine and my sister started for the car. After a few steps she realized that mother was not with her. Turning back toward the grave, she saw my mother kiss her first two fingers and place them on my father's name etched in the gray granite. She heard Mom say, in a voice thick with feeling, "I'll always love you Dick Exley. I hope to see you soon. It won't be long now." Barely two weeks later, we buried her body beside the remains of the man she loved more than life.

So how does anyone create a marriage like that? Based on their example, I can only conclude that marriage has to be built on something more than love for each other. That "something more," in their case, was a shared faith in the Lord Jesus Christ. It sustained them when the inevitable tough times came. That's not to say that love doesn't play a part for it does, a big part! You have to love your spouse more than you love yourself, you have to choose your spouse's needs over your own (Ephesians 5:33). And you have to be able

BASED ON THEIR EXAMPLE, I CAN ONLY CONCLUDE THAT MARRIAGE HAS TO BE BUILT ON SOMETHING MORE THAN LOVE FOR EACH OTHER. THAT "SOMETHING MORE," IN THEIR CASE, WAS A SHARED FAITH IN THE LORD JESUS CHRIST.

to communicate honestly. Or to use my mother's words, "You have to be able to talk about everything." Not just the easy things, but everything—your secret dreams, your hurts, your hopes, your disappointments, and even your fears. By talking things through instead of blaming each other and retreating into silence, you keep the channels of communication open even as you strengthen each other and your marriage.

Finally, you have to be willing to forgive each other. No one goes through life unscathed. Sooner or later you will wound the person you love the most or he/she will wound you. In that moment everything within you will cry out for revenge. You will be tempted to make your beloved suffer the way you have suffered. Or maybe you will be tempted to retreat inside yourself and make a shrine out of your hurts.

Be careful. If you insist on holding onto your hurts, your marriage will wither and die, becoming just an empty shell. Unresolved issues are like pieces of misplaced furniture in the soul of your marriage. You may never speak of them but every time you try to get close to each other you bump into them. The only way to get rid of those pieces of misplaced furniture is to let go of your hurts and forgive your spouse.

Did Mom and Dad wound each other? I'm sure they did although I can't recall a particular incident. They were always careful not to quarrel in front of us kids. Still Mom could be stubborn and Dad had mastered the art of pouting so I'm sure they had their moments, but they refused to go to bed mad. They realized that unresolved anger opens the door to the enemy and they never wanted to give him a foothold in their marriage (Ephesians 4:26-27). Early in their marriage they mastered the holy art of forgiveness and as the years passed it became the balm that healed their wounds and nurtured their love, enabling them to cherish each other all the days of their lives. Truly, theirs was a marriage for the ages.

Chapter 6
Bump, Bump, Bump . . .

"Richard, 'Motor Mouth,' always joking, always laughing, always talking, always willing to be the butt of our jokes, was dead. I'd asked him lots of times how he was doing, but I guess I had never asked him in such a way that made him want to tell me."

I n his book, *Come Share the Being,* Bob Benson writes, "We bought an old building and remodeled it for offices and warehouse space. The electrician who did the work was named Richard. He was such a talker that after a while somebody in the building started calling him 'Motor Mouth.' He always had a smile and a ready answer to any question, serious or joking. He was a joy to have in the building. In a year or so we were making some additional changes that would require wiring and I asked if anyone had called Richard.

"Somebody said, 'Didn't you hear about Richard?'

"'No, I didn't.'

"'Well, about two months ago his partner went by the trailer park to go to work with him and Richard said, 'I'll just meet you up at the job in about twenty minutes.'"

33

"'And Richard went back to the trailer. He had been arguing with his wife and went back to the bedroom and came back and touched her on the shoulder as she stood at the sink. She turned just in time to see him pull the trigger of the pistol he had pressed against his head.'

"LIFE IN A WAY IS LIKE THOSE ELECTRIC BUMPER CARS AT THE AMUSEMENT PARK. WE JUST RUN AT EACH OTHER AND SMILE AND BUMP AND AWAY WE GO.

"Richard, 'Motor Mouth,' always joking, always laughing, always talking, always willing to be the butt of our jokes, was dead. I'd asked him lots of times how he was doing, but I guess I had never asked him in such a way that made him want to tell me.

"Life in a way is like those electric bumper cars at the amusement park. We just run at each other and smile and bump and away we go.

"How are you doing—

—bump, bump,

"Hi, Motor Mouth—

—bump, bump,

"'Great, fantastic—

—bump, bump, bump.

"And somebody slips out and dies because there is no one to talk to.

Bump, bump, bump."[3]

Makes you think doesn't it?

I can't help wondering how many people I've bumped into, how many times I've asked how they were doing, but not in a way that made them want to tell me. How many of them slipped

34

out into the night and died, just a little on the inside, because they had no one to talk to? I mean *really* talk to.

What a haunting picture of our broken world. Masses of hurting people pretending to have it all together while dying on the inside. They hide their hurts and loneliness beneath a superficial gaiety because they're afraid to appear needy. Yet, even as they pretend with such clever and convincing aplomb, they are desperately hoping that we won't be taken in by their empty act, that we won't let them get away with it.

Who, you may be wondering, am I talking about? You may even think I am overstating my case, that you don't know anyone like that.

I beg to differ.

Look around you; I mean really look. What do you see? Probably lonely hurting people within arm's reach, maybe right there in your own family. A spouse you've been too busy to love, a teenager you've never taken time to understand, a child who hardly knows you. Or maybe it's the person you work with. The one you've written off as antisocial, the troublemaker. Do you have any idea why he's so angry, so defensive? What about the misfit you worship with, the person who is always on the outside looking in, the gal nobody likes. You know, the one who talks too loud, the one who tries too hard.

Bump, bump, bump . . .

Dr. Elton Trueblood contends that, "Somewhere in the world there should be a society consciously and deliberately devoted to the task of seeing how love can be made real, and demonstrating love in practice."[4]

Isn't this what Jesus was talking about when He said, "...I am giving you a new commandment: Love each other. Just as I have loved you, you should love each other. Your love for one another will prove to the world that you are my disciples" (see John 13:34-35 NLT)?

OFTEN THE PEOPLE WHO NEED OUR LOVE THE MOST ARE THE VERY PEOPLE WHO ARE THE MOST UNLOVABLE.

I'll admit that it's not easy to love like that. Often the people who need our love the most are the very people who are the most unlovable. Don't give up. When it seems impossible to love that obnoxious person, ask Jesus to help you look beyond their behavior, to help you to see that even when their actions are hostile and defensive they are often crying out for love. Like the wealthy, self-sufficient divorcee in Katherine Anne Porter's *Ship of Fools*, they cry, "Love me. Love me in spite of all! Whether or not I love you, whether I am fit to love, whether you are able to love, even if there is no such thing as love, love me!"[5]

Maybe you've been hurt. Maybe it seems you have loved in vain. Take heart, all is not lost. Even if no one responds to your love, you are better for having loved. The very act of loving has enriched you, made you more like Christ. And, when you least expect it, love works its miracle and another cynical person is made new, another bitter heart is healed. But it almost never happens instantly.

Bobby is a case in point. His mother found herself pregnant as young teenager. He was the unplanned, unwanted, and unnamed baby. The identity of his biological father remains a mystery to this day. Over the next five or six years, his mother gave birth to five more children. No one knows for sure who their fathers were.

His mother usually spent her nights in sleazy bars. Meanwhile Bobby was the six-year-old back at the garage apartment taking care of his baby brothers and sisters, sometimes for days on end. As bad as that was, it was worse when his mother came home, often with a boozing boyfriend. Not infrequently

36

they involved Bobby in their sex games. One night a drunken lout sodomized Bobby while his mother giggled.

Eventually Bobby and his siblings were placed in the state foster care system. It was a revolving door. Bobby would just start to feel secure when he would be shuffled to another family. In one foster home Bobby and his siblings were forced to eat out of dog dishes. In another they were hardly fed at all.

Bobby's greatest shame as a child was wetting the bed. He did so until he was almost thirteen years old. His foster parents tried everything to break him of that habit: scolding, pleading, shaming, and finally beatings. One foster mother printed a sign in bold black letters on a big square of cardboard: "This Boy Still Wets the Bed." She hung the cardboard sign on a rope around his neck and forced him to stand on the front porch while his classmates walked by on their way to school. After that he was teased unmercifully. His classmates called him Bobby Bedwetter!

It is little wonder that he was diagnosed as unable to give or receive love? He was damaged goods having been sexually abused repeatedly and shuffled from one foster home to another—what else could you expect? His sixth grade teacher wrote on his report card that he needed to be institutionalized. What he really needed was love—God's unconditional love expressed through a compassionate adult or adults.

The damage Bobby suffered took place over a decade and he would require years of unconditional love to effect his healing. There were however critical events in that long process. For instance, when he was twelve years old a childless middle-age couple adopted him. They gave him his very own room with a brand new Roy Rogers bunk bed. As bedtime approached that first night he was deeply troubled. Finally he burst into tears and blurted out to his adopted Mom. "I wet the bed every night. I'll ruin those new sheets and mattress. I always do."

To his amazement his adoptive mom put her arms around him and said, "Bobby, your dad and I love you no matter what. If you wet the bed, we'll change the sheets. Honey, you're home now. You just go to sleep and dream sweet dreams."

That night Bobby fell asleep in a peace he had never known. The next morning he awoke in a dry and warm bed. He never wet the bed again.

> **ARE YOU GOING TO ALLOW GOD TO LOVE THIS BROKEN, HODGE-PODGE OF HUMANITY THROUGH YOU OR ARE YOU GOING TO PLAY IT SAFE?**

Of course the deep psychological wounds he had suffered were not so easily healed, but over time, love—God's love expressed through flawed human beings—did its healing work. Today, Dr. Robert Peterson is a husband and a father, a successful pastor, a published author, and a much in-demand speaker.[6]

As I stated earlier, love often works its miracle when you least expect it and another damaged person is made new, another bitter heart is healed. You can take a chance on love or you can go through life with your guard up, keeping people at arms' distance. What's it going to be? Are you going to live a bumper car existence—bump, bump, bump—or are you going to let your guard down and take a chance on being hurt? Are you going to allow God to love this broken, hodge-podge of humanity through you or are you going to play it safe? Who knows whose life you might save if you dared to take a chance on love— Richard's? Motor Mouth's? Bobby's? Maybe your own.

[3] Benson, Bob and Benson, Michael w., "Disciplines for the Inner Life" (Waco: Word Books, 1985), pp. 311-312.

[4] Trueblood, Elton, quoted in "When the Walls Come Tumblin' Down" by Gordon C. Hunter, (Waco: Word Books Publisher, 1970) p. 26.

[5] Katherine Anne Porter, "Ship of Fools," (Boston: Little Brown & Co., 1962).

[6] Dr. Robert A. Peterson, "The Theater of Angels" (Covenant Books, 2015).

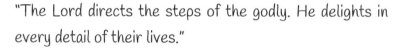

Chapter 7

An Original by Yahweh

"The Lord directs the steps of the godly. He delights in every detail of their lives."

—Psalm 37:23 NLT

My heart was heavy as I entered the small bedroom that served as my study. In January I had been released from my position as youth pastor and it was now June. In the ensuing months I had sent resumes to several churches without a single positive response. Having nearly depleted our savings, I was beginning to feel desperate. I couldn't help but wonder if there was any place for me in the ministry.

I lit the kerosene lamp sitting on the corner of my desk before taking a seat. Leaning back in my chair, I watched the steam rising from my rapidly cooling cup of coffee while replaying the last five or six months in my mind. In late December we had been vacationing with friends in Colorado when we received a long distance telephone call from Brenda's mother. She informed us that the doctors had discovered a grapefruit-sized tumor in her uterus. Surgery was scheduled in two days so we cut our vacation short and rushed back to Houston.

The day of the surgery arrived and we sat quietly in the family room awaiting the outcome. No one mentioned the "C" word but it was on all of our minds. Finally the surgeon came in with a good report. The grapefruit-sized tumor was not malignant. As a precaution he had removed both of her ovaries but he didn't think there was anything to be concerned about. To be safe he was sending them to the lab to be biopsied.

Three days later the hammer fell—both ovaries were cancerous. As soon as Hildegarde recovered from surgery she would have to begin a series of radiation treatments at M.D. Anderson Cancer Hospital. We were devastated. It sounded like a death sentence to us. In 1975, 95 percent of the women suffering from ovarian cancer died in five years or less. It seemed so unfair. Hildegarde was only forty-nine years old—far too young to die.*

While we were still reeling from Hildegarde's diagnosis, we received more bad news. The Sunday following her surgery our pastor unexpectedly announced his retirement. He then went on to inform the congregation that Brenda and I were resigning as youth pastors effective immediately. We were stunned. He had not discussed his immediate retirement or our termination with us. Complicating things was the fact that when he invited us to serve with him it was with the understanding that when he retired he would recommend that the church call us to be their next senior pastor. Obviously that wasn't going to happen now.

Following the benediction, I remained seated on the front pew trying to wrap my mind around what had happened while Brenda went to pick up our four-year-old daughter from Children's Church. One of the board members sat down beside me and asked if I was interested in being considered for the position of senior pastor. Being young and naïve I said, "Absolutely."

There was no way I could have imagined the firestorm my decision would unleash. There's nothing to be gained by delving into the painful details. Let it suffice to say it was messy. When the congregation voted, I fell nine votes short of having the necessary two-thirds majority to be elected pastor. Brenda and I were deeply disappointed and hurt. We felt betrayed by the pastor and confused by the entire situation. Still, I was ready to move forward, being sure that there was any number of churches that would be interested in having me as their pastor.

Five months later, I was no longer so sure. In fact I was filled with self-doubt and wondered if I was washed up in the ministry at the age of twenty-eight. Of equal concern was my relationship with the Lord. I still loved Him but I no longer felt I could trust Him. If the truth be told I felt like He had let me down. I couldn't help asking where He was when I needed Him.

For a few minutes I sat at my desk with my face buried in my hands weeping silently. With a groan I rolled out of my chair and lay face down on the floor. Burying my face in the red and black shag carpet (this was the seventies), I bared my heart to the Lord. I told Him everything—how alone I felt, how unfairly I had been treated, and how it seemed He had forsaken me. Desperately I cried out to Him. "Speak to me Lord, speak to me!"

In an instant my mind went back to a Wednesday evening in November of the previous year. A group of us were praying together when a thought sprang full-blown into my mind: *Read Isaiah 41:9-13.* It could not have been any clearer had someone handed me a note with that message printed on it. Opening my Bible I read:

"I took you from the ends of the earth, from its farthest corners I called you. I said, 'You are my servant; I have chosen you and have not rejected you.' So do not fear, for I am with you; do not be dismayed, for I am your God. I will strengthen you and help you; I will uphold you with my righteous right hand. For I am the LORD your God

who takes hold of your right hand and says to you, 'Do not fear; I will help you.'"

When I first read that passage, I found it interesting, even inspiring, but certainly not earth shattering. In fact I had forgotten all about it until that very moment. Given my current state of mind, and what had happened in the ensuing months, I now saw that whole experience in a totally different light. Weeks before Brenda's mother was diagnosed with ovarian cancer, weeks before we were dismissed from our ministry position, God gave us a word to prepare us for what was coming and a word to sustain us through the storm that was to follow.

"'You are my servant; I have chosen you and have not rejected you. So do not fear, for I am with you; do not be dismayed, for I am your God'" (Isaiah 41:9,10).

WAVE AFTER WAVE OF GOD'S PRESENCE WASHED OVER ME, HEALING MY WOUNDED SOUL, ASSURING ME THAT THERE WAS STILL A PLACE FOR ME IN MINISTRY.

Although the prophet Isaiah first spoke those words hundreds of years ago, they now resonated within my soul. God had not forsaken me. I wasn't washed up in the ministry. God would help us!

I don't know how long I lingered in prayer that evening but I do know wave after wave of God's presence washed over me, healing my wounded soul, assuring me that there was still a place for me in ministry. Heretofore I had been rather discriminating in the churches where I sent my resume. The church had to be located in a city near a college or university so I could finish my education. The congregation had to be large enough to support a fulltime pastor and they had to provide a decent parsonage. Now none of that seemed important. I told God I would go anywhere He wanted to send me—anywhere.

The next morning I telephoned the Assembly of God in Craig, Colorado. Previously I had dismissed them with hardly a thought. They were a small congregation located in extreme northwestern Colorado without a college or university within 200 miles. Their total annual income for 1974 was barely $14,000 and the parsonage was small—less than 1000 square feet. None of that mattered—not now. If Craig, Colorado, was where God wanted us then that was where we would go.

Following my telephone call, the official board invited us to come for an interview and to preach a trial sermon. Without a moment's hesitation we accepted their invitation. We took three days to drive the 1350 miles from Houston, Texas. While in route we received a message from a church in El Paso, Texas, inviting us to "tryout" for their church. Interesting isn't it? Before surrendering unconditionally to the Lord we had gone five months and sent out a score of resumes without receiving a single positive response. But once I surrendered unconditionally we received two invitations in just a matter of days. Truly the steps of those who delight in the Lord are ordered of Him (Psalm 37:23).

The interview and the trial sermon at the Assembly of God in Craig went very well. The pastoral election was scheduled immediately following my sermon and I felt certain the congregation would call me to be their pastor. When we left Houston I was fully prepared to accept that call should we be elected. Now I wasn't so sure. I wasn't prepared to make a decision until we had fully explored the possibilities offered by the church in El Paso. Although we informed the congregation of our dilemma they still elected us with a unanimous vote. I promised to give them a decision within ten days.

Early the next morning we set out for El Paso, Texas, where we interviewed with the official board and preached a trial sermon. On the surface it appeared to be a no brainer. We connected with the congregation, which was significantly larger than the one in Craig, as was the church's annual income. The four-bedroom parsonage was spacious and up to date and the salary they offered was considerably more than what the church in Craig was offering, plus I would be able to complete my degree at the University of Texas at El Paso.

Although that church seemed to offer everything we were looking for, neither Brenda nor I felt good about accepting their offer. No matter how hard we tried we simply could not get any peace. Once we made up our minds to decline their invitation a great weight seemed to lift. Going to Craig was risky—the congregation was small with a long history of internal conflict. Financially they were barely solvent and we would have to trust God week by week for our income. Nonetheless, when we decided to accept their invitation a great peace enveloped us. And why not? Hadn't the Lord said, "I am the LORD your God who takes hold of your right hand and says to you, 'Do not fear; I will help you'" (Isaiah 41:13)?

We served the church in Craig for just over five years. During that time the congregation experienced significant growth making it necessary to sell the existing church building and relocate. The congregation purchased nine acres of prime property and built a 13,000-square-foot multipurpose building with a seating capacity in the auditorium for nearly 400 people, plus offices, classrooms, nursery, and kitchen.

God blessed our ministry in ways we could never have imagined. Both Brenda and Leah, our daughter, remember our time in Craig as their favorite time in ministry. Nonetheless, following the completion of the new facilities I began to sense that my tenure was drawing to a close. The thought of sending out resumes and searching for a new pastorate felt overwhelming. Finally I told the Lord, "If I am supposed to make a pastoral change, a church will have to call me."

I realize there are well-known pastors, who are frequently contacted by churches seeking their services, but I was not a well-known pastor and no congregation had ever sought me out. I was a little-known pastor serving a relatively small congregation on the backside of the desert. There wasn't much chance a church was going to contact me. Not unless God moved in a truly remarkable way. Nonetheless, a few days later I received an unsolicited telephone call from the chairman of the pulpit committee representing Christian Chapel in Tulsa, Oklahoma. What made that telephone call so amazing was the fact that I had never preached in Oklahoma nor did I know anyone connected with Christian Chapel.

So how did I come to the attention of the pulpit committee? Did God speak to them in a dream or a vision? Did they read a book I had published? Had one of them heard me preach at the Church of the Comforter while they were vacationing in Colorado? God could have used any of those scenarios, but He didn't.

Here's what happened: Nearly fifteen years earlier, a relatively young wife and mother died leaving a husband and two children. Steve, her teenage son, was devastated by her death and in his grief he sought the comfort of his pastor. Soon he was taking meals with Pastor Groff and his family on a regular basis. Finally he simply moved in with them, becoming part of their family. Although Pastor Groff eventually left Tulsa to serve churches in Texas and Oregon, Steve remained close to him and his family. Steve continued to live in Tulsa and was now serving on Christian Chapel's pulpit committee. Knowing that Pastor Groff was well connected, he decided to call him and ask if he knew anyone he would like to recommend as a possible pastoral candidate. Pastor Groff recommended me.

So how did Pastor Groff know me? Another interesting story and more evidence of how God works behind the scenes to perfect His will in our lives. I met Tex (Pastor Groff) in 1974 while serving as a youth pastor in the Houston area. He was the President of the greater Houston area Assemblies of God Ministerial Association and he was responsible for leading our monthly meetings. One month he invited a cancer survivor to share her story. During her narrative she said, "Some people have trouble believing God can forgive them. Not me. I'm struggling to forgive God for the terrible things that have happened to me—being raped by two men and stricken with cancer.

What followed was nearly four hours of intense dialogue (think heated arguments) in which several area pastors rebuked her for her outrageous comments while others wanted to pray for her. A number of pastors were outraged that Tex had invited her to speak. Not a few of them called the District Office to lodge complaints. When I learned that Tex was getting a lot of heat I decided to call him and see if I could buy him lunch and encourage him.

> I MAY HAVE DOUBTED MYSELF, EVEN WONDERING AT TIMES IF THERE WAS ANY PLACE FOR ME IN THE MINISTRY, BUT TEX NEVER LOST FAITH IN ME.

He readily accepted my invitation and that was the beginning of a lifelong friendship. I soon learned that Tex had a history of befriending young ministers and in short order he took me under his wing. In the ensuing months we became close friends and when I was dismissed from my position as youth pastor he was there to encourage me. I may have doubted myself, even wondering at times if there was any place for me in the ministry, but Tex never lost faith in me. Later, when ministry took each of us to distant states, we remained in touch. He was my friend and mentor.

Looking back I cannot help but wonder how different my life and ministry might be had I not made that telephone call to Pastor Groff in the spring of 1974. At the time my only motivation was to be an encouragement to him. There was no way I could have known that the Lord was going to use our relationship to bring me to the attention of the pulpit committee from Christian Chapel six years later. I can't help thinking that before Christian Chapel had need of a pastor God had already set in motion the circumstances and events that made it possible for me to become their shepherd.

Christian Chapel was a relatively new church plant being only six years old. Most of the congregation was well educated and under forty years of age, with a liberal sprinkling of Oral Roberts University professors and students. Several members of the pulpit committee were professors at ORU and they wanted a pastor who was published, something of a rarity for Assemblies of God pastors in those days. I qualified, having published a number of magazine articles and my first two books while serving the Church of the Comforter in Craig, Colorado. Tex encouraged them to call me, telling them I was anything but your "typical" Assemblies of God minister.

The congregation was in crisis. The founding pastor was a man of great vision, an unusually gifted teacher, but not the best administrator. In its first six years the congregation grew from a handful of people meeting in his living room to more than 400 worshippers on Sunday mornings. Then things begin to unravel. There was difficulty with the pastoral staff, there were serious financial problems, and people begin leaving in droves. Soon Sunday morning attendance dropped below 100. Although the congregation was only six years old and had no facilities of their own they were more than $700,000 in debt. Finally the founding pastor resigned.

The pulpit committee was fully transparent with me regarding these matters. If I was going to become their pastor they wanted to make sure I knew what I was getting into. Although the circumstances were dire, I was not intimidated. Two things gave me confidence: 1) Isaiah 41—the word God gave me in November 1974—"I am the LORD your God who takes hold of your right hand and says to you, 'Do not fear; I will help you.'" 2) The extraordinary way the pulpit committee came to contact me. I should not have even been on their radar screen. Yet they called me within two weeks after I told the Lord if I was supposed to make a pastoral change a church would have to contact me. That was a God thing!

We were elected in August 1980 and the twelve years I served as the Senior Pastor of Christian Chapel were the most exciting years of our entire ministry. Almost immediately God intervened to deliver the congregation from their financial bondage. We were in default on our mortgage on forty acres of undeveloped land but before the mortgage holder could repossess the land the Lord provided a buyer who purchased it for $720,000. After paying off the original mortgage, the realtor's fee, and all of Christian Chapel's other indebtedness, we had a balance of $80,000. All of that happened before our first anniversary as pastor!

We established a crisis pregnancy ministry to help young women in crisis and a licensed adoption agency to help families who wanted to adopt a child. In the ensuing ten years more than 100 babies were saved from abortion and several families were able to adopt children. The Lord granted me favor with the seminary at Oral Roberts University and I was invited to serve as a pastoral leader in their field education program. Later God moved in a remarkable way enabling us to launch a national radio ministry called "Straight from the Heart." Our attendance grew to more than 1000 worshippers on Sunday mornings and we were forced to go to three Sunday morning services. In the mid-80s we experienced a supernatural move of the Holy Spirit with accompanying signs and wonders (see Acts 5:12-16).

Sometimes as I reflect over my life in ministry I play the "what if" game. What if Pastor Groff had not opened his heart and his home to Steve following his mother's death? What if they had lost contact with each other after Pastor Groff moved from Tulsa? What if I hadn't unexpectedly attended the Greater Houston Area Assemblies of God Ministerial Association meeting when the speaker created such a controversy? What if I hadn't called Pastor Groff to encourage him? What if he hadn't taken me under his wing? What if Steve hadn't called and asked him for a recommendation? What if . . .

Not infrequently the destiny of God's chosen ones hinge on such seemingly insignificant and random events. Some people call those "chance" encounters coincidences. I prefer to think of them as God incidences! As the psalmists said, "The Lord directs the steps of the godly. He delights in every detail of their lives" (Psalm 37:23 NLT). God's fingerprints are all over our lives. Every detail has been shaped and fashioned by Him. Open the robe of your life and look at the label. You are "An Original by Yahweh."

As I consider my life I am continually amazed at God's faithfulness. Time and time again He would have been justified in giving up on me but He never did. At times my faith failed and I felt like God had let me down. He never held that against me. 1975 was one of those times. In my lowest moment the Holy Spirit visited me, renewing my faith, and setting in motion the remarkable events that opened doors of ministry that continue to this very day. Well did the Lord say, *"You are my servant; I have chosen you and have not rejected you. So do not fear, for I am with you; do not be dismayed, for I am your God"*(Isaiah 41:9-10).

Maybe you are in a difficult place right now. If so, you are in good company. Even the most cursory overview of Scripture will reveal that all believers face challenges. Those God intends to use in special ways usually experience the greatest challenges. Joseph went to prison, Moses spent forty years on the backside of the desert, David was a fugitive hunted by King Saul, Daniel

NOT INFREQUENTLY THE DESTINY OF GOD'S CHOSEN ONES HINGE ON SUCH SEEMINGLY INSIGNIFICANT AND RANDOM EVENTS. SOME PEOPLE CALL THOSE "CHANCE" ENCOUNTERS COINCIDENCES. I PREFER TO THINK OF THEM AS GOD INCIDENCES!

went to the lion's den, and Paul had a thorn in his flesh. The challenges we face do not come from God. They are designed by the enemy to short-circuit God's purpose in our lives, but God has a better plan. He takes the very thing the enemy intends to use to destroy us and uses it to develop our character and our faith. Out of the deepest trials come the most faithful servants. God is preparing you for something special!

---

* Hildegarde is now ninety-one years old and she has never had a reoccurrence of cancer of any kind. God healed her!

Chapter 8

God's Grace is Always Greater than Our Sin

Now you know the worst thing I ever did, but more importantly you know the best thing God ever did for me. He forgave me and gave me another chance!

I recently read about a psychiatrist who asks each new client three questions. 1) What is the worst thing you have ever done? 2) What is the worst thing that ever happened to you? 3) What is the proudest moment of your life?

If you are like me you would probably like to skip over the first two questions and go directly to the third one. All of us like to remember our achievements, those bright and shining moments when we outdid ourselves. Yet, for many of us, even those highlights are tainted with the shame of past sins or the pain caused by some unspeakable tragedy. Many of us cannot accept our achievements because we are haunted by the thought that if others knew the whole truth about us they would know what a phony we are. Maybe that's why that psychiatrist wants his clients to remember the worst thing they have ever done. Maybe he realizes we can't really accept our achievements until we have made peace with our past.

IT MAY BE HELPFUL
TO REMIND
OURSELVES THAT
EVEN THE HEROES
OF FAITH DID NOT
GO THROUGH LIFE
UNSCATHED.

If that's the case, then the first step is to come to grips with our past—both the evil we have done and the evil we have suffered. No one likes to remember their sins but we must if we ever hope to be rid of them. Pretending they don't exist is futile.

It may be helpful to remind ourselves that even the heroes of faith did not go through life unscathed. Normally we like to remember their proudest moments, but it may be equally beneficial to recall their devastating sins. Not as a way of excusing the evil we have done, but as a way of reminding ourselves that God's grace is always greater than our sin.

So what was the worst thing Abraham ever did, or David, or Peter, or Paul? As far as I'm concerned the worst thing Abraham ever did was to disinherit Ishmael (Genesis 21:8-11). Only God knows what psychological wounds the boy suffered as a result of his father's rejection. Little wonder that he became a wild donkey of a man living in hostility toward all his brothers (Genesis 16:12). David was guilty of adultery and murder and his sins ripped his family apart. Amnon raped his stepsister Tamar turning her into a desolate woman (2 Samuel 13:1-20). Absalom waited two years before taking his revenge. In a well-conceived plot, he lured Amnon to Baal Hazor near the border of Ephraim where he murdered him (2 Samuel 13:23-29). Later Absalom led an armed revolt against his father David and was killed (2 Samuel 15-18) breaking his father's heart (2 Samuel 18:24-33). Peter denied the Lord three times (Luke 22:54-62), while Paul was a blasphemer, a persecutor, and a violent man (1 Timothy 1:12-15). If God could forgive them, if He could use them in spite of their blatant carnality, then there's hope for us no matter what we have done (see 1 Timothy 1:16).

Although I have been a believer since childhood, I have to acknowledge that I have done things that can only be described as evil—things I don't want to remember, things I wish I could forget. Almost all of them involved hurtful things I did and said in a moment of anger.

As a teenager I had a quick temper, a smart mouth, and a soft heart. I could become angry in a heartbeat. In an instant I was saying and doing things I would deeply regret when my anger passed. Filled with remorse, I sought for ways to make amends. Unfortunately not even the most sincere apologies could undo what I had done.

> IF GOD COULD FORGIVE THEM, IF HE COULD USE THEM IN SPITE OF THEIR BLATANT CARNALITY, THEN THERE'S HOPE FOR US NO MATTER WHAT WE HAVE DONE.

Once, in a fit of temper, I smashed my fist through the hollow core door of my bedroom. I offered to buy a new door but my father wouldn't allow it. He said, "I want you to see that hole in your door every time you go into your bedroom. When you look at it I want you to realize how destructive your temper is." Every day for nearly three years I was forced to look at that fist-sized hole, but I never once saw how destructive my anger was. As a result I continued to hurt those I loved the most.

As an adult I was never physically violent toward another person, nonetheless my volatile temper and angry words left a path of destruction in my wake. My anger grievously wounded my wife, in time killing her love for me. It terrorized my daughter, turning our home into a scary place where she felt it necessary to watch every word. She said that living with me was like walking on eggshells. Although I could be loving and kind, she never knew what might set me off.

As you have probably surmised there are any number of incidents involving my wife and daughter that might qualify as the worst thing I ever did. Thankfully God has healed the deep wounds my anger inflicted on them and healed our family, therefore I choose not to revisit those painful memories. Instead I want to focus on the damage I inflicted to the psyche of a young man named Terry. It shames me to recall what I did to him, but self-honesty forces me to do so. I cannot pretend it didn't happen, nor dare I attempt to justify my behavior. My only hope lies in honestly confessing my sin and receiving the Lord's forgiveness.

It embarrasses me to realize that I never took the time to learn much about him. I never bothered to learn who his parents were, where he was born, or how he happened to be in Craig, Colorado. I knew he was single and working in the local coal mine. That was the extent of my knowledge. Plus the fact that he was housesitting for a couple that had gone south for the winter, not that they really needed anyone to housesit, considering their daughter and her husband lived nearby. Most likely Terry didn't have a place to live and they took compassion on him, letting him live in their home.

Terry and I became acquainted following a Sunday morning service at the Church of the Comforter where I was serving as pastor. He was probably twenty-one or twenty-two years old and a new believer. I took him under my wing and began to disciple him. Things went well for several weeks. Terry and I studied the scriptures together and he was growing in the Lord. Brenda and Leah liked him and he began taking meals with us from time to time. The only fly in the ointment was his immaturity and lack of personal discipline. Although he had a good job at the coal mine, he hated it. He missed work so often that the company placed him on probation. Any further absences and he would be terminated. I talked to him like a Dutch uncle and he promised me he wouldn't miss any more work.

A few days later I noticed Terry's car parked in front of a parishioner's house when he should have been at work. I pulled into the driveway and got out of my car. Hearing voices in the backyard I headed that way. Sure enough Terry was engaged in an animated conversation with a couple from our church. I was furious. Terry had given me his word, he had promised me that he wouldn't miss any more work and now he was playing hooky again.

Stepping into the backyard, I let him have it. "Aren't you supposed to be at work?" I demanded, anger making my voice harsh. He started to say something but I cut him off. "You lied to me! You promised me that you wouldn't skip any more work and now you've broken your word." Once I got started I couldn't seem to stop. I continued to berate him, oblivious to his humiliation and the embarrassment of the couple whose backyard I had invaded.

Once my anger spent itself, I realized what I had done. I had grievously wounded a young believer, shaming him in front of his friends. I tried to convince myself that it was for his own good, but in my heart of hearts I knew better. If I had truly been acting in his best interests I would have handled things differently. I would have spoken to him in love not anger. And I would have addressed the issues privately, just between him and me.

I knew what I had to do. I would go to him and apologize. I would do everything in my power to right the terrible wrongs I had done. I would heal the deep wounds I had inflicted to his soul and to our relationship. And I did just that. I apologized profusely, but the damage was irreparable. At least I couldn't repair it. Now he was afraid of me. The love and trust we had once shared was shattered and in its place was a grievous wound.

I continued to reach out to him over the next few weeks but we never really connected. He stopped attending church, at least he stopped attending our church. Nor did he come by my office to study the scriptures or come by the house to share a meal. When we did interact it felt stiff, contrived, somehow artificial. Gradually we lost touch. To this day—more than thirty years later—I don't have any idea what happened to him.

Perhaps he found another pastor and another church—some godly man or woman whom the Lord used to heal his wounded soul and restore his faith. Possibly not. I fear I may have hurt him in ways that destroyed his faith. I have, with unspeakable sorrow, reflected on the words of Jesus: "If anyone causes one of these little ones—those who believe in me—to stumble, it would be better for them to have a large millstone hung around their neck and to be drowned in the depths of the sea. Woe to the world because of the things that cause people to stumble! Such things must come, but woe to the person through whom they come!" (Matthew 18:6-7 NIV).

> NOW YOU KNOW THE WORST THING I EVER DID, BUT MORE IMPORTANTLY YOU KNOW THE BEST THING GOD EVER DID FOR ME. HE FORGAVE ME AND GAVE ME ANOTHER CHANCE!

And now you know the worst thing I've ever done—I may well have destroyed a young believer's faith, causing him to stumble, maybe losing his soul for eternity. I can't think of anything worse than that. If I got what I deserve I would have a large millstone hung around my neck and be drowned in the depths of the ocean. Thank God, ". . . he (the Lord) does not treat us as our sins deserve or repay us according to our iniquities. For as high as the heavens are above the earth, so great is his love for those who fear him; as far as the east is from the west, so far has he removed our transgressions from us" (Psalm 103:10-12 NIV).

Someone has said that justice is getting what you deserve. Mercy is not getting what you deserve and grace is getting what you don't deserve. Justice would have put a millstone around my neck and cast me into the ocean. That's what I deserved. But instead of justice I received mercy and grace. Grace gave me what I desperately needed but did not deserve—forgiveness and another chance. Rather than casting me out on the scrap heap of life, the Lord allowed me to remain in ministry. Unbelievably, He continued to trust me to care for the souls of His people.

Now you know the worst thing I ever did, but more importantly you know the best thing God ever did for me. He forgave me and gave me another chance!

What about you? What is the worst thing you ever did? What is the one thing you hope no one ever discovers about you? Whatever it is—God's grace is greater still. God doesn't want to punish you. He doesn't want to reject you. More than anything, He wants to hear your confession, forgive your most grievous transgression, and give you another chance. No matter what you've done. No matter how insidious your sin, God's grace is greater still.

Chapter 9
Making Peace with Your Past

The real question isn't, "What's the worst thing that's ever happened to you?" but, "What will you do? Will you trust the Lord to heal your hurts, to redeem your troubles, and to fulfill His purposes in your life, or will you take matters into your own hands?"

Return with me to the psychiatrist who asks each of his new clients three questions. 1) What is the worst thing you have ever done? 2) What is the worst thing that ever happened to you? 3) What is the proudest moment of your life?

Of those three questions, I find this second one the most difficult. Not because nothing bad has ever happened to me, but because the disappointments and hurts I've suffered seem rather inconsequential when viewed in light of the things others have experienced. What is the disappointment of having a manuscript you've labored over for months repeatedly rejected compared to the devastation of divorce? Once I was "fired" from my position as youth pastor, several times I interviewed and preached trial sermons for churches only to have the congregation call another candidate, but what is that compared to having a child in prison or addicted to drugs?

Death is about as bad as it gets, but there are deaths and then there are "deaths." The death of a beloved parent or a dear friend—both of which I have experienced—is a grievous loss, but it pales in comparison to watching helplessly as your six-year-old son loses his life to the ravages of leukemia. That's what happened to Randy and Vicky and it just about killed them. Another dear friend lost his young wife and the mother of his four children to cancer. In the ensuing months he nearly lost his mind as he tried to come to grips with the reality of life without her.

Yet, as terrible as death is, there may be some wounds that are worse, wounds so grievous they leave freezer burns on your soul. I'm thinking of the child who is abused by a trusted parent, or another authority figure, leaving her world shattered. Try as she might she can't escape her shame; it taints every waking moment and undermines all her relationships. Years later she is still haunted, still tormented by that tragic experience.

Then there's the man or woman who is betrayed by a trusted friend or a beloved spouse. Like David he cries, "If an enemy were insulting me, I could endure it; if a foe were raising himself against me, I could hide from him. But it is you, a man like myself, my companion, my close friend, with whom I once enjoyed sweet fellowship as we walked with the throng at the house of God" (Psalm 55:12-14).

NO ONE GOES THROUGH LIFE UNSCATHED. SOME HURTS ARE WORSE THAN OTHERS, TO BE SURE, BUT EVERYONE GETS HURT SOONER OR LATER.

No one goes through life unscathed. Some hurts are worse than others, to be sure, but everyone gets hurt sooner or later. Out of the pain and darkness our heart cries, "God, can You redeem this tragedy?"

When I find myself wrestling with that question, when I'm confronted with hurts so deep that I'm tempted to wonder if even God can bring something good out of my hopeless mess, my thoughts inevitably turn toward a pastor who is a dear friend of mine. He's a robust man with a ready smile and a contagious joy. To look at him you would think he had lived a trouble free life. Nothing could be farther from the truth.

His father was a hard-drinking man; a mean drunk, if you know what I mean. My friend distinctly remembers his father's drunken rage and his mother's terrified screams. Being too small to intervene, all my friend could do was cower in fear. For years he was haunted by the memory of the night his father murdered his mother, while he and his brother huddle help-lessly in the next room. Subsequently his father was arrested, tried, convicted, and sentenced to prison. He and his siblings went to live with relatives.

My friend lost both his father and his mother in a single night, and in the worst possible way. Nonetheless, God, who is "a father to the fatherless" (Psalm 68:5), comforted him. As he grew into adulthood, he felt a call on his life and prepared for the ministry. While serving his first church, he was privileged to lead his brother to the Lord. Shortly thereafter his father was released from prison and contacted him.

As he prepared to meet with his father, his emotions were all over the place. Sometimes he felt like a little boy again, sick with fear. At other times he was consumed with rage, with a desire to make his father pay. Of course there were times he wished his father would just disappear. What if his church found out what his father had done? It could ruin his ministry— or at least that's what the enemy tried to tell him.

The first meeting between father and son was hardly prom-ising. Although they were civil to each other it was clear that they were both uncomfortable. Nonetheless they agreed to meet again and thus began a series of meetings where, little by little, they were able to begin building a relationship of sorts. Finally came the moment my friend had been dreading—his father asked him if he could come to church. Reluctantly my friend agreed, although it was the last thing he wanted to do.

The following Sunday, when he stepped into the pulpit, he saw his father slip into the church and take a seat on the back row. He tried to ignore him while he preached, but it proved impossible. Again and again his eyes were drawn toward the solitary figure on the last pew. How small he looked now, how forlorn, how lost.

FATHER AND SON KNELT TOGETHER AT THE FOOT OF THE CROSS AND JESUS DID WHAT ONLY HE CAN DO—HE MADE ALL THINGS NEW!

Against his will, he felt compassion fill his heart and when he gave the invitation, he found himself praying earnestly for his father to respond. At last his father did and as he made his way toward the front of the church, something broke in my friend's heart. Stepping out from behind the pulpit he met his father at the altar. Father and son knelt together at the foot of the cross and Jesus did what only He can do—He made all things new!

If God could do that for my friend and his father then you can be sure He can redeem the worst thing that has ever happened to you!

The real question isn't, "What's the worst thing that's ever happened to you?" but, "What will you do? Will you trust the Lord to heal your hurts, to redeem your troubles, and to fulfill His purposes in your life, or will you take matters into your own hands?" How you answer that question is critically important for it will determine both your spiritual and emotional wholeness, as well as your destiny so choose wisely.

Chapter 10
My Proudest Moment

To write Bunko Babes, Leah had to battle a chronic and often debilitating illness, while being a wife and the mother of two small children. Still, she did it. Against all odds she wrote a novel and tonight I'm basking in the joy of her moment. My daughter is a published author!

Return with me one final time to the three questions that the psychiatrist asks each of his new clients. 1) What is the worst thing you have ever done? 2) What is the worst thing that ever happened to you? 3) What is the proudest moment of your life? Since we've already addressed the first two questions, let's turn our attention to the final question: "What is the proudest moment of your life?"

When I think of my proudest moment several memories come to mind. In the first, it is Christmas season and I see my wife, Brenda, standing in the checkout line at the Wal-Mart in Fayetteville, Arkansas. She greets the woman in front of her—an elderly lady of indiscriminate age, attired in stylish but well-worn clothes—and they chit-chat as they work their way toward the cash register. In a moment of vulnerability the lady confides to Brenda, "I hope I've added right. I only have $15 and I'm afraid my groceries will come to more than that."

Nervously, she places her few items on the checkout counter and clutches her purse. Catching the checker's eye, Brenda tells her to put the lady's groceries on her bill. Surprised and touched, the elderly lady protests, "You needn't do that honey. I can manage. If you want to help someone, give that money to a homeless shelter. Or maybe buy some homeless person a cup of coffee."

Despite her objections, Brenda insists on paying for her groceries and as she shuffles into the night, both Brenda and the checker dab at their eyes. Now as far as I'm concerned, that's the real Christmas spirit and truly a moment to be proud of!

In the second, it's a blustery winter evening as I pull into the parking lot in front of the Barnes and Noble bookstore in Tulsa, Oklahoma. Through the plate glass window I can see that a crowd has gathered and I feel my heart swell with pride. Our daughter's first novel has just been released and Barnes and Noble is hosting her first book signing. Picking up my digital camera from the back seat, I make my way toward the front door.

TO WRITE *BUNKO BABES* SHE HAD TO BATTLE A CHRONIC AND OFTEN DEBILITATING ILLNESS, WHILE BEING A WIFE AND THE MOTHER OF TWO SMALL CHILDREN. STILL, SHE DID IT. AGAINST ALL ODDS SHE WROTE A NOVEL.

Standing at the edge of the crowd, I shoot several pictures as Leah signs books and banters with those who have come to get their book autographed. She looks dazzling, as does Brenda, who is chatting with several of our friends who have come to help us celebrate. I should join them but I want to savor this moment a minute more. Writing a novel is a major accomplishment. Getting it published an even bigger one. I should know, having written a number of books myself. But in many ways what I have done pales in comparison to what Leah has accomplished. To write *Bunko Babes* she had to battle a chronic and often debilitating illness, while being a

64

wife and the mother of two small children. Still, she did it. Against all odds she wrote a novel and tonight I'm basking in the joy of her moment. My daughter is a published author!

In my next memory it is late spring, 1992. Our entire family—parents, siblings, spouses and children—have journeyed to Austin, Texas, where we attend the commencement exercises for the University of Texas. The graduation ceremony is tedious for the most part, and the afternoon drags on. Finally the PhD candidates are called. One by one they receive their degrees and are hooded. Finally I hear them call, "Robert James Exley." My chest swells with pride as I watch my youngest brother become the first person in our family to earn a doctorate. Now I am out of my seat and heading for the center aisle where I join him in a joyful embrace. I tell you the absolute truth: I couldn't have been happier, or prouder for that matter, if I had earned that doctorate myself.

Now another memory comes into focus and I see my sister lying on the bed beside our aged father. The doctors have given Dad no more than four weeks to live. Rather than put him in a hospice facility, Sherry has taken a leave of absence from her position as the administrative assistant to the president of the company, in order to help mother care for our father. Being the youngest child, and the only girl, she and Dad have always had a special relationship, making his imminent death especially difficult for her. Still, she serves without flinching, tucking her sorrow away in some secret place to be dealt with later, when Dad no longer needs her. In the few days I've been here, I've watched her fluff Dad's pillow, bring him fresh water, help him turn over to minimize the risk of

SHE PERFORMS EVEN THE MOST MENIAL TASK WITH A GRACE THAT TRANSFORMS IT INTO AN ACT OF LOVE. HER TIRELESS EFFORTS MAKE DAD'S LAST DAYS NOT ONLY BEARABLE, BUT ALSO BLESSED. TRULY SHE IS A SISTER TO BE PROUD OF!

bedsores, bathe him, and even empty his bedpan. Although her heart is breaking, she never complains. She performs even the most menial task with a grace that transforms it into an act of love. Her tireless efforts make Dad's last days not only bearable, but also blessed. Truly she is a sister to be proud of!

Indulge me one last time and then I'll be done. Now I see my brother Don preaching to several hundred missionaries in the chapel at Central Bible College in Springfield, Missouri. His anointed words lay bare the hurts and hopes of every missionary present. He is one of them. He understands them as only another missionary can. He's saying the things they've always felt, but never been able to put into words. When he finishes his message, I watch in amazement as scores of hurting missionaries fill the altars. God has used him to touch something deep within and many of them will never be the same. Carefully I make my way to the platform where Don is standing. For a moment I just stand there, nearly in awe of the anointing that continues to rest upon him. Finally, I wrap my arms around him and say, "I am so proud to be your brother."

Why, you may be wondering, do my proudest moments revolve around the achievements of those I love? Before I try to answer that question, let me confess that it hasn't always been that way. In fact, there have been seasons in my life when I was so full of myself that there was no room in my world for anyone else. Still, the Lord refused to give up on me. Patiently He worked with me, chipping away at my self-centered pride. Year, after year, after year, until, at last, something of His likeness began to be formed in me. Now I can truly rejoice with those who rejoice (at least most of the time), even if their achievements dwarf my own, which they almost always do.

And if compliments come my way, I'm always careful to pass them on to the One to whom all glory belongs. It's a discipline I learned from Corrie ten Boom. When she received a compliment she would say, "Thank you. I'll put that in my bouquet." When asked to explain she said, "I think of every compliment as a flower. At the end of the day I arrange them into a bouquet and present them to Jesus."

Presenting them to Jesus is truly my proudest moment!

Chapter 11
Bank Failures and Bailouts

By giving people a hand out rather than a hand up, we have created dependency and a sense of entitlement. Rather than helping the poor achieve the American Dream, we have simply locked them into a cycle of poverty.

A s President George W. Bush's second term was drawing to a close, the United States experienced the greatest financial meltdown since Black Tuesday, nearly seventy years earlier. Some of the biggest investment banks failed and Congress passed a 700 billion dollar bailout to prevent a total financial collapse. Nearly ten years later many of us are still asking, "How could something like that happen? Who's to blame? What's to prevent it from happening again?"

Affixing blame, however, is simply an exercise in futility unless it focuses on learning from our mistakes and not just denigrating those who are most responsible. In truth, there is enough blame to go around. Some of the most obvious culprits—self-serving CEOs, greedy speculators, mortgage banks pushing subprime loans with adjustable rate mortgages, unprincipled real estate agents, naive homebuyers, and shortsighted politicians. They all share in the responsibility to one degree or another.

DANCING IN THE DARK

Obviously economics are not my forte, and the intricacies of the ongoing worldwide economic crisis are beyond me, so what I say here should be interpreted in light of that. Still, having offered that disclaimer, I would like to venture an opinion in regard to what should be done; not simply to solve the present crisis but to minimize the risk in the future.

First, given man's fallen nature and the inherit perils of power; some form of accountability (regulation) is absolutely mandatory. Left to his own devices a man (or a corporation) will almost always look out for himself first. Well it has been said, "Power corrupts and absolute power corrupts absolutely." That's true whether we are talking about union bosses, CEOs, mortgage bankers, politicians, or the person in the mirror.

WE MUST RETURN TO SOUND BIBLICAL PRINCIPLES WHEN CONDUCTING BUSINESS, ESPECIALLY WHEN IT COMES TO LENDING MONEY AND CHARGING INTEREST.

Secondly, we must return to sound biblical principles when conducting business, especially when it comes to lending money and charging interest. The Bible calls excessive interest usury and it is strictly forbidden in scripture. Nehemiah 5:11 declares, ". . . let the exacting of usury stop! Give back to them immediately their fields, vineyards, olive groves and houses, and also the usury you are charging them. . . ."

By throwing credit cards at people and then charging exorbitant and compounded interest, the banks have made debt slaves of millions of Americans. By making sub-prime loans that convert into usurious adjustable rate mortgages, the banks made foreclosures inevitable. It appears that mortgage banks hoped to make a killing on such loans by collecting fees up front, collecting usurious rates of interest when the ARM kicked in, and finally by foreclosing on properties that had appreciated when the borrower could not repay his mortgage. The only fly in the ointment was the greed of the lenders. Apparently they never anticipated the excessive number of foreclosures and the impact they would have on the housing market and on their balance sheets. Perhaps they should have read Proverbs 28:8, "He who increases his wealth by exorbitant interest amasses it for another. . . ."

Thirdly we must re-examine our responsibility to the poor. The "Great Society" envisioned by President Lyndon Johnson is simply not working. History has shown that although his intentions may have been noble, his plan was flawed. By giving people a hand out rather than a hand up, we have created dependency and a sense of entitlement. Rather than helping the poor achieve the American Dream, we have simply locked them in a cycle of poverty.

> BY GIVING PEOPLE A HAND OUT RATHER THAN A HAND UP, WE HAVE CREATED DEPENDENCY AND A SENSE OF ENTITLEMENT. RATHER THAN HELPING THE POOR ACHIEVE THE AMERICAN DREAM, WE HAVE SIMPLY LOCKED THEM IN A CYCLE OF POVERTY.

Good intentions are not enough. Our relationship to the poor must be guided not only by compassion, but also by scripture. The poor in the scripture were not those who would not work, but those who had no way of providing for themselves. This included the widows, the orphans, and the handicapped. Even these, if they were physically able, were expected to help provide for themselves. At harvest time they went behind the gleaners picking up what was deliberately left behind. Leviticus 19:9-10 declares, "When you reap the harvest of your land, do not reap to the very edges of your field or gather the gleanings of your harvest. Do not go over your vineyard a second time or pick up the grapes that have fallen. Leave them for the poor and the alien."

The principle is clear: those of us who have been blessed must make sure that the poor (the widows and the orphans) are given an opportunity to share in the blessing. We are not to harvest it for them but we are commanded to give them an opportunity to share in the harvest.

How that works in the twenty-first century remains to be seen, but I am convinced that if we can get the guiding principles right, the strategic details can be fleshed out. I know I am being simplistic, but I would like to see welfare linked to work. Our inner cities are in desperate need of cleaning up and renovating. Welfare recipients could learn a trade while helping renovate their neighborhoods and building playgrounds and parks. They could develop a work ethic, take pride in their accomplishments, contribute to their neighborhoods, and provide for themselves and their families. Now that's the real American Dream; not something for nothing but an opportunity to make something of yourself.

In closing let me remind you that no matter what happens in the days ahead our best hope, maybe our only hope, is Jesus Christ. The psalmist put it this way:

Blessed is the man who fears the Lord, who finds great delight in his commands. His children will be mighty in the land; the generation of the upright will be blessed. Wealth and riches are in his house, and his righteousness endures forever. Even in darkness light dawns for the upright, for the gracious and compassionate and righteous man. Good will come to him who is generous and lends freely, who conducts his affairs with justice. Surely he will never be shaken; a righteous man will be remembered forever. He will have no fear of bad news; his heart is steadfast, trusting in the Lord. His heart is secure, he will have no fear; in the end he will look in triumph on his foes. He has scattered abroad his gifts to the poor, his righteousness endures forever; his horn will be lifted high in honor. (Psalm 112:1-9 NIV)

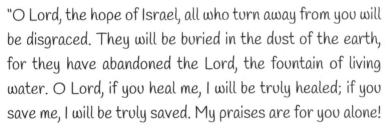

Chapter 12

One Nation under God

"O Lord, the hope of Israel, all who turn away from you will be disgraced. They will be buried in the dust of the earth, for they have abandoned the Lord, the fountain of living water. O Lord, if you heal me, I will be truly healed; if you save me, I will be truly saved. My praises are for you alone!

—Jeremiah 17:13–14 NLT

Two hundred and forty-one years ago, the Continental Congress was meeting in Philadelphia for the purpose of drafting the Declaration of Independence—a document that would ultimately give birth to the United States of America. Although the resolution was formally adopted on July 4, 1776, it was not until July 8 that two of the states authorized their delegates to sign it, and it was not until August 2 that the signers met in Philadelphia to actually put their names on the Declaration.

Each of the fifty-six men who signed it knew they were committing an act of treason against the king—an act punishable by death. Still, with a firm reliance on the protection of God Almighty, they mutually pledged to each other their lives, their fortunes, and their sacred honor. Nine died of wounds or hardships during the Revolutionary War. Five were captured and imprisoned, in each case with brutal treatment. Several lost wives, children, or entire families. One lost his thirteen children. Two wives were brutally treated. All were at one time or another the victims of manhunts and driven from their homes. Twelve signers had their homes completely burned. Seventeen lost everything they owned. Yet not one defected or went back on his pledged word. Because of their vision, their courage, and their sacrifice, we are privileged to live in the United States of America!

STEPHAN HOPKINS, ELLERY'S COLLEAGUE FROM RHODE ISLAND, WAS A MAN PAST 60. AS HE SIGNED WITH A SHAKING PEN, HE DECLARED: "MY HAND TREMBLES, BUT MY HEART DOES NOT."

William Ellery, a delegate from Rhode Island, watched with interest as each delegate signed the document—a supreme act of personal courage. Although some of the delegates signed their names quickly, Ellery said he could discern no real fear in any man. Stephan Hopkins, Ellery's colleague from Rhode Island, was a man past 60. As he signed with a shaking pen, he declared: "My hand trembles, but my heart does not."

The question I would like you to consider is simply this: What kind of nation did those 56 men envision? Does the 2017 version of the United States of America bear any resemblance to what they had in mind when they decided to risk their fortunes and even their lives? Do you think that in their wildest imaginings they could have imagined that the Constitution and the Bill of Rights would be used to remove prayer and Bible reading from public schools, justify abortion on demand, legalize same-sex marriage, and give special rights to gays, bisexuals, and those who identify themselves as transgender? Do you really think they could have envisioned that the Supreme Court would invoke rulings removing displays of the Ten Commandments from courtrooms, schoolhouses, and other municipal buildings? I think not—but that is exactly what has happened.

I am convinced, by both history and faith, that the United States of America was ordained by the providence of God. I haven't always believed this. Like many of you, I am a product of the public education system—an educational system that in the last half-century has consistently ignored, or misrepresented, a significant portion of our American history. For instance, the public educational system taught me that the vast majority of the Founding Fathers were deists—that is they believed in God the creator but they did not have a personal relationship with Jesus Christ.

> I AM CONVINCED, BY BOTH HISTORY AND FAITH, THAT THE UNITED STATES OF AMERICA WAS ORDAINED BY THE PROVIDENCE OF GOD.

That's simply not true. Fifty-two out of the fifty-six men who signed the Declaration of Independence were committed Christians! Not deists as historical revisionists like to claim, but orthodox Christians. Like all of us they were flawed human beings with feet of clay, but that in no way nullifies their faith in Jesus Christ. Consider Thomas Jefferson, who wrote, "I too have made a wee little book, from the same materials, which I call the *Philosophy of Jesus*. It is a paradigma of his doctrines, made by cutting the texts out of the book [Bible], and arranging them on the pages of a blank book, in a certain order of time or subject. A more beautiful or precious morsel of ethics I have never seen. It is a document in proof that I am a real Christian, that is to say, a disciple of the doctrines of Jesus. . . ."[7]

Although George Washington did not sign the Declaration of Independence, he is considered the father of our country and he was our first president. He wrote in his personal prayer book: "Oh, eternal and everlasting God, direct my thoughts, words and work. Wash away my sins in the immaculate blood of the lamb and purge my heart by the Holy Spirit. Daily, frame me more and more in the likeness of thy son, Jesus Christ, that living in thy fear, and dying in thy favor, I may in thy appointed time obtain the resurrection of the justified unto eternal life.

"IT CANNOT BE
EMPHASIZED TOO
STRONGLY OR TOO
OFTEN THAT THIS
GREAT NATION WAS
FOUNDED, NOT BY
RELIGIONISTS
[PLURALISM], BUT BY
CHRISTIANS; NOT ON
RELIGION, BUT ON
THE GOSPEL OF
JESUS CHRIST!"

Bless, O Lord, the whole race of mankind and let the world be filled with the knowledge of thy son, Jesus Christ."[8]

Patrick Henry, the man who said, "Give me liberty or give me death," also wrote, "It cannot be emphasized too strongly or too often that this great nation was founded, not by religionists [pluralism], but by Christians; not on religion, but on the gospel of Jesus Christ!"[9]

The founders were knowledgeable in the Scriptures and turned to them not only for personal guidance and strength, but also for wisdom as they struggled to birth a nation based on spiritual principles. For instance, our three branches of government were based on Isaiah 33:22: "For the Lord is our judge (judicial branch), the Lord is our lawgiver (legislative branch), the Lord is our king (executive branch)." Tax exemptions for churches came out of Ezra 7:24: "You are also to know that you have no authority to impose taxes, tribute or duty on any of the priests, Levites, musicians, gatekeepers, temple servants or other workers at this house of God."

"Political Science professors at the University of Houston wondered if there was something unique about the government of the U.S. They gathered 15,000 quotes from the founders and located where all of them came from. They then boiled that down to 3,154 quotes that had significant impact on the founding of America. It took them ten years to finish the project, but they found that the three men most quoted by the Founding Fathers were Blackstone, Montesquieu, and John Locke. They also found that the Bible was quoted 4 times more often than Montesquieu, 12 times more often than Blackstone, and 16 times more often than Locke.

"Additionally, 34 percent of all quotes were from the Bible, and another 60 percent of the quotes were from men who were using the Bible to arrive at their conclusions. Added together, 94 percent of all the quotes of the founders had their origin in the Bible, which shows the importance of God's Word in their lives and of this Nation's founding."[10]

Did the public education system tell you that immediately after adopting the Declaration of Independence, the Continental Congress created the American Bible Society and voted to purchase and import 20,000 copies of Scripture for the people of this nation? Probably not, but that is exactly what they did.[11] Given that fact, the founders must have turned over in their graves when 10-year-old James Gierke of Omaha, Nebraska, was prohibited from reading his Bible silently during free time at school . . . [in fact] he was forbidden by his teacher to open his Bible at school and was told doing so was against the law."[12]

Did the public education system tell you that prayer was what finally enabled the delegates meeting in Independence Hall in Philadelphia in 1787 to create the Constitution of these United States? Probably not. History, however, records that on June 28, 81-year-old Benjamin Franklin addressed the convention:

". . . The small progress we have made after four or five weeks [is] melancholy proof of the imperfection of the Human Understanding." Rather than mere human understanding, the delegates needed something more: ". . . the Father of lights to illuminate our understandings!" He reminded the delegates that during the Revolutionary War they had prayed regularly to God in that very Hall: "Our prayers, Sir, were heard, and they were graciously answered." All of them could remember God's intervention on their behalf, and to that intervention they owed their victory over Great Britain. "And have we forgotten that powerful friend? Or do we imagine that we no longer need his assistance? I have lived, Sir, a long time, and the longer I live, the more convincing proofs I see of the truth—that God governs in the affairs of men. And if a sparrow cannot fall to the ground without his notice, is it probable that an empire can rise without his aid? We have been assured, Sir, in the sacred writing, that 'except the Lord build the House they labor in vain that build it.' I firmly believe this; and I also believe that without his concurring aid we shall succeed in this political building, no better than the builders of Babel." Franklin then suggested daily prayers, led by one or more Philadelphia clergymen. As a result of those prayers our constitution was written.[13]

Given our nation's rich spiritual heritage how did we get here? How did we get to the place that everything imaginable, every unspeakable degeneracy, every shameful debauchery, is not only tolerated, but celebrated, while Christians and Christianity are denigrated at every turn? There is any number of explanations, but one of the root causes is the misinterpretation and misapplication of the phrase "the separation of church and state." For instance, those who oppose any public display of Christianity have used the "separation argument" to secure such absurd rulings as the 1981 *Collins v. Chandler Unified School District* ruling that said, "Freedom of speech and press is guaranteed to students unless the topic is religious, at which time such speech becomes unconstitutional."[14]

GIVEN OUR NATION'S RICH SPIRITUAL HERITAGE HOW DID WE GET HERE? HOW DID WE GET TO THE PLACE THAT EVERYTHING IMAGINABLE, EVERY UNSPEAKABLE DEGENERACY, EVERY SHAMEFUL DEBAUCHERY, IS NOT ONLY TOLERATED, BUT CELEBRATED, WHILE CHRISTIANS AND CHRISTIANITY ARE DENIGRATED AT EVERY TURN?

Would it surprise you to learn that nowhere in the Constitution or in the Amendments thereof do the words "a wall of separation between church and state" appear? Rather they are part of a letter that President Jefferson wrote to the Baptist Association of Danbury, Connecticut, on January 1, 1802, assuring them of a wall separating church and state that would prevent the Federal government from interfering in the affairs of the church. Jefferson never intended to exclude the church from the public square or from using its influence to shape the nation's morals and/or public policy. In fact, he would be appalled at how his words have been misinterpreted and misapplied. It was not until 145 years later that it was applied as a principal of law in the 1947 *Everson v. Board of Education* case. Since then, the Court has used it for a myriad of rulings that have reversed long-standing national traditions and brainwashed entire generations of American citizens.

Contrary to prevailing public opinion, our Founding Fathers never thought their personal faith could or should be separated from their public life. John Jay, the first Chief Justice of the United States Supreme Court, believed that if we were to preserve our Nation we must select Christians as our national leaders. "Providence," he said, "has given to our people the choice of their rulers and it is the duty as well as the privilege and interest of our Christian Nation to select and prefer Christians for their rulers."[15]

His personal faith in the Lord Jesus Christ is clearly evident in his Last Will and Testament: "Unto Him who is the author and giver of all good, I render sincere and humble thanks for His merciful and unmerited blessings, and especially for our redemption and salvation by his beloved Son."[16]

Apparently John Jay wasn't the only founder who felt it was imperative to elect Christians to lead this new nation, for immediately following the signing of the Declaration of Independence, the Founding Fathers returned home and started writing their state constitutions. What they wrote clearly reflected their strong Christian faith and the role it played in government. For instance, Delaware's constitution said: "Every person . . . appointed to any office or place of trust . . . shall . . . make and subscribe the following declaration, to wit: 'I, (name), do profess faith in God the Father, and in Jesus Christ His only Son and in the Holy Ghost, one God, blessed for evermore; and I do acknowledge the holy scriptures of the Old and New Testament to be given my divine inspiration.'"[17]

North Carolina made an even stronger statement: "No person, who shall deny the being of God, or the truth of the protestant religion, or the divine authority either of the Old or New Testaments, or who shall hold religious principles incompatible with the freedom and safety of the state, shall be capable of holding any office, or place of trust or profit in the civil department, with this state."[18]

In an address to military leaders, John Adams, our second president, who also served as chairman of the American Bible Society, said, "We have no government armed with the power capable of contending with human passions, unbridled by morality and true religion. Our constitution was made only for a moral and religious people. It is wholly inadequate to the government of any other."[19]

It is impossible for any thinking person to deny how radically different the moral values of the twenty-first century are from those held by the Founding Fathers. They recognized the wisdom of Scripture and humanity's absolute dependence on God Almighty, especially in the discharge of government. In 2017, if a person appeals to the Scriptures or his religious faith in a discussion regarding politics or government he is considered a religious fanatic or worse yet, an intolerant bigot. So how did we get here?

In 1963, the Supreme Court issued a ruling in *Murray v. Curlett* arguing that the Founding Fathers wanted a "wall of separation between church and State;" therefore, the government should be neutral to religion in schools, and as a result the Warren Court ruled that there would be no prayer in school or Bible reading. The court's "majority ruling" reasoned that being neutral or not favoring one religion over another was the same as not allowing religious practices in school. Justice Potter Stewart, the one dissenting vote blasted the ruling saying, "It led not to true neutrality with respect to religion, but to the establishment of a religion of secularism."[20]

William J. Murray, the student in *Murray v. Curlett* school prayer case, writes in his book *Let Us Pray*, 'The original First Amendment guarantee to every citizen, of the right to free religious expression without consequence or state interference, was transformed. This remarkable process, which took many years and many court decisions, turned the First Amendment inside out."[21]

In 1980, *Stone v. Graham* outlawed the display of the Ten Commandments in our public schools. In its ruling the Supreme Court said: "If the posted copies of the Ten Commandments are to have any effect at all, it will be to induce the schoolchildren to read, meditate upon, perhaps to venerate and obey, the Commandments. However desirable this might be as a matter of private devotion, it is not a permissible state objective under the Establishment Clause of the Constitution."

When you take God out of government—as has been systematically happening since the 1960s—you destroy a nation's moral compass. Without moral absolutes government has no consistent basis for making and enforcing laws. Laws become the expressions of political whim and you end up with the absurd. For instance in Fargo, North Dakota, an expectant mother was put in jail to keep her from endangering the child in

WITHOUT MORAL ABSOLUTES GOVERNMENT HAS NO CONSISTENT BASIS FOR MAKING AND ENFORCING LAWS.

her womb through her excessive drinking. Yet the same court that put her in jail to protect her child from Fetal Alcohol Syndrome released her from jail so she could have her child put to death by abortion.

Given the absurdity of these and a myriad of other similar rulings, is it any wonder our nation is in the condition it is? We have sown to the wind and we are reaping the whirlwind (Hosea 8:7). The sexual revolution has produced an epidemic of sexually transmitted diseases. More than 20 STDs have been identified and they affect an estimated 19 million men and women in this country each year. The annual treatment cost of STDs in the United States is estimated to be in excess of $14 billion. After steadily rising for five decades, the share of children born to unmarried women in the United States has crossed a threshold—more than half of births to American women under 30 occur outside marriage. Then there is abortion. To date we have killed 58 million children before birth. Drug addiction is rampant and mass murders have become so common we are becoming desensitized to them. And now there appears to be a war on the police.

As tragic as the moral and spiritual condition of our culture is, it is not unexpected. Any reasonably knowledgeable student of Scripture knows the degeneracy of our present age was predicted long ago.

2 Timothy 3:1-5 says: "But mark this: There will be terrible times in the last days. People will be lovers of themselves, lovers of money, boastful, proud, abusive, disobedient to their parents, ungrateful, unholy, without love, unforgiving, slanderous, without self-control, brutal, not lovers of the good, treacherous, rash, conceited, lovers of pleasure rather than lovers of God—having a form of godliness but denying its power. Have nothing to do with such people" (2 Timothy 3:1-5 NIV).

The Apostle Paul could have been describing our culture when he penned Romans 1:28-32: "Furthermore, just as they did not think it worthwhile to retain the knowledge of God, so God gave them over to a depraved mind, so that they do what ought not to be done. They have become filled with every kind of wickedness, evil, greed, and depravity. They are full of envy, murder, strife, deceit, and malice. They are gossips, slanderers, God-haters, insolent, arrogant, and boastful; they invent ways of doing evil; they disobey their parents; they have no understanding, no fidelity, no love, no mercy. Although they know God's righteous decree that those who do such things deserve death, they not only continue to do these very things but also approve of those who practice them" (Romans 1:28-32 NIV).

Please do not misunderstand me. I love the United States of America and I thank God for the privilege of being born here. We are of all people most blessed. But that does not make me blind to the fact that as a nation we have forsaken the Lord. We have called evil good (Isaiah 5:20) and made a mockery out of the biblical values upon which our nation was founded. The only thing that stands between the United States and the judgment of Almighty God is the prayers of God's holy people. I challenge you to fall on your knees and intercede for our country with humility and repentance.

> THE ONLY THING THAT STANDS BETWEEN THE UNITED STATES AND THE JUDGMENT OF ALMIGHTY GOD IS THE PRAYERS OF GOD'S HOLY PEOPLE.

Let Daniel be your example. Although he lived in the sixth century before Christ, in many ways his early experiences parallel our own. He was a citizen of Judea, whose capital was Jerusalem, and he was one of God's chosen people. By all accounts he was a godly young man, unfortunately that did not spare him from the plight that befell his country. Judea had forsaken the Lord and as a result they suffered the judgments of God. King Nebuchadnezzar and the Babylonian army invaded Judea. They sacked and burned the city of Jerusalem, plundered the land and took thousands of Judeans into exile in Babylon including Daniel.

Yet Daniel remained faithful to His God. Even in Babylon he remembered Jerusalem and prayed for the restoration of Judea and the rebuilding of the holy city. He says, ". . . I turned to the Lord God and pleaded with him in prayer and petition, in fasting, and in sackcloth and ashes" (Daniel 9:3).

His prayer was characterized by two great truths. 1) His confidence in the faithfulness of God—"I prayed to the LORD my God: 'Lord, the great and awesome God, who keeps his covenant of love with those who love him and keep his commandments,'" (Daniel 9:4). 2) His consistency in taking responsibility for the sinfulness of his people including the rulers, the priests and prophets, and ordinary citizens. Hear his confession: "I prayed to the LORD my God and confessed: '. . . We have sinned and done wrong. We have been wicked and have rebelled; we have turned away from your commands and laws'" (Daniel 9:5).

God's faithfulness gave Daniel the confidence to intercede, to trust God to intervene, in spite of the sinfulness of the people of Judea. Their collective sinfulness gave him the humility to pray with fasting, and in sackcloth and ashes. He never tried to rationalize or make excuses for their wickedness, rather he confessed with brutal honesty, throwing himself on the mercies of God.

"Lord, you are righteous, but this day we are covered with shame—the people of Judah [the United States] and the inhabitants of Jerusalem [Washington DC] and all Israel [the United States], both near and far . . . We and our kings [Presidents], our princes [elected officials] and our ancestors are covered with shame, LORD, because we have sinned against you . . . Lord, in keeping with all your righteous acts, turn away your anger and your wrath from Jerusalem [Washington DC], your city, your holy hill. Now, our God, hear the prayers and petitions of your servant. For your sake, Lord, look with favor on your desolate sanctuary. Give ear, our God, and hear; open

your eyes and see the desolation of the city that bears your Name. We do not make requests of you because we are righteous, but because of your great mercy. Lord, listen! Lord, forgive! Lord, hear and act! For your sake, my God, do not delay, because your city and your people bear your Name" (Daniel 9:7-8,16-19 NIV).

Daniel's prayer was answered and that gives me hope for the United States. After 70 years ". . . the LORD moved the heart of Cyrus king of Persia to make a proclamation throughout his realm and also to put it in writing" (Ezra 1:1). His proclamation permitted the Judean exiles to return to their country and to rebuild the temple in Jerusalem. Furthermore, "...in any locality where survivors may now be living, the people are to provide them with silver and gold, with goods and livestock, and with freewill offerings for the temple of God in Jerusalem" (Ezra 1:4).

Still, I can't help wondering if it is too late for the United States? I hope not but I must confess that I am not optimistic. It is hard for me to imagine a scenario where the Supreme Court would reverse the numerous rulings that have been adversarial toward Christian values. Given current attitudes regarding morality, homosexuality, abortion, and same-sex marriages, it's hard for me to envision society returning to biblical values. There's no politician or political party that can make America great again—only God can do that. America's only hope is a spiritual awakening that will transform the hearts and minds of its citizens.[22]

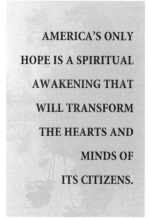

AMERICA'S ONLY HOPE IS A SPIRITUAL AWAKENING THAT WILL TRANSFORM THE HEARTS AND MINDS OF ITS CITIZENS.

"O LORD, if you heal me, I will be truly healed; if you save me, I will be truly saved. My praises are for you alone!" (Jeremiah 17:14 NLT).

[7] Adams, Dickinson W., ed. *Jefferson's Extracts from the Gospels: "The Philosophy of Jesus" and "The Life and Morals of Jesus."* Princeton, N.J.: Princeton University Press, 1983, pp, 364-365.

[8] www.foundingfatherquotes.com/quote/676.

[9] *The Trumpet Voice of Freedom: Patrick Henry of Virginia,* www.americas-foundingfathers.wordpress.com/2010/11/26/

[10] Os Hillman, "Change Agent: Engaging Your Passion to Be the One Who Makes a Difference" (Creation House, 2011) pp. 128-129.

[11] Dave Miller, Ph.D., "Much Respect for the Quran—Not Much for the Bible" (Apologetics Press. http://www.apologeticspress.org/APContent.aspx?category=7&article=1525&topic=44).

[12] IFA Newsletter, February 1989, "Fifth Grader Sues for Right to Read Bible."

[13] John Eidsmoe, "Christianity and the Constitution" (Grand Rapids: Baker Books, 1987), Kindle edition location 45.

[14] *Collins v. Chandler Unified School District;* 644 F. 2d 759, cert. denied, 454 U.S. 849, (1981).

[15] www.faithofourfathers.net/jay.html

[16] American Minute with Bill Federer, May 17 John Jay first Supreme Court Chief Justice, President of Bible Society

[17] The Avalon Project: Documents in Law, History, and Diplomacy, Yale Law School, Lillian Goldman Law Library, Constitution of Delaware, 1776.

[18] *The Founding Faith Archive,* North Carolina Constitution 1776.

[19] The Quotations Page, www.quotationspage.com, Quotation #14102 from *Classic Quotes:*

[20] http://www.free2pray.info/2schoolprayerrulings.html

[21] Ibid.

[22] When Pastor Joe Wright of Central Christian Church in Wichita, Kansas, was invited to pray to open the new session of the Kansas Senate some years ago everyone was expecting the usual generalities, but they were wrong.

Pastor Wright prayed: "Heavenly Father, we come before You today to ask Your forgiveness and to seek Your direction and guidance. We know Your Word says, 'Woe to those who call evil good' (Isaiah 5:20), but that is exactly what we have done. We have lost our spiritual equilibrium and reversed our values. We have exploited the poor and called it the lottery. We have rewarded laziness and called it welfare. We have killed our unborn and called it choice. We have shot abortionists and called it justifiable. We have neglected to discipline our children and called it building self-esteem. We have abused power and called it politics. We have coveted our neighbor's possessions and called it ambition. We have polluted the air with profanity and pornography and called it freedom of expression. We have ridiculed the time-honored values of our forefathers and called it enlightenment. Search us, oh God, and know our hearts today; cleanse us from every sin and set us free. Amen."

Chapter 13

Unintended Consequences

Liberal politicians, jurists, and even educators insist that there are no moral absolutes—creating a society where each person is a law unto himself.

Sometimes good people make poor choices that result in unintended consequences. Maybe you've done that. I know I have. Sometimes principled people make misguided decisions that produce unintended consequences. The more powerful the people making the decisions, the more far reaching the consequences—even the unintended ones.

I suspect this is what happened in the case of *Roe v. Wade*, the infamous 1973 Supreme Court decision that legalized abortion on demand. I cannot imagine that the seven Supreme Court justices who voted to legalize abortion intended to set in motion forces that would result in nearly fifty-eight million babies being put to death before birth, but they did. I cannot believe cruelty was the motivating factor or that they harbored a hatred of children. Laying aside the finer points of law, which in this case seem misinterpreted to me, I truly believe

THE MORE POWER-FUL THE PEOPLE MAKING THE DECI-SIONS, THE MORE FAR REACHING THE CONSEQUENCES—EVEN THE UNIN-TENDED ONES.

DANCING IN THE DARK

they were motivated by a misguided compassion. They wanted to help women and thought they were, but they were wrong.

Laying aside the deaths of fifty-eight million innocent children for a moment, let's consider some of the other unintended consequences. The decision to have an abortion is gut-wrenching. It is usually made when the pregnant woman is in a crisis and more often than not leaves her psychologically damaged for life. The law may tell her she has the right to choose to have her baby put to death before birth, but in her heart of hearts she knows it is wrong, and she has to live with that knowledge.

Linda Cochrane eloquently expresses the unrelenting pain of abortion's aftermath when she writes: "If abortion is so right, why am I feeling guilty and seeking help from psychiatrists and feminist therapists? If abortion is so right, why am I needing increased amounts of alcohol and drugs to numb the pain? If abortion is so right, why am I so depressed that I think of suicide as a way out? If abortion isn't the death of a baby, why am I grieving?"[23]

Another victim of abortion says, "When I was eighteen years old . . . I had an abortion . . . and the last two years of my life have been a nightmare. . . . Sometimes I just lie in bed all day long, too depressed to get up. I buy baby clothes and toys. In fact, I have a room full of baby accessories. I see children everywhere I go . . . I don't feel any less guilty today (two years later) than the day I had the abortion. My memories haven't faded . . . I've tried alcohol, drugs, and relationships. Nothing will ever take away my loss or the memories, not even for a little while."[24]

ABORTION IS AN ACT OF VIOLENCE AGAINST BOTH THE MOTHER AND HER UNBORN CHILD.

This being the case we can only conclude that abortion is an act of violence against both the mother and her unborn child. The psychological damage the mother suffers as a result of aborting her baby is an unintended consequence of the most grievous kind. That's why pro-life organizations all over the country now provide post-abortion healing groups.

Another unintended consequence is the Social Security crisis. If the present trend continues, we will see an increasingly disproportionate number of workers trying to underwrite the social security program. In 1980 there were 3.5 workers for every retired person. By the year 2020 that number will be 2, and by 2040, it will only be 1.5. One does not have to be an economics expert to understand that will not work.

An equally tragic, but much less obvious consequence— unintended of course—is the unparalleled increase in domestic violence and child abuse in the wake of that misguided decision forty-four years ago, not to mention the random killing sprees on school campuses, in shopping malls, and now in churches.

Anyone who watches the national news knows that mass murder in the United States has increased exponentially in recent years. The graphic images are indelibly imprinted on our minds. Who could ever forget the sight of frightened students fleeing from Columbine High School where two classmates gunned down twelve students and one teacher, or the emergency vehicles and grieving parents surrounding a one-room Amish School house in Lancaster, Pennsylvania, where five school children, all girls, were killed execution style by Charles Carl Roberts IV? Then there's the image of thousands of Virginia Tech students at a candlelight vigil following the murder of thirty-two of their classmates by Seung-Hui Cho.

There's more, many more. On March 20, 2009, Robert Stewart entered a nursing home in Carthage, N.C., and opened fire on residents, killing seven of them along with one nursing home employee. And on April 3, 2009, Jiverly Wong, armed with two handguns, went on a killing rampage at an immigration center in Binghamton, N.Y. According to police reports, he fired

98 shots, killing 13 people before taking his own life. Let me mention one more—the Sandy Hook Elementary School shooting in Newtown, Connecticut. On December 14, 2012, Adam Lanza shot and killed twenty-six people, including 20 first grade children before taking his own life.

Of course murder is nothing new. From the time Cain killed Able until now the human race has a long history of cold-blooded atrocities. Still, there seems to be something different, something more sinister about the random killings being perpetrated by these troubled young men. For the most part their killing sprees were not prompted by religious fanaticism or political ideology or even personal revenge. Their victims were strangers by and large—innocent victims—and seemed to be chosen at random.

Mark Kopta, chairman and professor in the department of psychology at the University of Evansville in Indiana, has researched extensively the country's mass killings, which he defines as attacks leading to the deaths of at least five people, including the killer's suicide. He found three incidents in the United States fitting this profile between 1930 and 1970. Three more followed over the course of the 1970s. In the 1980s, however, there were ten such incidents of mass murder. The 1990s had seventeen. A report released by the FBI stated that between 2000 and 2006 there were on average 6.4 mass shootings a year. From 2007 to 2013 that number rose to an average of 16.4 a year. Since the beginning of the new millennium, 486 people have been killed in such shootings with 366 of the deaths in the past seven years (2000-2013).

So what's going on? Why this sudden rise in mass killings? Are they just a statistical fluke or might they be an unintended consequence of *Roe v. Wade*?

There are no easy explanations, no pat answers. The conditions conspiring to produce these troubled young men are varied and complex. The entertainment industry continues to produce video games, music, and movies that glorify violence. Liberal politicians, jurists, and even educators insist that there are no moral absolutes—creating a society where each person is a law unto himself. Corruption in high places, within business, government, and the church, has produced a jaded cynicism in young and old alike. Then there's the economic meltdown of recent years and the resulting despair. Finally there is rampant divorce and the resulting dissolution of the traditional family, creating a generation of lost souls.

> AMERICA MADE A COVENANT WITH DEATH ON JANUARY 22, 1973 WHEN THE UNITED STATES SUPREME COURT RULED 7-2, IN THE NOW INFAMOUS *ROE V. WADE* DECISION LEGALIZING ABORTION ON DEMAND, AND WE ARE NOW REAPING THE UNINTENDED CONSEQUENCES.

While all of these are contributing factors I do not believe they are the root cause. In my opinion the root cause is spiritual rather than sociological or even psychological. America made a covenant with death on January 22, 1973 when the United States Supreme Court ruled 7-2, in the now infamous *Roe v. Wade* decision legalizing abortion on demand, and we are now reaping the unintended consequences. When the highest court in the land rules that killing the child in your womb is an acceptable way of dealing with your unplanned pregnancy, we shouldn't be surprised when children reared in a culture of death turn to murder and suicide when life becomes overwhelming.

What, you may be wondering, can we do? How can we reverse this tragic trend? Since the root cause is spiritual it demands a spiritual response.

1) Intercession: Since we do not contend with physical foes, but spiritual ones, our weapons must be spiritual rather than the weapons of the world (2 Corinthians 10:3-5). In prayer we must

bind the spiritual forces that are operating behind the scenes and only then can we see men and women set free. Remember, Jesus said that before we can spoil the strong man's house we must first bind him (Matthew 12:29). We must bind the spirit of death and we can only accomplish this through intercessory prayer.

2) Evangelism: Those who do not know Christ, even those who have become mass murderers, are not our enemies but our mission. We are called to love them into the Kingdom.

3) Reformation (Spirit directed social action): As evangelism redeems the individual, so Spirit-directed social action redeems the institutions of society, restoring them to their God-given purpose.

Remember, we are not holy warriors doing battle with those whose values and lifestyles are different from ours, but holy lovers who turn the other cheek, who go the second mile, who do unto others as we would have them do unto us. No matter how strident those who hate the cause of Christ become, let us always live lives that reflect the love of Him who laid down His life for us.

One last thing—some of you may be living with the unintended consequences of a poor choice you made years ago. Try as you might you cannot forgive yourself or move on with your life. I bring you good news! Christ has redeemed us from the curse of our sinful mistakes by suffering the curse for us (see Galatians 3:13-14). You can't undo the past. Not even God can do that, but His forgiveness does unlock the future. Since He has forgiven you, you are now free to forgive yourself.

---

[23] "Post-Abortion Syndrome," an article in the advertising supplement of an Oklahoma City newspaper, produced and paid for by Life Issues, Inc. January 1989, p. 9.

[24] "Memories of My Abortion," an article in the advertising supplement of an Oklahoma City newspaper, produced and paid for by Life Issues, Inc. January 1989, p. 9.

Chapter 14

The Painted Parable

Without Christ we are all part of that anonymous crowd—nameless, faceless people, lacking distinction and detail. But when we turn to Him, He covers the canvas of our lives with the bright colors and intricate details of abundant life. He touches our mistakes, even our sins, with His grace and they become part of the finished painting—a portrait of love.

Several years ago Brenda and I were browsing in a subterranean flea market when my attention was drawn to an unusual painting. At first I couldn't decide what it was that so captivated me. The artist was good but not great. His technique was just that—technique, nothing more. Still I lingered, studying the painting.

Brenda had moved on, her attention drawn to something in another booth and now she was calling to me. I turned to go and then I saw it, out of the corner of my eye. Although the picture was painted in great detail every face was blank—every face was featureless! Finished but faceless! How had I missed that?

93

My mind was whirling. This was more than just a painting. It was a message. The artist was trying to tell us something about himself, or maybe about us, and he did it the only way he knew how. He painted a parable.

Thinking about it now I can only conclude that the painting was prophetic, giving us a glimpse of life in the twenty-first century. Of all the symbols he might have used to depict the lives we live without Christ, none is more accurate than the sad and eloquent anonymity he captured in the featureless faces in his painting. We are many things—we are restless, we are often angry, we are sometimes cruel, we are often in great pain—but surpassing all of this is our individual and collective anonymity. Utilizing email, twitter, instant messages, blogs, and text messaging we manage the transfer of information faster than ever before—but we communicate less. We don't talk to each other; we don't connect. We are faceless people living among other faceless people.

So what happened? How did we end up this way—alienated and alone?

Well it has been said, "When man fell in the garden he fell away from God, he fell against his neighbor, and he fell apart on the inside." Sin ruins our relationships! Like Cain we might well lament, ". . . my punishment is greater than I can bear. Behold thou has driven me out this day from the face of the earth; and from thy face shall I be hid; and I shall be a fugitive and a vagabond in the earth . . ." (Genesis 4:14).

Paradoxically this haunting emptiness, this alienation, is also our best hope because it draws us back to God. Yet we fight it. We stubbornly cling to our independence with one hand, while reaching for God with the other hand. Or maybe it is fear more than stubbornness that keeps us from embracing Him. Fear that if we surrender to Him He will erase our individuality and turn us into a Christian clone with a featureless face. As one self-deprecating wit said, "I may not be much but I'm all I've got. If I lose 'me' I won't have anything at all."

Some see God as a schoolteacher with a giant eraser, wanting nothing more than to wipe out our individuality. May I suggest another possibility? Maybe instead of thinking of God as a schoolteacher with a giant eraser, we should think of Him as an artist—a watercolor artist. Is it possible that He wants to finish what He started when He created us? Maybe He wants to make each one of us into a unique masterpiece.

My friend Max Davis says, "A watercolor work reflects every, and I mean every, single bit of contact the painter makes with the canvas. Each stroke of the brush leaves an imprint just like each experience in this life leaves an imprint on us. You can't hide anything or cover it up in watercolor. You have to blend in the mistakes. You can't undo them, so you use them to make the work stronger. Mistakes become part of its character—making it unique."

Without Christ we are all part of that anonymous crowd—nameless, faceless people, lacking distinction and detail. But when we turn to Him He covers the canvas of our lives with the bright colors and intricate details of abundant life. He touches our mistakes, even our sins, with His grace and they become part of the finished painting—a portrait of love.

> HE TOUCHES OUR MISTAKES, EVEN OUR SINS, WITH HIS GRACE AND THEY BECOME PART OF THE FINISHED PAINTING—A PORTRAIT OF LOVE.

Across the years, I've witnessed God's artistic touch displayed in some of the most unlikely people, and in the most unexpected ways. Take Sterling for instance. He was newly converted and out on bail when he came to my office for pastoral counseling. Haltingly he told me his story. He never knew his father, and his mother abandoned him when he was

95

just a child, not yet three years old. A kindly aunt took him in and reared him as her own. Still, her love could not heal the wound his mother's rejection had inflicted. By the time he was fourteen years old he was a confirmed alcoholic.

His self-destructive lifestyle soon landed him in reform school. Unfortunately, rather than reforming him it only intensified his anger, and upon his release he immediately reverted to his incorrigible behavior. From petty crimes he graduated to more serious offenses and soon he was serving a sentence in the state penitentiary, then another.

Now he was in trouble again. Only this time a miracle happened. While incarcerated in the county jail awaiting bail, he started reading the Bible, which gave birth to faith and he was born again. Now he wanted to know if he could attend the Church of the Comforter where I served as pastor. I assured him that he would be welcomed with open arms. Soon he was deeply involved in the life of our fellowship, including a growth group that I led every Thursday evening. I will never forget the night he told our group that he finally felt loved, for the first time in his life, by God and by us.

The wheels of the criminal justice system grind slowly and months passed before Sterling went to trial. Given his faithfulness and the growth in his walk with the Lord, it was easy to forget that he was an ex-con, out on bail, awaiting trial. We became good friends and he shared meals with our family nearly every week. He taught me to play backgammon. Leah, our seven-year-old daughter, thought of him as a favorite uncle. He was always helping around the church and our congregation loved him.

Late in December he returned to my office, deeply agitated. "Pastor," he said, "my trial starts in a few days. When it does it will be in the newspaper and everyone will know what I've done."

He stumbled to a stop and the silence became almost unbearable before he finally spoke again.

"I'm scared, really sacred. Not so much of prison, I've been there before, but of being rejected by my church family. I'm afraid they won't have anything more to do with me when they realize I'm charged with raping my sixteen-year-old step-daughter."

Although I was shocked, this being the first time he had mentioned his alleged crime, I tried to cover my revulsion. My mind was racing. I couldn't help thinking how foolish I had been to invite him into our home. I had put my wife and daughter at risk. Yet I knew he wasn't the same man who had attacked his step-daughter. He wasn't just an ex-con with a rap sheet as long as my arm. He was a new man, he was born again. I reminded myself, ". . . that anyone who belongs to Christ has become a new person. The old life is gone; a new life has begun!" (2 Corinthians 5:17 NLT).

Having regained my equilibrium somewhat I hastened to assure him that our congregation would stand with him, and he seemed somewhat comforted when he left. After he was gone, I began to have some serious doubts of my own. Rape is a heinous crime, especially when it involves children, and ours was a young congregation with several families having daughters. My own daughter was only seven, and I couldn't help being concerned for her. Sterling was my friend, he shared meals with our family, I knew him personally; yet I was assailed with misgivings of my own. If I felt that way how was our congregation going to feel? As I thought about it, I concluded that Sterling's concern was probably more legitimate than I had let on.

At the conclusion of service, the following Sunday evening, I felt impressed to share Sterling's story with the congregation. Better to hear it from me, I reasoned, than to read about it in the newspaper. As I spoke, a somber silence settled over the congregation and I began to wonder if I had made a mistake. I finished my remarks by saying, "I assured Sterling that his past is dead and buried. Whatever he did or didn't do isn't going to change how we feel about him. We know that he is a new man in Christ Jesus and that old things—his old nature and his old habits—have passed away and that everything was made new when he was born again."

For what seemed a long time, no one moved, no one made any attempt to reassure him. He was sitting near the front and he seemed to shrink within himself as it appeared his worst fears were about to be realized. Then Mary stood up and started down the aisle.

I was filled with misgivings as I watched her walk toward him. She had been sexually molested as a child, and at the age of eighteen she got pregnant after being raped. Although she was a married woman now, with teen-age children of her own, she continued to battle the demons from her past and it didn't usually take much to shatter her fragile equilibrium. I couldn't help thinking this might well push her over the edge.

She stopped in front of Sterling, and I held my breath. Slowly she reached down and took his hand. "Jesus loves you Sterling and so do we." Her voice cracked as a wave of emotion washed over her. "The past doesn't matter. You're forgiven. We're family!"

IT WAS A HOLY MOMENT. LOVE, GOD'S LOVE, TRIUMPHED OVER THE HARSH REALITIES OF HUMAN WEAKNESS.

Tears spilled from Sterling eyes and his shoulders shook with silent sobs. Suddenly it seemed that everyone was talking at once and crowding around him to affirm their love and support. It was a holy moment. Love, God's love, triumphed over the harsh realities of human weakness.

Although God took the sin ruined canvas of Sterling's life and turned it into a masterpiece of grace, Sterling still had to deal with the consequences of his criminal behavior. At his trial, some weeks later, he was found guilty of rape and given a lengthy sentence in the state penitentiary. God had forgiven Sterling, but life hadn't.

I watched with a heavy heart as he was handcuffed and led away following his sentencing. In spite of my most determined efforts to remain positive, I couldn't help wondering how he would fare in prison. Was his faith strong enough to sustain him or would fall back on the habits of a lifetime? My fears proved ungrounded. To my great joy he continued to grow in the Lord. He enrolled in a three-year Bible School correspondence course. Upon completing it he became an assistant to the prison Chaplain and a Bible study leader for his fellow inmates. Like an artist, God continued to fill the canvas of Sterling's life with the bright colors and intricate patterns of abundant life! His once featureless face was now filled with the likeness of Christ. If God could make something beautiful out of Sterling's ruined life, just imagine what He can do for you!

Chapter 15

Nothing in My Hand

As I thought of standing before God Almighty I wasn't thinking of the hundreds of sermons I had preached, or the books I had written, or the people I had led to Christ, or the money I had given to the work of the Lord. Instead a single phrase kept repeating itself over and over again in my head. "Nothing in my hand I bring. Simply to thy cross I cling. O Lamb of God I come, I come." My only hope, my only security was in what Christ had accomplished on that old rugged cross!

Several years ago Brenda and I were flying into Nashville, Tennessee, for the Christian Booksellers convention when our plane was struck by lightning knocking out one of the jet engines. When lightning hit the plane there was a loud bang, a blinding flash of light and then the cabin lights went out. Brenda screamed, "We're going down!" Fortunately she was wrong. Although we temporarily lost one engine the pilot was able to safely land the plane. Other than being a little shook up we were none the worse for wear.

Another time we were on our final approach into DFW and just about to touch down when the pilot suddenly aborted the landing. Instead of touching down he put the MD-80 into a steep climb. In an instant the cabin went deathly quiet. Glancing around I saw the tension I felt mirrored in the faces of the passengers around me. We were all wondering what had happened. Maybe another plane had taxied onto the runway and thanks to the pilot's quick action we had narrowly averted a deadly collision. Hopefully it was nothing more serious than that, but we had no way of knowing.

For several minutes we continued to climb before circling the airport as the tension in the passenger cabin mounted. Finally the pilot came on the intercom. "As we were about to touch down a warning buzzer sounded in the cockpit signaling that our landing gear was not locked in position. Discretion being the better part of valor, I decided to abort the landing until we can get this figured out. Hopefully the warning buzzer simply malfunctioned but we need to make sure our landing gear is properly deployed before we attempt to land. We are going to fly by the control tower and some of the traffic controllers are going to use binoculars to try and see if our landing gear is down."

That whole process required fifteen or twenty minutes and during that time my imagination was working overtime. If the landing gear was not properly deployed or if was not locked in position we would have to make some kind of emergency landing—not a pleasant prospect. Worst-case scenario, some of us might die.

MY ONLY HOPE, MY ONLY SECURITY WAS IN WHAT CHRIST HAD ACCOMPLISHED ON THE CROSS!

Rather than put that thought out of my mind, I embraced it. I considered the possibility of my own death. As I thought of standing before God Almighty, I wasn't thinking of the hundreds of sermons I had preached, or the books I had written, or the people I had led to Christ, or the money I had given to the work of the Lord. Instead a single phrase kept repeating itself over and over again in my head. "Nothing in my hand I bring. Simply to thy cross I cling. O Lamb of God I come, I come." My only hope, my only security was in what Christ had accomplished on the cross!

Once more the intercom came to life and the pilot told us the control tower had confirmed that the landing gear was in position. He didn't think there would be a problem landing but for safety's sake he told us to assume the crash position as we made our final approach. The next four or five minutes were some of the longest of my life. Over and over again I kept repeating, "Nothing in my hand I bring. Simply to thy cross I cling. O Lamb of God I come, I come." Finally the wheels touched the tarmac and the landing gear held. We were safely on the ground and the passengers erupted in a huge cheer.

Looking back I don't suppose we were ever in any real danger in either of those instances but they were harrowing at the time. More importantly they caused me to think about that day when I will stand before God Almighty to give an account for how I've lived my life. Hebrews 9:27 declares, ". . . it is appointed unto men once to die, but after this the judgment" (KJV).

Having been reared in a strict Pentecostal tradition I grew up feeling I could never measure up, that I could never witness enough, pray enough, or do enough to earn God's favor. As a consequence, I lived much of my early life on tiptoe, never fully secure in my salvation. Some of my friends simply gave up after deciding there was no way they could meet God's impossible standard. Who, they reasoned, could ever be perfect as God is perfect (see Mt. 5:48)?

Given my legalistic background it was pretty remarkable that I had reached a point in my walk with the Lord where I could trust only in the finished work of Jesus Christ. As a teenager any sinful failure, no matter how insignificant or inadvertent, caused me to fear I had lost my salvation. I identified

103

with Martin Luther who saw his sin and failure to keep the Law so clearly, that his fear of Christ the Judge grew exponentially. Although I never experienced the depth of condemnation and suicidal depression that dogged him for so many years, I did live with an abiding guilt. Like a low-grade fever, it robbed me of my spiritual vitality.

During his lectures on Paul's Epistle to the Romans in 1515-16, Luther finally found the assurance that had eluded him for years. He discovered (or recovered) the doctrine of justification by faith alone. In Romans, Paul writes of the "righteousness of God." Luther had always understood that term to mean that God was a righteous judge who demanded human righteousness. Now, he understood righteousness as a gift of God's grace.

It was this same truth that delivered me from my debilitating preoccupation with my performance and the inevitable condemnation it produced. Based on my performance I always fell short of God's righteous requirements. But what I could not do for myself Jesus did for me. By living a sinless life He completely fulfilled all the requirements of God's holy law; something I could never do. When we trust Him alone for our salvation He imputes His perfect righteousness to us. According to 2 Corinthians 5:21 (KJV), "[God] hath made him [Jesus] to be sin for us, who knew no sin; that we might be made the righteousness of God in him."

WHAT I COULD NOT DO FOR MYSELF JESUS DID FOR ME. BY LIVING A SINLESS LIFE HE COMPLETELY FULFILLED ALL THE REQUIREMENTS OF GOD'S HOLY LAW.

So how was Jesus made to be sin for us? By sinning? Absolutely not! "[He] has been tempted in every way, just as we are—**yet he did not sin**" (Hebrews 4:15, emphasis mine).

Jesus was made to be sin for us by an act of God! Father God collected all the sins of Adam's lost race—past, present, and future—and imputed them to Him. That was the cup Jesus

104

couldn't bear to drink, the cup He begged the Father to take from Him (Matthew 26:36-43). In its dark dregs was the poison that was destroying those who were created in His image. There was rebellion in it and lust, and profane passions. It was filled to the brim with all manner of evil—treachery and deceit, pride and power, racism and genocide, adultery and murder. Sickness and disease were there, as was death. Everything that Jesus hated was in that cup, everything that He had come to destroy. Although it repulsed Him, He submitted to the Father's will. He drank the cup and when He did He took upon Himself all the sins of our fallen race. He who had never sinned was made to be sin for us.

So how are we made the righteousness of God in Him? How are we made perfect like our heavenly Father is perfect (Matthew 5:48)? How are we made holy as He is holy (1 Peter 1:15)? Not by living a sinless life for that is impossible (1 John 1:8,10). Not by living righteously, for Isaiah says all our human righteousness is nothing but filthy rags as far as God is concerned (Isaiah 64:6).

> JESUS WAS NOT MADE TO BE SIN BY SINNING AND WE WILL NOT BE MADE RIGHTEOUS BY OUR RIGHTEOUS ACTS.

Jesus was not made to be sin by sinning and we will not be made righteous by our righteous acts. Even as God imputed to Jesus all the sins of Adam's lost race, making Him to be sin for us, so He imputes the sinless life of Jesus to us through faith and we are made the righteousness of God in Him. "For God took the sinless Christ and poured into him our sins. Then, in exchange, he poured God's goodness into us" (2 Corinthians 5:21 TLB)!

We call this justification—right standing before God. Our right standing before God is not based on what we do for Him, but on what Jesus has done for us through His sinless life, His sacrificial death, and His glorious resurrection. "Therefore, since we have been made right in God's sight [justified] by faith, we have peace with God because of what Jesus Christ our Lord has done for us" (Romans 5:1 NLT).

Some misguided souls think that since our right standing before God is based on the righteousness of Jesus rather than our performance we can live a sinful, self-indulgent life. Not true. "If we deliberately keep on sinning after we have received the knowledge of the truth, no sacrifice for sins is left, but only a fearful expectation of judgment and of raging fire that will consume the enemies of God" (Hebrews 10:26-27).

For the most part the strict Pentecostal culture in which I was reared no longer exists. Being free from the constant condemnation we battled is a good thing, but in the process it appears we have lost our fear (reverence) of God. Many post-modern believers have little or no sense of sin. Everyone does what is right in his or her own eyes without fear of the consequences. Political correctness and tolerance are the highest virtues in the modern church. Same sex couples claim to be Christians, professing believers live together before marriage and often birth children out of wedlock without shame. More and more ministers are performing same sex marriages and churches are even ordaining gay and lesbian ministers. As Jude warned, "ungodly people have wormed their way into your churches, saying that God's marvelous grace allows us to live immoral lives. The condemnation of such people was recorded long ago, for they have denied our only Master and Lord, Jesus Christ" (Jude 4 NLT).

So where do we go from here? How do we recover a holy fear (reverence) of God and a sense of sin?

First we must have a revelation of God's awesome holiness. Not simply an intellectual appreciation for the doctrine of His holiness, but an encounter with the One who is altogether holy beyond anything we can imagine. An encounter like the one

Isaiah had when he entered the temple following King Uzziah's death. He saw the ". . . Lord, high and exalted, seated on a throne; and the train of his robe filled the temple" (Isaiah 6:1). Angelic beings were crying, "'Holy, holy, holy is the LORD Almighty . . .' at the sound of their voices the doorposts and thresholds shook and the temple was filled with smoke" (Isaiah 6:3-4).

By all accounts Isaiah was a good man and highly respected, but when he came face to face with the holy God he was literally undone. "Woe to me!" he cried. "I am ruined! For I am a man of unclean lips, and I live among a people of unclean lips, and my eyes have seen the King, the LORD Almighty" (Isaiah 6:5).

Early one Sunday morning in July, 1984, I entered my study to prepare my heart for the morning service. As I was sitting at my desk, I received an open vision. In this vision I saw the Church in what at first appeared to be a large banquet hall. Believers were laughing and talking, eating, and fellowshipping. I saw myself walking among them, from table to table. What I overheard was deeply disturbing. There was little or no conversation relating to spiritual matters. Instead, there was foolish talk and coarse jesting, profanity, sexual innuendo, and suggestive stories.

Looking up, I saw Jesus standing in the foyer with a pained expression on His face. It was then I realized that this was no banquet hall, at least not in the ordinary sense, but the parlor in a house of prostitution. Then I heard the church worshipping. Yet it was strange, different. One moment they were laughing and jesting profanely, and the next they were speaking in tongues and prophesying. It was both disconcerting and encouraging, and I rushed to tell Jesus that things weren't as bad as they might appear.

As soon as I reached Him I said, "Jesus, I know that things look bad but I have heard them worshipping, praying, even prophesying in Your name."

Without a word, He grabbed His stomach and doubled over. Then He began to weep, great groaning sobs racked His body. Only then did I realize that it was worse than I had thought. Instead of being comforted by the fact that His people were manifesting spiritual gifts, even as they sat in a house of prostitution, He was heartbroken. The vision faded and I was left sitting at my desk, alone, weeping, under great conviction.

Later that morning I shared that vision with our congregation. As I did, a nearly overwhelming sense of God's holiness filled the auditorium and the fear of the Lord gripped the congregation. While I was still speaking men and women ran to the front of the auditorium and fell on their faces before the Lord, crying out in repentance. Nearly three hours later they were still there. Secret sins were confessed, spiritual strongholds were broken and lives were transformed!

A revelation of God's holiness inevitably leads to a realization of personal sin. Once we see God high and lifted up in all of His glory we cannot help but be undone. Like Isaiah we will cry, "Woe is me!" Thankfully the Lord does not leave us there, overwhelmed by our sin. Instead He takes our guilt away and makes atonement for our sin. "Then one of the seraphim flew to me with a burning coal he had taken from the altar with a pair of tongs. He touched my lips with it and said, 'See, this coal has touched your lips. Now your guilt is removed, and your sins are forgiven.'" (Isaiah 6:7).

But what happens if we continue in our sin? What happens if we dismiss our sin without a second thought, as if we will not have to give an account to a holy God? Hebrews 10 makes our fate clear: "For anyone who refused to obey the law of Moses was put to death without mercy on the testimony of two or three witnesses. Just think how much worse the punishment will be for those who have trampled on the Son of God, and have treated the blood of the covenant, which made us holy, as if it were common and unholy, and have insulted and disdained the Holy Spirit who brings God's mercy to us . . . It is a terrible thing to fall into the hands of the living God" (Hebrews 10:28,29,31 NLT).

It is popular today to discount any thought of impending judgment. But to do so one has to ignore a vast amount of scripture, much of it spoken by Jesus Himself. He referred to hell and judgment, directly or indirectly, more than seventy times. Admittedly some of those references are repeats where the Gospel writers are describing the same events, but most aren't.[25]

Let me be clear. God has appointed a day when He will judge the living and the dead. Paul says, "He has set a day when the entire human race will be judged and everything set right. And he has already appointed the judge, confirming him before everyone by raising him from the dead" (Acts 17:31 MSG).

Judgment day is certain. God's requirements are unattainable. We cannot save ourselves. That's what drove Martin Luther to the point of suicide—his total inability to measure up to God's holy requirements and thus his fear of God's impending wrath. That's what caused Jonathan Edwards' congregation to swoon in fear and fall to their knees wailing and trembling as he preached his famous sermon, "Sinners in the Hands of an Angry God." But that's also what brought them to salvation. They realized they could not save themselves. Jesus was their only hope.

Based on your performance you will always fall short of God's righteous requirements. But what you cannot do for yourself, Jesus did for you. By living a sinless life He completely fulfilled all the requirements of God's holy law; something you can never do. When you trust Him alone for your salvation God imputes Jesus' perfect righteousness to you. Romans 5:19 declares, "For just as through the disobedience of the one man [Adam] the many were made sinners, so also through the obedience of the one man [Jesus] the many will be made righteous."

We are called to live a godly life and abstain from fleshly lust that war against the soul (1 Peter 2:11) even though it is the righteousness of Christ that justifies us. A godly life is irrefutable evidence that the righteousness of Jesus has been imputed to us. What makes us righteous, however, is not our lifestyle, but the sinless life and the perfect righteousness of Christ that has been credited to us through faith in His finished work. Succinctly put: the security of our salvation is in the finished work of Jesus Christ. The proof of our salvation is in the godly life we live. The key to living an overcoming life is to focus on what Jesus has done for you rather than on what you are doing for Him.

THE SECURITY OF OUR SALVATION IS IN THE FINISHED WORK OF JESUS CHRIST. THE PROOF OF OUR SALVATION IS IN THE GODLY LIFE WE LIVE.

---

[25] Timothy J. Stoner, "The God Who Smokes," (Colorado Springs: NavPress, 2008), p. 247.

Chapter 16

Can You Make the Preacher Cuss?

Never have I witnessed a more complete transformation than what Bob experienced. Salvation totally changed his character but his personality remained pretty much the same. He was a true man of God but he still enjoyed giving me a hard time.

Lil's Café was a noisy place when I walked in, as it was most mornings at this time. Glancing around for a place to sit, I spotted Bob, the local crop duster. There was an empty chair at his table so I headed his way. He was a hard drinking man and a womanizer, estranged from his third wife. As far as I was concerned that made him a "lost sheep" and the object of the Lord's special attention. Knowing he was a hard case, I had appointed myself the Lord's helper. I was just twenty-one years old and serving my first church. My early months in the pastorate had been mostly unfruitful and I was desperately in need of a convert. After giving my situation considerable thought I had set my sights on Bob. If he came to Jesus it would be the talk of the town.

For some reason he seemed to have taken a dislike to me and he never missed an opportunity to needle me. This morning was no exception. Hardly had I taken my seat before he started in.

Smirking at me, he asked, "How can you tell when a preacher is lying?" Without giving me a chance to respond he said, "When his lips are moving."

He bellowed with laughter and slapped the table spilling my coffee. Looking around to make sure he had an audience he turned his attention on me once more. "Easy money," he said. "I think that's what I'm going to call you—Easy money."

When I just sipped my coffee without responding he started in again. "Sure wish I was a preacher and only had to work one hour a week!"

That did it. Although I knew better, I couldn't seem to help myself. "Well, Bob," I said, and paused as the buzz of conversation quieted around the room. "If you were as smart as I am, as creative, as talented, and as good looking, you wouldn't have to work like a slave to make a living. Of course you're not, so I guess you've got a hard row to hoe."

When I finished Bob had a startled look on his face and for a few seconds no one said anything, then the whole café seemed to erupt with laughter. From across the room someone piped up, "Looks like he's got you there, Bob." Someone else said, "You're doomed to a life of hard labor. Good looking you ain't!" There was more good-natured ribbing as Bob gulped down his coffee and made his way out the door.

Although I had obviously gotten the best of him I wasn't feeling good about it. How would I ever win him to Christ if I let him get under my skin like that? While I was still musing on my irresponsible behavior one of the local businessmen sat down in the chair Bob had vacated. Giving me a friendly smile he said, "You know what's going on don't you?"

I shrugged my shoulders, "Maybe, maybe not. I guess he just doesn't like me."

"It's himself he doesn't like, but that's not the point. Bob bet several of us that he could make you cuss. If he is successful we have to pay him $50.00. If he can't make you cuss he has to attend your church this coming Sunday. If he can't get you to cuss by tomorrow you will be seeing him in church come Sunday."

Walking the two blocks from Lil's Café to the parsonage I found myself chuckling on the inside. Had Bob known my background he would never have made that bet. I was reared in a strict Christian home. I can't recall hearing either of my parents use a slang word, let alone a curse word. To be absolutely honest I don't think I had ever uttered a cuss word; I wasn't even sure if I knew any. Bob had set himself up for failure without even knowing it.

Of course Bob lost that wager and the next Sunday evening he joined us for worship. In those days our Sunday evening attendance usually numbered less than a dozen, meaning Bob stuck out like a sore thumb. At the conclusion of my sermon, I invited the congregation to join me at the front of the church to receive communion. For Bob's benefit I was careful to explain that our congregation practiced open communion and that you did not have to be an official member of our local fellowship to share the Lord's Supper with us.

Not wanting to appear like an outsider, Bob joined the rest of the congregation when they came forward and knelt at the altar to receive the emblems of our Lord's body and His blood. When I served him, I made it a point to tell him that the apostle Paul warned us that if anyone partook of the bread or the cup in an unworthy manner that he was eating and drinking judgment on himself (see 2 Corinthians 11:27-29). After the benediction, I couldn't help noticing that Bob had left the communion elements untouched.

Fast-forward with me a couple of days. It was about 7 o'clock on Tuesday evening. Brenda and I were watching television in the parsonage, which was located next door to the church. For several minutes I had been feeling a prompting to go to the church. It made no sense, so I tried to ignore it. When that feeling persisted, I decided to head next door. If nothing else, I could spend some time praying in the empty sanctuary.

As I descended the porch steps and turned toward the church, Bob's pickup slid around the corner and skidded to a stop. Leaping out, he hurried to the front door of the church and started jerking on the door handle, trying to get in. Once I got the door unlocked, he pushed by me and ran to the altar where he fell on his knees.

For the next fifteen or twenty minutes he wept and confessed his sins, calling on the name of Jesus. When he finally finished he looked up and gave me a huge smile. Noticing the communion service sitting on the communion table behind me he asked, "May I receive communion now?"

Without a moment's hesitation, I selected the elements and knelt down beside him. Breaking the bread I said, "On the night Jesus was betrayed He took bread and broke it and blessed it saying, 'Take eat, this is my body which is broken for you." Together, Bob and I ate the bread.

Holding the cup I said, "In the same manner Jesus took the cup saying, 'This is my blood of the new testament which is shed for the remission of your sins. Drink ye all of it.'" Together, we lifted our cups and drank.

Later, Bob shared the details leading up to his remarkable conversion. For two days the Holy Spirit convicted his heart, ever more intensely. Finally, while he was eating dinner at Lil's Café on Tuesday evening, the Spirit of the Lord came upon him in such a powerful way that he felt that if he didn't give his life to Jesus that very moment he might well be lost for eternity. Throwing some money on the table, he rushed from the cafe and drove directly to the church. Looking me in the eye he said, "I don't know what I would have done if you hadn't been here to let me in the church. Broke the door down probably. I was that desperate!"

A couple of days later Bob and I were having coffee at Lil's Café when he said, "I've decided to go get my wife and kids and bring them back to Holly."

Bob and his wife had been separated for several months so I ask, "How does Diane feel about moving to Holly?"

"I haven't told her."

Knowing how headstrong Bob could be, I tried to reason with him, but gently. "Do you think it's a good idea to spring this on her? Maybe you should call her first and tell her what's happened to you and see if she's willing to move to Holly?"

Shaking his head, Bob said, "It will be better if I tell her in person."

"Well you should at least let her know you're coming."

"No," he said. "I've made up my mind. I'm just going to show up."

It was more than 400 miles from Holly to Olathe, Colorado, where Diane lived. I was young and inexperienced but even I knew letting Bob go alone wouldn't be wise. He was just a baby Christian and the enemy could throw a lot of temptation at him, especially if Diane wasn't interested in reconciling with him and moving to Holly. I knew we had to be there to support him.

Early the next morning the three of us set out for Olathe. Bob drove his pickup and Brenda and I followed in our Dodge R/T. Eight hours later, after crossing the continental divide and descending Monarch Pass, we drove into a dusty farmyard just outside of Olathe. Brenda and I stood a little behind Bob as he mounted the wooden steps and knocked on the door. A vivacious young woman, dressed in faded blue jeans and a T-shirt, opened the screen door.

"Bob Arnold," she exclaimed in surprise, "what are you doing here?"

"I got saved on Tuesday night," he announced, then gesturing toward Brenda and me he continued, "and this is my preacher and his wife. I've come to get you and the kids and bring you back to Holly so you can get saved."

Brenda and I were stunned. Bob hadn't spoken to this woman in months and without any preamble he told her that he was taking her and the kids back to Holly so she could get saved! Diane just stood there with her mouth hanging open. Finally she managed to invite us in.

Diane and Brenda hit it off instantly and in a manner of minutes they were talking like lifelong friends. When bedtime came nothing had been resolved and Brenda and I were only too happy to head for the back bedroom leaving Bob and Diane alone in the living room to work out their situation. Bob must have been persuasive because early the next morning Diane asked Brenda to help her pack her meager possessions for the move to Holly. By mid-afternoon Bob's pickup was piled high with their scanty belongings. We must have looked like a caravan of Okies headed for California when we finally pulled onto Highway 50 headed for Holly. I was in the lead in my Dodge R/T, Brenda and Diane followed in Diane's old clunker with the two children, and Bob brought up the rear in his overloaded pickup truck.

It was nearly four o'clock on Sunday morning when we finally made it to Holly. The fact that Diane and the children

116

were with us was still hard for me to believe. When we left Holly on Thursday I didn't think there was a way in the world she would reconcile with Bob. "O ye of little faith." The best was yet to come. When I finished my sermon the next morning and gave the invitation Diane walked down the aisle and knelt at the altar and received the Lord Jesus as her savior.

Brenda and I spent the next two years disciplining them. They became our dearest friends and we did everything together. Bob and I continued to meet for coffee at Lil's Café, we read and discussed the scriptures continually, and prayed together often. Diane and Brenda took turns preparing meals and we ate together several times each week. Many a night the telephone would ring about ten o'clock. When I answered it Bob would say, "Diane just baked some bread. Get a bottle of grape juice and come over and let's have communion."

When we arrived at the tiny airport, where Bob and Diane lived in a doublewide mobile home, the kids would already be in bed. The four of us would go into the living room and kneel around the coffee table. Diane would place a small loaf of home baked bread on the coffee table and I would pour grape juice in the Melmac cups. Bob and Diane would confess their temptations and their failures then we would share communion and that living room would become a holy place.

Never have I witnessed a more complete transformation than what Bob experienced. Salvation totally changed his character but his personality remained pretty much the same. He was a true man of God but he still enjoyed giving me a hard time. He was a pilot with extraordinary skills and his crop dusting was legendary. When Brenda's parents came to visit us I took her dad into the country to watch Bob fly. We got out of the car so we could see better and I walked down the road to wave at Bob. When he saw me he dove his plane at me and I flung myself into the muddy bar ditch beside the road. Bob thought that was hilarious. Brenda's dad got a kick out of it too! Like I said his personality remained pretty much the same.

Bob has remained my dear friend and brother in Christ for nearly fifty years. Although we live hundreds of miles apart we still talk often. Each week he sends Richard Exley Ministries a $30 contribution. On the memo line on the check he always writes, "For Jesus' use only." More importantly he prays for me every day!

In case you're wondering . . . he never made this preacher cuss.

Chapter 17

I's Needs Some Wools, Man

Try as I might I cannot make His words mean anything other than what He said. "I needed clothes and you did not clothe me" (Matthew 25:42). That's plain enough. Each homeless person represents Jesus. To ignore them is to ignore Him. "Whatever you did not do for one of the least of these, you did not do for me" (Matthew 25:45).

It was early December and winter had Tulsa, Oklahoma, by the throat. Night after night temperatures plunged into the low teens, occasionally dropping into the single digits. Add the wind chill factor and it was dangerously cold, especially for the homeless who, because of overcrowding at the homeless shelters, had been forced to seek refuge under bridges and in abandoned automobiles. According to the television news, places like Mother Tucker's Rescue Mission and the Salvation Army were turning people away because they had no more room.

Although I had no firsthand knowledge of what it was like to be homeless, I had experienced it vicariously through the local television news. Normally that would have been the end of it— a momentary compassion quickly forgotten. In the past, I put their sad plight out of my mind as soon as the sports news came on. Not this time. Several days passed and I was still troubled by what I had learned. Each time I worshipped, or went to prayer, I found myself obsessing about their desperate situation. Yet, what could I do? I was only one man with limited resources. Besides whose fault was it anyway—their own most likely. They were probably reaping the consequences of their own irresponsible choices . . . or so I told myself.

Although I tried to put their dire plight out of my mind a passage of scripture I had read countless times haunted me. In Matthew's gospel, chapter 25, Jesus said:

"I was hungry and you gave me nothing to eat, I was thirsty and you gave me nothing to drink, I was a stranger and you did not invite me in, I needed clothes and you did not clothe me, I was sick and in prison and you did not look after me. They also will answer, 'Lord, when did we see you hungry or thirsty or a stranger or needing clothes or sick or in prison, and did not help you?' He will reply, 'Truly I tell you, whatever you did not do for one of the least of these, you did not do for me'" (Matthew 25:42-45 NIV).

EACH HOMELESS PERSON REPRESENTS JESUS. TO IGNORE THEM IS TO IGNORE HIM.

Try as I might I could not make His words mean anything other than what He said. "I needed clothes and you did not clothe me" (Matthew 25:42). That was plain enough. Each homeless person represented Jesus. To ignore them was to ignore Him. "Whatever you did not do for one of the least of these, you did not do for me" (Matthew 25:45).

That being the case, why did I spend the better part of a month wrestling with the Lord in my spirit? Why did I stubbornly refuse to give my double-breasted, 100% wool, navy blue overcoat to a homeless person when I felt compelled by the Lord to do so? I'll tell you why. That overcoat was my favorite. It was the best coat I had ever owned. I didn't want to give it away, to anyone, and certainly not to some homeless person I didn't even know. Yet, I have to admit that I was deeply troubled by my self-ishness and the thought that I was displeasing the Lord.

Things came to a head one morning during prayer with the pastoral staff. It seemed as if the Lord said to me, "This has gone on long enough. I want you to give your overcoat to a home-less person and I want you to do it this morning!"

Although I had a busy morning I immediately left the church office and drove home. Brenda walked in while I was rummaging in the coat closet. "What are you doing home in the middle of the morning?" she asked.

"I've come to get my double-breasted, navy blue overcoat. God told me to give it to a homeless person."

"What are you talking about? You don't even know a home-less person."

Frustrated I replied, "God will show me who to give it to."

"And if He doesn't?"

"He will!" I snapped, anger coloring my words.

Stubbornly Brenda persisted, "And if He doesn't show you who to give it to?"

"Well, then I will just donate it to Mother Tucker's Rescue Mission," I replied, taking my coat from the closet. Brenda just shook her head as I headed out the door.

Twenty minutes later I exited the Broken Arrow Expressway toward downtown Tulsa. For several minutes I drove the nearly deserted streets and alleys looking for homeless people. In the television specials they seemed to be all over this area but now it was deserted. To my chagrin I couldn't find a single one. I had been so confident when I told Brenda that God would direct me, that He would show me who to give my coat to. Now her words seemed to taunt me, "And if He doesn't?"

Reluctantly I drove toward Mother Tucker's Rescue Mission. It looked like plan "B" was my only option, but I have to admit I was more than a little disappointed. If God was really directing me to give my favorite coat to a homeless person why couldn't I find that person?

After parking in front of Mother Tucker's Rescue Mission I stepped out of the car. When I did the cold wind pierced me like a knife. Involuntarily, I tugged up the collar of my overcoat and tried to burrow into its warmth. Thank God I've got a home, I thought. Life on the streets would be deadly in this weather.

"I's needs some wools, man."

His voice was raspy, harsh sounding, and when I turned to see who had spoken, he began pleading. "I's needs some wools bad. I's freezin in dis col."

He stood there shivering, as I looked him up and down. I guessed him to be about forty, but he looked older. His lips were cracked from the cold, and his skin was chapped and raw. The jacket he was wearing had a broken zipper and was badly worn, especially at the elbows where the lining was showing through. Underneath he wore a cardigan sweater over a faded flannel shirt.

I wish I could tell you that I immediately realized he was the homeless person I had been looking for; the one to whom I was supposed to give my coat, but I can't. Instead of compassion, I felt contempt. In disgust I turned my back on him and opened the rear door of my car. When he saw me take my navy blue overcoat out of the car his eyes lit up with desire. Ignoring him,

I started walking toward the front door of the mission. He followed me, pleading, "I's needs some wools, man." As I placed my hand on the door handle it finally hit me. He was the answer to my prayer, the man God wanted me to give my coat to.

I stopped so suddenly that he bumped into me. Thrusting the coat at him I said, "Here, try this on. If it fits it's yours, but if it doesn't fit you I'm giving it to Mother Tucker."

In an instant he had that coat on and buttoned up. Not surprisingly, it fit perfectly. Stepping closer, I put the matching wool scarf around his neck and tucked it inside the front of his coat. Before I could step back, he wrapped his arms around me and pulled me to his chest in a bear hug. He smelled like booze and body odor and damp clothes, but I didn't mind. In that moment it felt as if God himself were hugging me.

Back in my car, I watched him walk down the street until he turned the corner and disappeared from sight. I have to admit I was feeling pretty good about myself. I couldn't help wondering how many people would give their favorite coat to a homeless person. Probably not many!

HE WRAPPED HIS ARMS AROUND ME AND PULLED ME TO HIS CHEST IN A BEAR HUG. HE SMELLED LIKE BOOZE AND BODY ODOR AND DAMP CLOTHES, BUT I DIDN'T MIND. IN THAT MOMENT IT FELT AS IF GOD HIMSELF WERE HUGGING ME.

I might have broken my arm patting myself on the back if the Lord hadn't interrupted me. Suddenly a question sprang full-blown into my mind: *Why didn't you offer to buy him breakfast?*

Why indeed? The truth be told it never occurred to me. I was so busy congratulating myself on my generosity that I hadn't given that homeless man a second thought. Chagrinned, I started the car and turned the corner determined to find him and buy him breakfast. To my dismay the sidewalk was deserted and although I spent the next ten minutes cruising the streets and alleyways in the immediate vicinity I never caught sight of him.

While I was castigating myself for my self-centeredness another question took hold of my mind. Two questions really: *Was that man a believer? Why didn't you tell him about Jesus?*

By now my smug self-righteousness was long gone. I was face to face with the truth about myself and it wasn't pretty. To my credit I gave my favorite coat to a homeless man, howbeit reluctantly, and only after the Lord had dealt with me for several days. Unfortunately that act of charity was outweighed by my spiritual blindness and insensitivity. I never bothered to learn his name, nor offered to buy him breakfast. Saddest of all, I never inquired about the condition of his soul, neither did I offer to pray for him, nor did I tell him about Jesus.

> TO THE WORLD'S WAY OF THINKING THAT HOMELESS MAN MAY HAVE BEEN A "NOBODY" BUT TO GOD HE WAS A PERSON OF INFINITE WORTH.

What did I learn from that experience? Several things. First I was reminded of how much Father God cares. That man needed a coat and God went to a great deal of trouble to make sure he got one. To the world's way of thinking that homeless man may have been a "nobody" but to God he was a person of infinite worth. I was also reminded of how God directs our steps if we will allow Him to do so. He had me in the right place at just the right time to give that man my coat.

Of course I learned some other things as well, mostly about myself, and they were not flattering. That experience showed me just how stubborn I am. God had to deal with me for several days before I was willing to part with my navy blue overcoat.

And when I finally found myself face to face with that homeless man, my first reaction was not compassion but disgust. I judged him without knowing anything about his situation. It also showed me how full of myself I was. I didn't even bother to learn his name or offer to buy him breakfast.

Maybe the most important thing I learned is that I can't allow the enormity of the world's need to intimidate me. In the past I often justified my lack of involvement by reasoning that I was only one man with limited resources. What could I do? Never again! Although I can't meet every need I will not let that keep me from doing what I can.

I agree with Norman Cousins who writes, "Certainly it is true that behind every human being who cries out for help there may be a million or more equally entitled to attention. But this is the poorest of all reasons for not helping the person whose cries you hear. Where, then, does one begin or stop? How to choose? How to determine which one of a million sounds surrounding you is more deserving than the rest? Do not concern yourself in such speculations. You will never know; you will never need to know. Reach out and take hold of the one who happens to be nearest. If you are never able to help or save another, at least you will have saved one."[26]

[26] Norman Cousins, **Human Options,** (quoted in Disciplines for the Inner Life, by Bob Benson and Michael W. Benson, Word Books Publisher, Waco, TX, 1985), p. 310.

Chapter 18

It's Not about Fishing

It took me nearly thirty years to figure it out but I've finally realized that when you take a child fishing it's not about fishing; it's about building relationships and making memories—memories they will cherish for a lifetime.

A s I write this I am sitting at my desk overlooking beautiful Beaver Lake. A hundred feet down the mountain from me, its crystal clear water sparkles in the morning sunlight, tempting me with thoughts of fishing. With an effort I turn my attention to the task at hand only to be sidetracked again. This time it is a framed photograph sitting on the windowsill to my left. Looking at it, my thoughts wander to a spring afternoon several years ago. . . .

Killing the outboard engine, I make my way to the fishing platform on the bow of my bass boat. After lowering the electric trolling motor, I maneuver the boat toward my favorite crappie hole. In a couple of minutes I have it positioned and I cast my red and white jig toward a pile of submerged brush near an outcropping of rocks. Before I can begin my retrieve, Alexandria, my three-year-old granddaughter, is pulling at my sleeve. "Papa," she says, "I want to fish."

I try to talk her into sharing my rod but she won't hear of it. She wants her own rig, so reluctantly I prop my rod against the side of the boat and tie another jig on a second pole. After casting it out I hand it to her and she immediately reels it in and hands it back to me to cast again. This time I show her how to let the jig drift to the bottom before beginning a slow retrieve. At her age she isn't going to master the art of fishing a jig, but I am hoping to distract her long enough to get in a little fishing of my own.

My jig has hardly hit the water before she is tugging on my sleeve again. "It no work, Papa," she says, frustration coloring her words. "It no work."

Glancing her way I see that her light rod is bent nearly double. Most likely she is snagged considering we are fishing in and around submerged brush piles. With that thought in mind I put my rod down once more and prepare to deal with her situation. As soon as I take hold of her rod I know it is no snag. The rod throbs in my hand as a heavy fish makes a determined run. Motioning for Alexandria to help me, I place the rod back in her hands while supporting her as she fights to land that fish. Determinedly she cranks the reel and after a couple of minutes a large crappie breaks the surface of the water near the boat. Reaching for the net I scoop it up and place it on the floor of the boat while Alexandria squeals with delight.

As crappies go it is huge—almost fifteen inches long and nearly as wide as a dinner plate. I want to put it in the live well, but Alexandria wants to pet it so I leave it on the floor of the boat. The next time I glance her way she is trying to feed it tiny bits of candy and I can't help thinking about another fishing trip, one I took with her mother when she (her mother) was barely six years old.

On that long ago day, Leah was nearly as hyper as Alexandria has been today. Every time I cast her line out, she would reel it right back in. Finally I threatened to make her sit in the car if she didn't leave her fishing rod alone. Grudgingly she placed it in the rod holder and sat down beside it to wait for a bite, but she couldn't be still. In short order she abandoned her rod in favor of the coffee can full of fishing worms. That was the last straw. Angrily I ordered her to sit in the car.

Driving home later that evening we hardly spoke. I had a nice stringer of rainbow trout but I could take no pleasure in them. Leah's rambunctious behavior had spoiled the day for me and my anger had ruined it for her. It was a long time before I took her fishing again. Needless to say, the emotional residue of that day has forever tainted her view of fishing.

Thinking about it now, I can't help comparing Alexandria's joyful laughter, and my own contentment, with the unhappiness that permeated that earlier fishing trip with Leah. Two fishing trips—so much alike and yet so different. As a young father I was so uptight, so intent on fishing that I ruined the whole experience for both of us. I had an opportunity to bond with Leah, to maybe help her fall in love with fishing, and I blew it.

WHEN YOU TAKE A CHILD FISHING IT'S NOT ABOUT FISHING; IT'S ABOUT BUILDING RELATIONSHIPS AND MAKING MEMORIES.

It took me nearly thirty years to figure it out, but I've finally realized that when you take a child fishing it's not about fishing; it's about building relationships and making memories. There will be plenty of time for fishing when the children are grown and gone but today is the only chance you will have to make this memory—a memory they will cherish for a lifetime.

Chapter 19
The Ministry of Presence

There is nothing, absolutely nothing, more powerful than prayer; yet suffering and grief can render it unreal at least for a time. That is not to say that there will never be a time for prayer in the sickroom, but only that the time will seldom come before we have listened deeply and with compassion to the honest concerns of the dying and their family members.

I t has been estimated that the average person can go through a twenty-year period without being exposed to the death of a single relative or friend. As a result, we do not know what the dying person or his family really feels, wants, or expects of us. Therefore we tend to avoid the dying and the bereaved. Even when we do force ourselves to "do our duty" (that is, even if we don't avoid them physically), we often isolate the bereaved emotionally by avoiding any reference to their illness or possible death.

One lady, a victim of cancer, told me that her pastor would breeze in and out of her room, chatting all the time, hardly giving her a chance to get a word in edgeways. He did ask how she was doing, but not in a way that encouraged her to respond honestly. After a few minutes, he would pray, and then he was gone.

A little of that goes a long way and she soon had all she could take. She determined that on his next visit she was going to tell him how she really felt. When he arrived she was ready. He breezed in with his usual chatter and superficial questions: "How are you feeling today? Did you sleep well? Are you having much pain?" Then she unloaded on him. Not in anger, just honestly. She told him that the pain was absolutely intolerable; that she was afraid of dying; that she prayed day and night but it seemed that God was gone, that He never answered her, never made His presence known. Her emotional outburst made her pastor uncomfortable and when she paused for a breath he said, "Let's pray."

"Don't do that to me," she said. "You're always using prayer like some kind of escape hatch. Every time I start to tell you what it's really like to be barely thirty, the mother of two young children, and dying with cancer, you want to pray. That's not real prayer. It's just religious words, a smoke screen, so you can make your escape. Today you are going to hear me out; you're going to walk with me through this valley of the shadow of death. That's what you're supposed to do, isn't it? Isn't that why you're here—so I don't have to face death alone?"

I share that incident not to discredit that pastor, or the ministry, but as a way of graphically illustrating a common but ineffective practice. It's not that we consciously misuse prayer, but when faced with impossible situations, we gravitate to it naturally, almost by second nature. Most of the time that's as it should be, but in situations like the aforementioned one it effectively isolates the dying person, and prayer was never meant to do that.

Timing and sensitivity are the keys here. Or as one grieving father said, following his son's untimely death, "I know all the 'right biblical passages.' . . . But the point is this: While the words of the Bible are true, grief renders them unreal."

The same thing can be said about prayer. There is nothing, absolutely nothing, more powerful than prayer; yet suffering and grief can render it unreal at least for a time. That is not to say that there will never be a time for prayer in the sickroom, but only that the time will seldom come before we have listened deeply and with compassion to the honest concerns of the dying and their family members.

Such a ministry is not without great cost. There's something painfully disturbing about watching a person die, whether it takes a few hours or several weeks. Death seems to mock us, to render our best efforts, our latest medical technology, even our most earnest prayers, impotent. It brings us face to face with our own mortality, a subject we've mostly been able to dismiss in the rush of living. But here in the sick room, it catches us by the throat, looks us in the eye, demands our full attention.

John Claypool, describing his own journey through the valley of the shadow of death as he watched his eight-year-old daughter battle acute leukemia, writes: "I perhaps need to confess to you that at times in the past few months I have been tempted to conclude that our whole existence is utterly absurd. More than once I looked radical doubt full in the face and honestly wondered if all our talk about love and purpose and a fatherly God were not simply a veil of fantasy that we pathetic humans had projected against the void. . . . There were the times, for example, when Laura Lue was hurting so intensely that she had to bite on a rag and used to beg me to pray to God to take away that awful pain. I would kneel down beside her bed and pray with all the faith and conviction of my soul, and nothing would happen except the pain continuing to rage on. Or again, that same negative conclusion tempted me when she asked me in the dark of the night: 'When will this leukemia go away?' I answered: 'I don't know, darling, but we are doing everything we know to make that happen.' Then she said: 'Have you asked God when it will go away?' And I said: 'Yes, you have heard me pray to him many times.' But she persisted: 'What did He say? When did He say it would go away?' And I had to admit to myself He had not said a word! I had done a lot of talking and praying and pleading, but the response of the heavens had been silence."[27]

> CAN YOU MINISTER COMFORT TO ME WHEN YOU KNOW YOU CAN'T REALLY CHANGE ANYTHING; WHEN ALL YOU CAN DO IS BE THERE WHILE I DIE, SO I DON'T HAVE TO FACE THOSE LAST HOURS ALONE?

This, I believe, was what Jesus was talking about when He asked James and John, "'Can you drink the cup I drink or be baptized with the baptism I am baptized with?" (Mark 10:38). Not, "can you drink your own cup of death;" not, "can you remain faithful unto death;" not, "can you die a martyr's death;' but, *can you walk with Me through My suffering and death?* Do you have the stomach for it? Can you minister comfort to Me when you know you can't really change anything; when all you can do is be there while I die, so I don't have to face those last hours alone?

"Will you be able to bear it when the Romans get done with their thorns and their whips; when My face is chalky white from loss of blood; when My back is raw ribbons of mutilated flesh; when I stagger, weak from more pain than I could have ever imagined it possible for a man to bear? Or will you turn away, unable to bear it? When you see Me writhing in excruciating pain, and you can't so much as cool My fevered flesh; when you hear My strangled cry of thirst; when you sense the darkness and aloneness that surrounds both inside and out; when you hear My soul's anguished cry, 'My God, My God, why have You forsaken Me?' will you comfort Me then?"

John was there to the bitter end, as was Mary, the mother of Jesus, and Mary Magdalene and a few others. Peter too, but at the far edge of the crowd, as far away as possible. Did they drink that cup as they so confidently said they could? Hardly. They sipped it maybe, choking on its painful dregs, gagging, so bitter was it, but they couldn't drink it.

It's interesting, isn't it, that the women outnumbered the men several times over? Not because women are braver than men, but because comfort comes more naturally for them. The women in Jesus' life understood that He would draw strength just from the sight of them, that their presence would be a comfort to Him. Besides, they wanted to be there; they couldn't imagine letting Him die alone.

The ministry of comfort, on the other hand, is especially hard for men, for those of us who are used to getting things done. It's hard on us to sit and wait—to watch, powerless, as death claims its prey. We want to do something, anything. We want to exert our authority, regain control of our world. But what can we do in such seemingly impossible cases? Pray maybe? Or pretend the one we love isn't dying?

Our need to do something, anything, is almost unbearable. Taking action gives us a feeling of being in control again. We're not, of course, but it seems we are—and that makes us feel better. Yet when we allow our discomfort to initiate action, we usually do the wrong thing.

For instance, when Jesus tried to tell the disciples of His impending suffering and death in Jerusalem at the hands of the chief priests, "Peter took him aside and began to rebuke him. 'Never Lord!' he said. 'This shall never happen to you!'" (Matthew 16:22).

How similar to the way we respond when the dying person attempts to talk about their impending death. They often say things like, "I don't have much to look forward to anymore," or perhaps something even more direct, "I think I am going to die soon." Unfortunately, many people respond by changing the subject or with such nonsense as: "Don't talk like that. You're going to live for years. Why, you'll probably outlive me." While the conscious intent may be to bring cheer, it seldom, if ever, works. Instead, such a response effectively isolates the patient, leaving him to face death alone.

The underlying motive, unconscious for the most part, is to escape our own pain that is brought on by the patient's candid discussion of his true feelings. We are not yet ready to honestly acknowledge either his impending death or our personal loss.

Go with me to Gethsemane, on the night of our Lord's betrayal. The scriptures record it this way: ". . . he (Jesus) began to be deeply distressed and troubled" (Mark 14:33). Hear Him as He speaks to Peter, James, and John: "My soul is overwhelmed with sorrow to the point of death. Stay here and keep watch" (v. 34). Which is to say: Don't leave Me alone with this. Stay with Me through these awful hours. I need you now as I have never needed you before.

Some days earlier He had ask them, "Can you drink the cup I am going to drink?"

"We can," they assured Him, but can they?

This is the moment of truth, and they can't drink it. The cup is too bitter, the pain too real. They can't even bear to look. They abandon Him—not literally, that comes later. Now they simply escape into the sweet oblivion of sleep. Three times He attempts to arouse them, three times He appeals to them for their support, but still they turn from the cup of His sufferings.

Mark says, "They did not know what to say to him" (Mark 14:40). How like most of us they were; or more likely, how like them we are. Wordless before such sorrow, tongue-tied and fumbling, never realizing that our presence is all He wants. Not words, not theological explanations, just our presence.

What am I trying to say? Simply this: when ministering to the grieving, meet them where they are. If they are expressing honest faith, reflect honest faith back to them. If they are raging, pouring out their hurt and anger, absorb their anger without rebuke. Don't censure them. And don't try to explain why this terrible tragedy has happened to them. Listen with love. Weep with them. Remember, it is all right to say you don't know. Life is filled with mystery, and faith doesn't mean we have all the answers as much as it means we trust God unconditionally even when there seem to be no answers.

No one wants to die alone. Ultimately all who look death in the eye—whether they are a terminally ill patient slowly dying or the grieving loved one—long for the comfort that only a compassionate person can give. When we reduce it to the lowest common denominator, what they want from us, what they expect from us, is nothing more or less than our presence.

> WHEN WE REDUCE IT TO THE LOWEST COMMON DENOMINATOR, WHAT THEY WANT FROM US, WHAT THEY EXPECT FROM US, IS NOTHING MORE OR LESS THAN OUR PRESENCE.

---

[27] John Claypool, "Tracks of a Fellow Struggler" (Waco: Word Publishers, Inc. 1974), p. 77.

Chapter 20
In Memory of George Gentry

On my very first visit, George said to me: "I hope you're not like that hospice Chaplain. Every time he comes to see me he falls asleep." I assured him I would do my best to stay awake. I only fell asleep once and just for a split second, but he caught me. I started to deny it, but he just smirked at me and I knew I couldn't fool him. We both laughed. I blamed it on his boring company and he told me I was just a worthless lay about.

George was my friend and I looked forward to spending an hour with him from 4 to 5 PM each Tuesday afternoon. He had been diagnosed with terminal cancer and that's what prompted my first visit, but his illness soon became secondary to the relationship we shared. That first afternoon, however, we were sizing each other up. He was tempted to view me as Joyce's preacher, while I was struggling to see him as a man in his own right and not just her son-in-law.

Joyce loved George and couldn't bear the thought of his impending death. Knowing that all things are possible with God, she was eager for me to pray with George for complete healing. However when I asked George if he would like me to ask Jesus to heal him he said, "Absolutely not. My times are in God's hands and I don't think we have any business interfering with what He has planned." I could have debated the finer points of divine healing but that seemed somehow inappropriate so I dropped the subject. I would ask him from time to time, in the ensuing weeks, if he had changed his mind. Without hesitation he would reply, "Let's leave things the way they are."

I soon found myself looking forward to Tuesday afternoon each week. Joyce would meet me at the door with a bottle of water and I would make myself comfortable while George expressed his views regarding the latest "liberal lunacy" while Fox News played in the background. Once he got that out of the way we turned to other topics, usually George's favorite—himself.

He was a fascinating storyteller, holding me spellbound week after week. I learned about his childhood and how many different schools he attended in a single year. He loved dogs and the Ozark Mountains in Arkansas. Hard work was second nature to him and he spent most of his adult life in construction work. No matter how tired he was at the end of the workday, he always had time to play with his children. He spoke often of his spiritual heritage—his grandmother was Pentecostal, but he grew up Baptist. Somewhere along the way he became discouraged with church, although he never doubted the reality of God or His unconditional love.

HE BECAME DISCOURAGED WITH CHURCH, ALTHOUGH HE NEVER DOUBTED THE REALITY OF GOD OR HIS UNCONDITIONAL LOVE.

Of course, I was concerned about his relationship with Jesus, especially given the condition of his health. He assured me that he had made his peace with the Lord and that Jesus was his personal savior. After four or five weeks of visits we began taking communion together. Joyce would join us, and a couple of times George's wife got home from work in time to share in that special time. Once, his granddaughter joined us. Each week at the Lord's Table we experienced forgiveness, regeneration, and the promise of eternal life all over again.

On my very first visit George said to me: "I hope you're not like that hospice Chaplain. Every time he comes to see me he falls asleep." I assured him I would do my best to stay awake. Next he told me he hoped I wasn't like his nurse who was always late. Once more I assured him I would do my best to be on time, but that I couldn't always control my schedule. I managed to be on time for the most part and if I was running a few minutes late I always asked my secretary to call. I only fell asleep once and just for a split second, but he caught me. I started to deny it, but he just smirked at me and I knew I couldn't fool him. We both laughed. I blamed it on his boring company and he told me I was just a worthless lay about.

Somewhere in those weeks and months we became good friends. We laughed a lot, shared the stories of our lives, argued politics in a good natured sort of way, prayed together, and talked about what it felt like to know you were dying. He was mostly free from pain and he was thankful for that. He hated the thought of leaving Susan and his family, but he was kind of excited about going to heaven. He dreamed about it once and in his dream, heaven was a lot like the Ozark Mountains only better, and he had a dog to go hiking with him. "Of course," he said, "God was very near in my dream and more real than I can explain."

SOMEWHERE IN THOSE WEEKS AND MONTHS WE BECAME GOOD FRIENDS. WE LAUGHED A LOT, SHARED THE STORIES OF OUR LIVES, ARGUED POLITICS IN A GOOD NATURED SORT OF WAY, PRAYED TOGETHER, AND TALKED ABOUT WHAT IT FELT LIKE TO KNOW YOU WERE DYING.

The last two or three times I visited him he was too weak to leave his bedroom so I pulled up a chair next to his bed. Talking was an effort and I had to lean close in order to hear him. I told him that I hoped that when my time came I could die with as much dignity as he was. That seemed to please him and he told me I probably couldn't because he was a better man than me. We both laughed until he started coughing.

The last time I saw George was Tuesday afternoon, December 18th. I think we both knew it was going to be our last visit. I was traveling to Pennsylvania to be with my daughter and her family, and he was going home to be with Jesus. George was not really a "touchy feely" type of guy, but he had grown accustomed to my goodbye hugs and seemed to enjoy them. Of course he would never say so. On that final afternoon I bent over George's bed, kissed him on the forehead and bid him Godspeed. At the doorway I paused and looked back at him. "Thank you, George," I said, my words thick with emotion. "Thank you for sharing your life with me. I am a richer man because of your friendship."

Chapter 21
Does Steel Float?

For those who refuse to give up, who dare to see with both eyes, there's something beyond the darkness, something beyond the pain and brokenness of our shattered world.

Most people can overcome any adversity if they can be assured of three things. First, they must know that God cares. Then, they must be convinced that He won't forsake them. Finally, they have to know that God will redeem their situation. As rational creatures, the thought that a tragic accident or some other life-altering event might be pointless is simply unbearable. But if we are convinced that God will ultimately bring good out of what looks for all the world like a senseless tragedy, we can somehow bear it.

Do you remember the time Jesus and His disciples were caught in a terrible storm? Mark records it: "A furious squall came up, and the waves broke over the boat, so that it was nearly swamped. Jesus was in the stern, sleeping on a cushion. The disciples woke him and said to him, 'Teacher, don't you care if we drown?'" (Mark 4:37-38).

"Don't you care?"

That's the question that haunts us when our secure world is suddenly shattered. We want to know that God cares.

I'm thinking of a young couple who spent two years on the mission field. While they were there, their second child was stillborn. It was a devastating blow. They were thousands of miles from family and friends, laying their lives on the line for the sake of the kingdom, doing exactly what God had called them to do, so why did their baby die? How many times, I wonder, did they cry, "Lord, don't You care?"

Theirs is an extreme case, I'll grant you, but it is not nearly as isolated as you might think. After more than four decades in the ministry, I've come to realize how many people live with unspeakable sorrow, how many people suffer in silence and hide their hurt behind a public smile. Over and over they have pled with me for an answer. "Does God care?" they ask, or, "Why doesn't God do something?"

It's not really answers they seek, but assurance. And in response, all I can do is point to the cross. There He is—God's Son—bleeding and dying because He cares!

Once we know God cares, then we want to be assured that He is with us. The sense of God's nearness is what kept my sister going when she was diagnosed with stage 3 cancer. The oncologist told her that it was untreatable and that she should go home and prepare to die. But she refused to accept that diagnosis and instead of preparing to die, she determined to live. It wasn't easy, but when she was tempted to despair, to give up the fight, she strengthened herself by focusing on the Lord's nearness.

WHEN SHE WAS TEMPTED TO DESPAIR, TO GIVE UP THE FIGHT, SHE STRENGTHENED HERSELF BY FOCUSING ON THE LORD'S NEARNESS.

I prayed with her nearly every day for more than four years. We prayed for a miracle of healing. We prayed for strength to get through all the surgeries and chemotherapy treatments. We prayed for God to redeem that tragedy, to bring good out of that terrible ordeal. All of that was meaningful to her but what quieted her spirit and strengthened her heart was when I prayed for God to be nearer to her than the breath she breathed and closer than life itself. As long as she could sense His near presence she could face her uncertain future with courage.

Like so many others who have endured unspeakable hardship, Sherry couldn't bear the thought that her suffering might be pointless. If she had to endure the ravages of chemotherapy and surgery, while looking the possibility of a premature death in the eye, she wanted to be assured that her suffering wouldn't be wasted. She clung tightly to Romans 8:28: "And we know that in all things God works for the good of those who love him, who have been called according to his purpose."

> UNFORTUNATELY, THE GOOD GOD IS WORKING THROUGH OUR SUFFERING IS OFTEN IMPOSSIBLE TO SEE IN THIS LIFE. STILL, THAT DOESN'T MEAN THAT GOD IS NOT AT WORK.

Unfortunately, the good God is working through our suffering is often impossible to see in this life. Still, that doesn't mean that God is not at work.

I'm thinking of a pastor whose only son committed suicide. One Lord's day, he entered the pulpit and announced his text. Visibly struggling, he read Romans 8:28. Holding up his Bible he said, "I cannot make my son's suicide fit into this verse. It's impossible for me to see how anything good can come out of it. And yet this verse supports me somehow, it enables me to go on living even though life doesn't seem to make any sense.

"It's like the mystery, the miracle, of the shipyard. Almost every part of our great ocean-going vessels is made of steel and if you take any single part, be it a steel plate out of the hull or the huge steel rudder, and throw it into the ocean it will sink. Steel doesn't float! But when the shipbuilders are finished, when the last steel plate has been riveted into place, then that massive steel ship will float. Steel doesn't ordinarily float, but when the ship builders are finished it does!

"Taken by itself my son's suicide 'won't float.' Throw it into the ocean of Romans 8:28 and it sinks. But when the divine shipbuilder is finally finished, when God has worked out His perfect design, even this senseless tragedy will make sense. It will float!"

IF YOU LOOK WITH THE EYE OF FAITH YOU WILL SEE JOY WHERE YOU WERE SURE THERE WAS NO JOY TO BE FOUND AND POSSIBILITIES WHERE YOU WERE SURE NONE EXISTED. YOU MIGHT EVEN SEE A MIRACLE IN THE MAKING, FOR WITH GOD NOTHING IS IMPOSSIBLE.

When you look around what do you see? Do you see shattered dreams, a failed business, family problems and an impending divorce? All of that is there plus a whole lot more. No one can deny that, but if that's all you see you're only seeing with one eye. If you open both eyes you will not only see what *is*—the tragedies of life—but what *can be*. If you look with the eye of faith you will see joy where you were sure there was no joy to be found and possibilities where you were sure none existed. You might even see a miracle in the making, for with God nothing is impossible (Luke 1:37).

When you're in Gethsemane the situation can look hopeless. No matter how desperately you pray things never seem to get any better. Worst of all, it feels like God has forsaken you. The sense of His nearness that once sustained you seems to have vanished. You are left to wander alone in the darkness, stumbling over the wreckage of your world, or so it seems. But you are only seeing with one eye. For those who refuse to give up, who dare to see with both eyes, there's something beyond the darkness, something beyond the pain and brokenness of our shattered world. Whether God saves us from our "Gethsemane" or allows us to walk the "Via

Dolorosa" (literally the sorrowful way) our ultimate deliverance is assured. "He who believes in me," Jesus said, "will live, even though he dies" (John 11:25).

Sometimes the future triumph is just around the corner. A young woman is instantly healed of stage 3 leukemia. A childless couple is given a miracle. After being told she would never conceive, she becomes pregnant and gives birth to a son. After prayer, a dear friend's blocked arteries are instantly opened—making bypass surgery unnecessary. Financial provision too—a struggling author receives several paying projects after praying for provision. A small congregation receives a one-time gift of $429,444.79 enabling them to finally move out of rented facilities where they have been holding services for ten years!

Sometimes it's a long way off, maybe even in the next life, but knowing it's coming gives us the strength to live with joy no matter how difficult our present circumstances. "Therefore we do not lose heart. Though outwardly we are wasting away, yet inwardly we are being renewed day by day. For our light and momentary troubles are achieving for us an eternal glory that far outweighs them all. So we fix our eyes not on what is seen, but on what is unseen. For what is seen is temporary, but what is unseen is eternal" (2 Corinthians 4:16-18).

Chapter 22

It May Be Winter, but Christmas is Coming

Think about it. In the winter of her life she had Christmas every day and so can you! Christianity does not make us immune to the vicissitudes and sufferings so common to this life, but it does empower us to live with meaning in the midst of unspeakable loss.

Winter is not what it used to be. I'm not talking about the weather patterns, but the impact of winter. One hundred years ago there was little or no electricity; few houses had central heat or indoor plumbing, automobiles were a rarity, and in winter fresh fruits and vegetables were almost nonexistent. Make no mistake—winters were hard. The snow piled up, travel was treacherous, houses were cold, the nights were long with little light, and people were often hungry. The only bright spot in that winter wasteland was Christmas. When my late father reminisced about his childhood, his memories of Christmas were special. He remembered few gifts but he did recall, with pleasure, hard peppermint candy, an orange, and Christmas dinner. The way he remembered it, it was the only meal the entire winter where there was more than enough food to go around.

In that context, C.S. Lewis' line, "It was always winter but never Christmas" is especially haunting. Think about it. Without electricity winter nights were long and dark. Without central heat houses were never really warm except right next to the pot-bellied stove. Communication was limited—only the most affluent had telephones, the mail was sporadic, travel of any distance difficult if not impossible, and there was seldom an abundance of food. Truthfully, Christmas was the only thing that made winter bearable, but what if there was no Christmas?

Times have changed; in the United States modern advances have lessened winter's impact. Most houses have central heat and indoor plumbing. Electricity makes night nearly as bright as day, snowplows clear the highways and only the severest winter storm impedes travel, and then only for a short time. Even the poorest families have cell phones, colored televisions, and access to the Internet. Yet, for many it is "always winter but never Christmas."

EVEN THE POOREST FAMILIES HAVE CELL PHONES, COLORED TELEVISIONS, AND ACCESS TO THE INTERNET. YET, FOR MANY IT IS "ALWAYS WINTER BUT NEVER CHRISTMAS."

Of course, I'm not talking about the weather but about life. For many, even in my relatively small circle of acquaintances, it is winter with no relief in sight. A young mother is spending Christmas alone with her two children because her minister husband divorced her after becoming involved with another woman. A family was forced into bankruptcy when their business failed. A grieving widow faces the holidays alone after losing her husband way too soon to the ravages of cancer. A husband and father lost his job when the company he worked for went out of business. Another friend received a negative diagnosis from his doctor. . . . Always winter but never Christmas!

That's the way it was in Bethlehem too. Life was brutal—poverty was widespread, disease rampant, the exposure of infants an accepted fact of life in the Roman world, women had no rights and were considered the property of their husbands, and Judea was an occupied country. The Jews had their own puppet king but he was just a figurehead. Rome was calling the shots, collecting the taxes and executing anyone who dared oppose them. It was always winter but never Christmas!

DON'T GIVE UP! GOD HAS A LONG HISTORY OF SHOWING UP IN THE VERY WORST OF TIMES.

You may know firsthand what I'm talking about. You're in the midst of a hard winter right now with no Christmas in sight. Don't give up! God has a long history of showing up in the very worst of times. Or maybe tough times simply make us more perceptive. Maybe He's been there all the time and it simply takes pain and suffering to open our eyes. Take a moment and examine your own life. Look back through the years and identify those times when you felt closest to the Lord. More than likely it was during the hard times, those times when it seemed it was always winter but never Christmas; at least that's been my experience.

My brother told me about a missionary's teenage daughter who was stricken with a grievous disease. Her digestive system stopped working and she was literally starving to death. To keep her alive the doctors inserted a shunt and begin feeding her through a tube. Her activities were severely restricted and she had to carry a feeding pouch at all times. With no hope of a cure it was a heartbreaking situation, but she managed it with surprising grace, trusting Jesus minute by minute to strengthen her.

After a couple of years the Lord instantaneously healed her. Overnight she was able to resume a normal life. Some months later she told her father, "I'm eternally grateful for my healing but there are times I miss the relationship I had with Jesus when I was so sick. He was my only hope and I clung to Him for dear life."

Think about it. In the winter of her life she had Christmas every day and so can you! Christianity does not make us immune to the vicissitudes and sufferings so common to this life, but it does empower us to live with meaning in the midst of unspeakable loss. Therefore I will praise the Lord in the hard times, knowing, ". . . that in all things God works for the good of those who love him, who have been called according to his purpose" (Romans 8:28).

Don't give up. It may be winter, but Christmas is coming!

Chapter 23

Wet, Cold, and Hungry

As we plowed resolutely forward, through the damp gray mist, I couldn't help thinking how foolish I had been. Alaska is still mostly wilderness and largely unforgiving. She does not suffer fools easily. No one should venture forth without proper survival gear. If we ran out of gas—a very real possibility if we were heading in the wrong direction— we might land on some uninhabited island, that is, if we didn't drift into the Gulf of Alaska.

Descending the stone steps leading to the waterfront of Sitka Sound, I waved a greeting to eighteen-year-old David, who was standing in the prow of a sixteen-foot rubber raft called a zodiac. Handing him the tackle box and fishing gear, Weldon and I climbed aboard. While he stowed the gear, I located the life vests and passed them out. Once we were situated, David started the outboard engine and nodded to his father, who pushed us away from the dock. Easing the zodiac around, David headed southwest toward the Gulf of Alaska. Our destination was a halibut hole near the tip of Viscary Island, about ten miles out.

Although the sun blazed brightly in the brilliant blue sky—a true rarity in southeast Alaska, which averages nearly 100 inches of rainfall a year—it was none too warm. Turning up the collar of my jacket against the chilly wind, I gave myself to the moment. The sun had burned the last of the persistent mist away, revealing towering, snow-capped mountains that jutted hundreds of feet into the sky. All around us were densely forested islands. There were no beaches, only rugged shorelines of jagged rocks where the ocean beat itself into a perpetual spray. Those islands—devoid of human habitation for the most part—were a small sprinkling of the more than 1000 that make up the Alexander Archipelago.

After about thirty minutes, Viscary Island came into view, and we eased around the point to the windward side. As we were rigging up, I noticed a heavy bank of clouds rolling in, totally obscuring Sitka. It became noticeably colder, and the first huge raindrops were pitting the ocean's gray surface by the time we got our lines into the water. Neither Weldon nor David seemed concerned, so I pushed my growing uneasiness to the back of my mind.

Settling down to wait for a fish to strike, I reminisced about my good fortune. For the past fourteen days I had been privileged to see much of the forty-ninth state while preaching a conference for ministers and leading a men's retreat at a fishing camp on Admiralty Island. To get to the fishing camp we had to be ferried by floatplane from Juneau—a breathing taking experience affording us a truly exquisite view of Mount Juneau and the Mendenhall Glacier.

Alaska is the land of the midnight sun and evening light lingered long past bedtime, giving the rugged terrain a softness it lacked when viewed in harsher light. Though human inhabitants were scarce, there was an abundance of wildlife. Occasionally we saw bears come down to the steam to feed, and once we spotted several humpback whales. Always we saw the bald eagles—sometimes near, sometimes far.

My reminiscing was cut short by the roar of the outboard engine. David had reeled in his line and stowed his fishing gear in order to give his full attention to maneuvering the zodiac. The wind was up, and the waves were visibly larger, making it a challenge to keep the raft positioned properly. I could not help noticing that there were no other fishermen in the vicinity. The two or three boats that were nearby when we arrived had apparently made a run for Sitka in hopes of beating the weather. Turning to Weldon I said, "It's getting pretty rough out here. Do you think we ought to call it a day and head in?"

He studied the sky for a minute before replying. "I think we'll be OK. This time of the year these storms usually blow over in an hour or two. Besides, we need to let the fog lift so we can see our landmarks to guide us back."

The wind continued to pick up, making it nearly impossible for David to keep the zodiac in position. Suddenly the sky seemed to crack open dumping a deluge of icy rain, cutting visibility to fifty feet or less. Though we were wearing slickers over our jackets, they were no match for the fury of the storm. In seconds we were drenched. When the storm showed no sign of letting up after ten minutes, we belatedly decided to make a run for home. My fingers were stiff with cold as I struggled to crank in nearly 300 feet of heavy line. Weldon was faring no better, but we eventually managed to get our gear stowed.

David turned the zodiac toward home as Weldon hunkered down on the bench in the prow. It was his job to locate our landmarks and make sure we didn't run aground on one of the islands. Straining to see through the driving rain, he covered his eyes with one hand, peering through the tiny slit between his first and second fingers. His other hand gripped a safety strap that was fastened to the bench on which he sat; a good thing, too, for the waves were huge and we were taking a fearful pounding. I was seated on the second bench in the center of the raft, a safety strap firmly gripped in each hand; still I was being thrown around. In a matter of minutes my buttocks were painfully bruised, and my shoulders felt like they were being jerked out of socket.

Finally when I was sure I could not endure the pounding a minute more, the storm began to ease a little. Weldon looked over his shoulder, smiled encouragingly, and gave me the thumbs-up sign. I managed to give him a forced smile in return. Then the engine coughed and almost died. Frantically, David worked the throttle, coaxing it to life once more. It responded with a roar, the prop biting into the frigid water, thrusting the zodiac into the teeth of the departing storm.

I heaved a sigh of relief. The possibility of spending a stormy night on an open raft in the Gulf of Alaska was more than a little unnerving. My relief was short-lived however. Our engine troubles were not over. Now the outboard sputtered and died.

I glanced a question David's way, but he just shrugged his shoulders noncommittally while working the starter. The engine turned over, but it would not fire. Finally he released the starter, lest he drain the battery, and an uneasy stillness settled over us.

The fury of the rain had passed, but a soundless drizzle, cold and merciless, continued to drip from the low-hanging gray clouds. Through the fog, I heard what sounded like surf pounding against the rocks. And a disconcerting sound it was, for without power we had no way of controlling the raft. If we drifted onto the rocks they would shred our rubber craft, plunging us into the frigid waters and pounding surf. Of course the alternative wasn't very comforting either. If we couldn't get the engine running, the tide could carry us into the wide expanse of the Gulf of Alaska. I could only imagine how difficult it would be to locate our small raft in conditions like these.

Weldon joined David at the rear of the zodiac, where the two of them conferred in hushed tones. Though I was no mechanic, it was obvious to me that they were not either. After several minutes they concluded that the engine had probably gotten wet and was drowning out. Since it was still raining steadily they decided against lifting the cover to try and dry the spark plugs.

For the first time I let my eyes roam over the zodiac, looking for survival gear. Nothing. No flare gun, no first aid kit, no packaged food, and no matches. Neither did I see a compass or a map.

Fear was like a cold knot in the pit of my stomach, and I couldn't help thinking how irresponsible we were to venture into the Gulf of Alaska so poorly prepared. Even if we got the engine started we were still in trouble. The fog lay like a damp shroud over the gray water, obscuring all but the most immediate objects. Without a compass we had no way of determining if we were heading back to Sitka or out to sea.

As I glanced toward the rear of the raft I saw David reach under the rear bench and pull out the gas tank. Lifting it up, he gave it a good shake before pronouncing it empty. "Don't panic," he said. "There's another gas tank under here."

Working quickly, he disconnected the fuel line from the empty tank and reconnected it to the second one. After giving the black bulb on the fuel line a half a dozen firm squeezes, he hit the starter button. The engine turned over but it didn't fire. Just when I was about to lose hope it roared to life. Grinning, David gave his Dad a high five.

As Weldon made his way back to the prow, I gave the second gas tank a surreptitious shake. It couldn't have been more than half full. Although I was thrilled to have the engine running again, we weren't out of the woods yet. We had a limited amount of fuel. Visibility was still extremely poor, and without a compass we had no idea in which direction we were heading. If we had to spend the night on the water we could be in real trouble. Without survival gear, hypothermia was going to be a problem as wet and cold as we were.

Glancing at my watch I noted the time. It was nearly 5:00 P.M., meaning we had now been on the water more than four hours. Although it took only thirty minutes to reach Viscary Island on our way out, we had now been battling the elements more than two hours in our attempt to return to Sitka.

As we plowed resolutely forward, through the damp gray mist, I couldn't help thinking how foolish I had been. Alaska is still mostly wilderness and largely unforgiving. She does not suffer fools easily. No one should venture forth without proper survival gear. If we ran out of gas—a very real possibility if we were heading in the wrong direction—we might land on some uninhabited island, that is, if we didn't drift into the Gulf of Alaska. With an effort I pushed those thoughts from my mind and concentrated on conserving what little body heat I had left.

For more than an hour we maintained our course without spotting any landmark even vaguely familiar. To my untrained eye, every rocky shoreline and every heavily wooded island appeared the same. Though the fog was lifting a little, I feared it was too late. It seemed to me that we were likely so far off course that even if full visibility returned we might not be able to locate our landmarks. Resolutely I began to steel myself to spend the night at sea. I was wet, cold, and hungry, but I was determined that I would survive. I had a wife and daughter to live for.

Belatedly I decided to pray. Bowing my head I cried, "Lord Jesus, have mercy on us. Save us. Come and guide us safely back to Sitka." Undoubtedly Weldon and David were praying also.

Almost immediately a fishing trawler emerged from a fog bank on a course that would intersect ours. Frantically we began waving to attract the captain's attention. Instantly the throb of the fishing boat's powerful engine fell off, and the captain brought her alongside our rubber raft. A crewman threw us a rope and we secured the raft.

"We got lost in the storm," Weldon told them. "We're trying to get back to Sitka. Are we headed in the right direction?"

"If you keep going the way you are heading you will eventually get there," the captain replied in a gravelly voice. "Of course you will have to go completely around the world. On the other hand, if you were to head in the opposite direction you could probably make it to Sitka in about thirty minutes."

Nodding toward the horizon where mountains draped in gray mist could now be seen against the sky, he added, "Just remember to keep those mountains to starboard, and you'll be all right."

Weldon thanked him and tossed the rope to the crewman, and we drifted away from the trawler. The throb of her engine resumed its earlier cadence, and we watched as she pulled away.

We reversed our direction and thirty minutes later we were tying up at the dock. Once more, the seas were calm and the sun was shining brightly, painting the waterfront in golden hues. As peaceful as it now was, it hardly seemed possible that we were ever in any real danger—but I know we were. In fact, had it not been for God's faithfulness to answer prayer, we might well be lost somewhere along the Inside Passage that links Sitka with the lower forty-eight states.

> HAD IT NOT BEEN FOR GOD'S FAITHFULNESS TO ANSWER PRAYER, WE MIGHT WELL BE LOST SOMEWHERE ALONG THE INSIDE PASSAGE THAT LINKS SITKA WITH THE LOWER FORTY-EIGHT STATES.

159

Some may scoff at the thought that the sudden appearance of that fishing trawler was an answer to prayer, suggesting it was more likely a simple coincidence. I can appreciate their skepticism. After all, the trawler was in position to intersect our path whether we prayed or not. Still, that doesn't change anything. God, who is beyond time, as we know it, has promised, "that before [we] call, [He] will answer; And while [we] are still speaking, [He] will hear" (Isaiah 65:24).

Knowing where we would be at that exact moment, and knowing that we were going to pray for help, God had already arranged to have that fishing trawler in position. The Lord speaking to us in an audible voice, telling us to reverse our direction, would have been no greater an answer to prayer than that boat's sudden appearance.

These thoughts filled my mind as I climbed the stone steps toward the parking lot where our car awaited. In minutes I would be standing under the shower's hot spray scrubbing the cold from my aching body. In a couple of days all physical evidence of our ordeal would be gone, but in my heart the lessons I learned will remain—lessons that will serve me well as I prepare for life's inevitable storms.[28]

YOU CANNOT PREVENT THE STORMS OF LIFE—ACCIDENTS, DISEASE, DEATH, HEARTACHE, BROKEN RELATION-SHIPS, AND PERSONAL FAIL-URES—SO YOU MUST PREPARE FOR THEM.

Lesson #1: Realize that storms are inevitable. You cannot prevent the storms of life—accidents, disease, death, heartache, broken relationships, and personal failures—so you must prepare for them.

Lesson #2: Be prepared. You can prepare for the inevitable storms by practicing daily prayer, regular Bible study, worship, and fellowship before the storm strikes. Make sure you have spiritual and emotional survival gear on hand at all times.

160

Lesson #3: Realize that help is near even when you cannot see it. When trouble comes, the storm is often so severe that it blinds us to the help that is at hand. It feels like we are totally alone, abandoned by both God and man, but we are not. "God is our refuge and strength, a very present help in trouble" (Psalm 46:1).

---

[28] Richard Exley, *Strength for the Storm* (Nashville: Thomas Nelson Publishers, 1999), pp. xi-xxi.

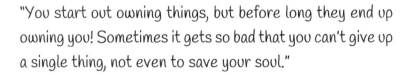

Chapter 24
The White Elephant

"You start out owning things, but before long they end up owning you! Sometimes it gets so bad that you can't give up a single thing, not even to save your soul."

I don't like to think of myself as a materialistic person, but driving away from the Highway 12 East storage complex, I could hardly come to any other conclusion. For nine years I paid almost $40 a month to store things I hadn't used in nearly a decade. Still I continued to hang onto them. Not because I had any attachment to them, but because I had no way to get rid of them.

We donated several things to people we knew. For instance we gave a newlywed couple a dining room set and a chest of drawers. A few months later I invited a young church planter to meet me at the storage facility to see if there was anything he could use in setting up his church office. He selected a desk and some office equipment. We loaded the things he had chosen into his pick-up but I had no idea what to do with the rest of the stuff. It was junk mostly—a couple of battered book cases, a metal storage cabinet, and several boxes of things that we had carted all over the country in our forty plus years of marriage.

There was no organization in our area that would take the stuff so I kept paying rent to store it. Brenda finally decided enough was enough and called a dumpster service to come out and haul it off. That cost me $290! Add it up—nine years at $444 a year comes to $3,996 in rent plus the $290 to haul if off. $4,286 to store and dispose of junk! Now that's a true "white elephant" and hardly what I would call good stewardship.

Thinking about it as I drove home, three things came to mind. The first was the parable that Jesus told about a rich man. He said, "The ground of a certain rich man produced a good crop. He thought to himself, 'What shall I do? I have no place to store my crops.' Then he said, 'This is what I'll do. I will tear down my barns and build bigger ones, and there I will store all my grain and my goods. And I'll say to myself, "You have plenty of good things laid up for many years. Take life easy; eat, drink and be merry."' But God said to him, 'You fool! This very night your life will be demanded from you. Then who will get what you have prepared for yourself?' This is how it will be with anyone who stores up things for himself but is not rich toward God" (Luke 12:16-21).

MORE AND MORE PEOPLE ARE RENTING OFF SITE STORAGE TO STORE ALL THE THINGS THEY "OWN" AND FOR WHICH THEY HAVE NO PLACE AND OFTEN NO USE.

What a tragic picture and a prophetic one at that! The rampant consumerism of the twenty-first century is unparalleled in the history of the world. People live in huge houses with three car garages but have to park their cars in the driveway because their garages are overflowing with things they can't get in the house. Our addiction to things is further evidenced by the fact that one of the fastest growing businesses in the United States is storage rental. More and more people are renting off site storage to store all the things they "own" and for which they have no place and often no use. "But God said to him, 'You fool!'"

164

The second thing that came to mind was an incident related by an East German refugee. Her name was Sigi and I've never been able to get her words out of my mind. She told of being relocated to a detention camp by the Soviet Army as World War II was drawing to a close. Each family was allowed to take only what they could carry, and if they lagged behind they were shot.

This is where her story takes its most tragic turn. Scores of people simply could not part with their possessions. Rather than discard a single thing, they fell behind and were gunned down mercilessly.

"That's the danger of materialism," she said, with a conviction that left no room for debate. "You start out owning things, but before long they end up owning you! Sometimes it gets so bad that you can't give up a single thing, not even to save your soul."

Opening her Bible she read, "Then he [Jesus] said to them, 'Watch out! Be on your guard against all kinds of greed; a man's life does not consist in the abundance of his possessions'" (Luke 12:15).

> "YOU START OUT OWNING THINGS, BUT BEFORE LONG THEY END UP OWNING YOU! SOMETIMES IT GETS SO BAD THAT YOU CAN'T GIVE UP A SINGLE THING, NOT EVEN TO SAVE YOUR SOUL."

More than thirty years have passed since I heard Sigi speak, but I have never forgotten her words. I found myself replaying them in my mind as I drove home last week. Without a doubt they are more relevant today than they were the day she first spoke them. We are literally working ourselves to death to possess things for which we have no use, in order to impress people we don't even like.

The third thing I thought of was something Dr. Richard Swenson related in his book, *A Minute of Margin*. He wrote:

"Years ago in Siam, if the king had an enemy he wanted to torment, it was easy: give him a white elephant. The receiver of this gift was now obligated into oblivion. Any gift from the king obviously had to be cared for; it could not be given away without causing offense. Additionally, a white elephant was considered sacred and thus required the best nourishment and protection. Soon the extreme costs of caring for the gift drove the king's enemy to destitution."[29]

Recent studies indicate that we use about 20 percent of our possessions but we maintain 100 percent of them. Maybe it's time to get rid of the "white elephant" so we can get our lives back. The only way to combat this ever-expanding consumerism is to deliberately buy less and give more away. Remember, "godliness with contentment is great gain" (1 Timothy 6:6).

[29] Swinson, Richard, MD, *A Minute of Margin* (NavPress, P.O. Box 35001, Colorado Springs, Colorado, 2003), reflection #62.

Chapter 25
Ray and Patsy

I was so busy congratulating myself that I never even considered taking them to a restaurant for a bite to eat, nor did I offer to take them by the grocery store in case they needed to pick up a few things.

T he biggest challenge in my spiritual walk has been pride; or to put it more bluntly—arrogance. Considering how modest have been my achievements, you may find that a bit of a stretch. Experience, however, has taught me that success has only a small part to play in a person's susceptibility to this particular temptation. Even underachievers can find themselves beset with a disproportionate sense of self-importance. What makes pride so deadly is the fact that the arrogant person is usually unaware of his arrogance. He can spot it in a heartbeat in others but he's blind to it in himself—at least that's the way it was for me.

Two experiences from my past serve as a case in point. When I served as the lead pastor of Christian Chapel, the congregation honored Brenda and me each year on Pastor Appreciation Day. Parishioners sent us cards and letters and some even gave us small gifts. One year a lady brought me Max Greiner, Jr.'s casting of Jesus washing Peter's feet. To this day I treasure that gift, and it sits in a prominent place in my study, but I never bothered to learn that woman's name. I didn't give it a thought at the time, but now my thoughtlessness reeks of arrogance. I can only shake my head when I realize that I was so full of myself that I didn't have time to learn her name. Even worse is the fact that I didn't recognize the sad state of my soul until years later.

The second experience is even more telling. One night Brenda and I were driving out of the church parking lot following the evening service when we spotted Ray and Patsy standing on the sidewalk in front of the church. Everyone else had gone so I stopped and lowered the car window. In response to my questions they informed me that they had ridden a bus to church but had no way to get back home as the buses had stopped running at that late hour. I offered to drive them and they gratefully accepted.

As we were driving across town to the motel, where they lived in one small room and cooked their meals on a hot plate, I couldn't help thinking how different they were from the rest of our congregation. Christian Chapel was a "Yuppie" congregation and Ray and Patsy looked like homeless people—he with his bad teeth, out-of-style double-knit slacks, and scuffed shoes, and she in her too-small Salvation Army thrift shop dresses and taped up glasses. In spite of this they seemed unaware of the vast social chasm that separated them from the other parishioners.

Each week they marched to the front of the church and sat on the first row. When I entered the sanctuary at the beginning of service, Patsy never failed to greet me, calling out my name and waving. Ray just grinned. After the benediction they made a beeline for Brenda where they dominated her time, making it impossible for her to greet other parishioners. To her credit, Brenda never seemed to mind and she never looked past Ray and Patsy while they talked with her. She gave them her undivided attention, something I found nearly impossible to do.

What does all of this have to do with arrogance? I'm getting to that. Driving home that night, after leaving Ray and Patsy at the motel, I felt pleased with myself. Although I was the pastor of a significant congregation, the author of several books, and the host of a nationwide radio broadcast, I was willing to "humble" myself and drive them across town to their motel. I was so busy patting myself on the back that I never even considered taking them to a restaurant for a late dinner, nor did I offer to take them by the grocery store in case they needed to pick up a few things. Now that's arrogance, but again I never realized it until years later.

Thinking about it now, I'm tempted to get caught in the "if only" trap—if only I had been more caring, if only I had not been so full of myself, if only. . . .

Instead of allowing myself to go there, I remind myself that "if only" are the two saddest words in the human vocabulary. They focus on the past and the past can't be changed. Deliberately I replace "if only" with "next time." Next time I will be less full of myself. Next time I will be more sensitive to Ray and Patsy's needs. Next time I will insist on buying them dinner and at a decent restaurant. Next time I will see if there is anywhere else they need to go or anything else I can do for them. Next time I will do my best to make sure it is all about them and not about me.

"IF ONLY" ARE THE TWO SADDEST WORDS IN THE HUMAN VOCABULARY. THEY FOCUS ON THE PAST AND THE PAST CAN'T BE CHANGED.

Chapter 26
God and Caesar

As Christians we have a dual citizenship. We are citizens of the Kingdom as well as citizens of the United States. While our highest allegiance belongs to God, we have civic responsibilities that we owe the country of our birth. As Jesus said, "Render therefore unto Caesar the things which are Caesar's; and unto God the things that are God's.

I've lived long enough to have no illusions about politicians or political parties. In my lifetime I have seen a Republican president forced to resign rather than face impeachment and a Democratic president whose sexual philandering while in the White House has forever tainted his legacy. The bribes, the kickbacks, and the sexual scandals on both sides of the aisle are too numerous to detail and at times the level of incompetence has simply been staggering. I mention this, not to speak disparagingly of our elected officials, but only to remind you that there are no ideal candidates and no ideal parties. Even as we fulfill our responsibilities as citizens, our hope must always remain fixed on God and on God alone.

Some consider this presidential election the most critical in our nation's history. I don't know if I would go that far, but given the economic crisis, the ongoing threat of terrorism, the assault on Judeo Christian values, and the fact that the next president will appoint at least one Supreme Court justice and likely two or maybe even three, I think we can all agree that these are critical times. As Christians we have a dual citizenship. We are citizens of the Kingdom as well as citizens of the United States. While our highest allegiance belongs to God, we have civic responsibilities that we owe the country of our birth. Or as Jesus said, "Render therefore unto Caesar the things which are Caesar's and unto God the things that are God's" (Matthew 22:21).

> AS A CITIZEN OF THE KINGDOM WE HAVE A RESPONSIBILITY TO MAKE SURE OUR VOTE REFLECTS THE VALUES OF THE KINGDOM AND THE KING TO WHOM WE OWE OUR HIGHEST ALLEGIANCE.

As a citizen of the United States we have a responsibility to vote, to participate in the democratic process. As a citizen of the Kingdom we have a responsibility to make sure our vote reflects the values of the Kingdom and the King to whom we owe our highest allegiance. While there may be any number of issues on which Christians can vote either way, there are other issues on which the Scriptures are emphatically clear and in regards to these we must never compromise. Non-negotiable issues include the sanctity of life (i.e., abortion, euthanasia, embryonic stem-cell research, and human cloning) and the biblical view of marriage (i.e. between a man and a woman).

When both candidates profess to be Christians we must look beyond their words to their actions. Remember Jesus said, "Not everyone who says to me, 'Lord, Lord,' will enter the kingdom of heaven, but only he who does the will of my Father who is in heaven" (Matthew 7:21). We must ask ourselves if the positions each candidate takes on non-negotiable issues line up with the clear teaching of Scripture. We must examine their voting records to see how they have voted on these non-negotiable issues. While a non-Christian may take a biblical position on these issues, a Christian cannot take an unscriptural position without compromising his faith.

It's also important to consider who a candidate's friends and supporters are. As my Grandma Miller used to say, "Birds of a feather flock together." Ask yourself, *Who is Planned Parenthood (the largest abortion provider in the U.S.) supporting? Who is the LGBT coalition supporting? Who are those in favor of same-sex marriage supporting?*

Remember the next president will likely appoint at least one Supreme Court justice, perhaps two or even three. Without a doubt the selection will be based, not only on qualifications, but on ideology as well. These selections may well be more far-reaching than anything else the next president accomplishes and will shape the values of our nation for decades to come, so vote wisely.

One final thought. The level of animosity generated by this election is unlike anything I have seen in my lifetime. As Christians we must guard our hearts. Although we are called to stand for truth regardless of the cost, we must always walk humbly and in love. In the past we have spoken truth but without love and as a result we have been perceived as being harsh and judgmental. In a misguided attempt to rectify this, some Christians now refuse to address the issues at all. Both extremes miss the mark. Truth without love can be harsh and judgmental even as love without truth is permissive. But when we speak the truth in love it is transformational (see Ephesians 4:15).

> TRUTH WITHOUT LOVE CAN BE HARSH AND JUDGMENTAL EVEN AS LOVE WITHOUT TRUTH IS PERMISSIVE. BUT WHEN WE SPEAK THE TRUTH IN LOVE IT IS TRANSFORMATIONAL.

Regardless of who wins this election our responsibilities remain the same—to pray for our elected officials (1 Timothy 2:1-2), to act justly (Micah 6:8), to look after the orphans and widows (James 1:27), to make disciples (Matthew 28:19), to love

God with our whole heart and our neighbor as our self (Matthew 22:38-39) and to keep ourselves from being polluted by the world (James 1:27).

Chapter 27
Stubborn Love

Overcoming a transgression of that magnitude isn't easy, and he spent months battling guilt and depression. He couldn't forgive himself, so why should he believe that God would forgive him? He wanted to believe, but he didn't dare. Forgiveness seemed too good to be true.

Several years ago, a desperate man came to my office for counseling. Hardly had I closed the office door before he fell to his knees sobbing. For several minutes he wept before the Lord. Finally he was able to compose himself and only then did he share his dark secret.

He was a good man, a Christian, and he never intended to become trapped in sexual sin, but he had. His journey into sexual addiction started innocently enough with morning coffee at a nearby convenience store. Then he started browsing through the pornographic magazines on the counter while he drank his coffee. Then he purchased one, then another. They were "soft" porn to be sure but they fed his lust.

From that point, his story has an all too familiar progression. From magazines he went to x-rated videos, and then he secured the services of a prostitute. Of course, this degenerating progression didn't happen overnight. It took place over a period of months and with each step he told himself he would go no farther, but he seemed powerless to stop.

He lived in a self-made hell. There were moments of lustful pleasure, to be sure, but they were followed by debilitating shame; days and weeks of unspeakable regret. Yet even in his shame he was irresistibly drawn toward the very thing he hated. His desperate prayers seemed powerless against the demons within. Now he lived in secrecy and fear. What if someone saw him? What if his wife or someone from his church found out? His marriage suffered, as did his walk with the Lord. He wanted out, he wanted to stop, but he seemed powerless to do so.

Then his worst fears were realized. He contacted a sexually transmitted disease and possibly infected his wife. Thankfully it wasn't AIDS, but it still meant that he had to tell his wife so she could receive treatment if needed. What was going to happen now? Would she forgive him? Could she ever trust him again? How foolish, how insane, his sins now seemed.

After hearing his confession, I helped him identify his sinful failures and the steps necessary to rectify them. He had failed God, sinned against Him, and now he needed forgiveness and restoration. He had failed his wife, been unfaithful to her, broken their wedding vows, and now he had to acknowledge his sins against their marriage and seek her forgiveness as well. And he had sinned against himself, betrayed his own values, and dishonored everything he had once held sacred and dear.

Overcoming a transgression of that magnitude, isn't easy, and he spent months battling guilt and depression. He couldn't forgive himself, so why should he believe that God would forgive him? He wanted to believe, but he didn't dare. Forgiveness seemed too good to be true. Yet he couldn't live with his condemnation either. It drove him to despair, told him it was no use, that he would never be any different. And it became a birthing place for temptation. If he was never again to know the joy of his salvation, then why not plunge headlong into the pleasures of sin?

We battled those monsters together, using both prayer and the Word of God. First we reviewed what the scriptures taught about forgiveness—it is always God's will to forgive, He is faithful and He will never give up on us. I ask him to memorize and meditate on 1 John 1:9: "If we confess our sins, he is faithful and just and will forgive us our sins and purify us from all unrighteousness."

I helped him differentiate between the conviction of the Holy Spirit and the condemnation of the enemy. Second Corinthians 7:10 says, "Godly sorrow [conviction] brings repentance that leads to salvation and leaves no regret, but worldly sorrow [condemnation] brings death."

Holy Spirit conviction makes us painfully aware of our sinfulness, but even as it does, we are motivated to confess our sins and try again. We hear ourselves saying, "I know I've failed, but with God's help I will overcome."

Condemnation, on the other hand, drives us to despair. It tells us that we will never be any different, that God is sick of our repeated failures and ready to wash His hands of us.

Then he had to come to grips with his propensity toward sexual sin. There were certain things he couldn't do, certain places he couldn't go, not because they were sinful in themselves, but because of his susceptibility to pornography and sexual sin. For instance, he could not go into a convenience store where pornographic magazines were sold, the risk was simply too great. Nor could he go into any place that rented videos. Extreme? Perhaps, but we were dealing with matters of life and death: "If your right eye causes you to sin, gouge it out and throw it away. It is better for you to lose one part of your body than for your whole body to be thrown into hell" (Matthew 5:29).

Finally, there was his marriage. His wife was shattered. This wasn't the man she had married. That man was good and godly, incapable of the kind of things this man had done. Unspeakable things, evil acts beyond the realm of her understanding. And not only had he done them, not only had he confessed in sordid detail, but she carried in her own body the evil evidence. She had trusted him, never thought to question his late hours. She had believed him when he told her his preoccupation was job-related pressure. But now her trust was gone, crushed beneath the awful fact of his unfaithfulness.

Yet she wanted their marriage to work, she wanted to forgive him as badly as he wanted to be forgiven, but could she? Could she learn to trust him again, respect him as a godly man, as the spiritual leader in their home? These and a hundred more questions haunted her every waking moment.

The three of us worked our way through those issues, painfully, one at a time, and little by little their lives began to be restored. It was slow, and it was hard. There were several crises, moments when it didn't look as though they were going to make it, but by God's grace they did.

> GOD HAS A LONG HISTORY OF REDEEMING OUR SINFUL FAILURES, TURNING OUR WORST BLUNDERS INTO OPPORTUNITIES FOR PERSONAL GROWTH AND SPIRITUAL DEVELOPMENT.

Several years have passed since that fateful morning when he entered my office and confessed his sin. I'm thankful to report that God's grace was sufficient for that man and his wife. The road back was painful and long, requiring months of marital counseling and intense personal ministry, but it was well worth it. Today they are happily married and active in their church.

And theirs is not an isolated incident either. God has a long history of redeeming our sinful failures, turning our worst blunders into opportunities for personal growth and spiritual development. When I was a boy we used to sing, "It is no secret what God can do. What He's done for others, He will do for you." We don't sing that old song anymore but its truth still resounds in my soul. What God did for that desperate man and his shattered wife He will do for you!

"This is a trustworthy saying, and everyone should accept it: 'Christ Jesus came into the world to save sinners'—and I am the worst of them all. But God had mercy on me so that Christ Jesus could use me as a prime example of his great patience with even the worst sinners. Then others will realize that they, too, can believe in him and receive eternal life" (1 Timothy 1:15-16 NLT).

Chapter 28

Legacy

My father lived a rich life and his legacy lives on in his children and grandchildren who are all serving the Lord. Although he has been gone nearly ten years, his memory has not faded and when all of us kids get together, we always end up reminiscing about our rich spiritual heritage.

My father wasn't a man much given to words. As I reflect on my growing up years I can't remember a single time when he took me aside to impart a practical life lesson or some spiritual wisdom. Yet almost everything I know about life and godliness I learned from him. Not from what he said but from the way he lived his life.

Several memories come to mind. In the first, I see my father bending over a heap of rusting machinery in a junkyard. It is late, well past my bedtime, but I have been allowed to stay up in order to "help" my father. I am cold and tired but I am not about to complain. As I watch, the acetylene torch comes to life, piercing the darkness with a hissing blue flame. Wielding the cutting torch with practiced skill, my father dismantles the abondoned machinery, turning it into piles of scrap metal. Later we will load the scrap metal into my

ALMOST EVERYTHING I KNOW ABOUT LIFE AND GODLINESS I LEARNED FROM HIM. NOT FROM WHAT HE SAID BUT FROM THE WAY HE LIVED HIS LIFE.

Uncle's pickup and haul it to a dealer who will pay good money for it; money that my father will give to the Church's building fund, refusing to keep a single cent for himself although cash is in short supply at our house.

Now a second memory superimposes itself upon the first. My father is remodeling a small house for a young widow and her two children. Her husband died of a brain tumor leaving her virtually destitute. Following his death she was forced to move into more affordable housing. The only thing she could find was a small house that was in desperate need of repair.

Day after day, Dad would rush home from work, gulp down his supper, load up his tools, and work late into the night trying to turn that ramshackle house into a fit place to live. He replaced the plumbing, updated the electrical wiring, built cupboards for the kitchen and repainted inside and out. Of course Mom worked side by side with him and my brother and I cleaned up the trash and carried it out to the burn pile. When Dad was finally finished, that young mother and her two children had a small, but comfortable place to call home. More importantly they knew they were not alone, that God had not forgotten them.

When I was maybe fourteen years old Dad "loaned" our grocery money to a desperate couple in our church. They assured him they would return the money in short order but they were unable to do so. As a result our cupboards were bare— literally—and the folks had no money to buy groceries. Dad suggested that we eat cereal with water. Mom told him there was no cereal in the house. He then suggested that she make gravy with flour and water and we could eat bread and gravy. Struggling to control her emotions, Mom informed him that there was no flour and even if there had been there was no bread. By this time things were getting a bit testy so Mom and Dad left the house to continue their discussion. Being the oldest I was left in charge of my three siblings.

While the folks were gone the doorbell rang. When I opened the door Sister Ford, my Sunday school teacher, was standing there. Without giving me a chance to speak she asked, "Are your parents home?" When I shook my head, she said it didn't matter. Then she told me the Lord had awakened her early that morning and told her to buy us a bill of groceries. By now Don (my brother) had joined me at the front door. Without pausing for a breath, Sister Ford told us to carry the groceries into the house. We made several trips and by the time we finished, the table and the kitchen counters were piled high with sacks of groceries.

Hardly had she bid us goodbye before Mom and Dad returned. You can imagine their stunned disbelief when they saw sacks and sacks of groceries filling our kitchen. At first they were speechless, then they began praising the Lord! In an instant God turned their despair into rejoicing and their mourning into dancing. Although the family to whom Dad had "loaned" our grocery money was unable to repay us, God intervened on our behalf. Well it has been said, "If you help the poor, you are lending to the LORD—and he will repay you" (Proverbs 19:17 NLT)!

> WELL IT HAS BEEN SAID, "IF YOU HELP THE POOR, YOU ARE LENDING TO THE LORD—AND HE WILL REPAY YOU" (PROVERBS 19:17 NLT)!

Years later, my father befriended a cantankerous old man who was dying of cancer. During the last weeks of his life, Dad was almost the only person who spent time with him. His meanness had alienated his family and associates years ago and now he was reaping what he had sown. At first he resented my father's presence, and he did his best to offend him, but to no avail. No matter how ugly he acted or how spitefully he spoke, my father simply absorbed it without retaliating. Little by little Dad won his trust and a few days before he died Dad was able to lead him to the Lord.

As you can see my father lived a rich life and his legacy lives on in his children and grandchildren who are all serving the Lord. Dad was a man of his word. If he said he was going to do something you could count on it. By example he taught us to work hard and finish what we started. Although he has been gone nearly ten years, his memory lives on and when all of us kids get together, we always end up reminiscing about our rich spiritual heritage. We each have our own special memories, but we all share one memory in common—the sound of Daddy's voice lifted to God in prayer.

Distinctly I remember awaking in the predawn darkness and tiptoeing barefoot down the hallway that led to the living room. Standing just inside the door, I would listen to my father pray. Never have I felt more loved, or more secure, than when I heard him call my name to Father God in prayer.

NEVER HAVE I FELT MORE LOVED, OR MORE SECURE, THAN WHEN I HEARD HIM CALL MY NAME TO FATHER GOD IN PRAYER.

Sherry, my youngest sister, experienced that same feeling of security during family worship. She always sat on the couch, close to Dad, as he read the scriptures. When we knelt to pray, she would kneel in front of Daddy so when he knelt he couldn't help but kneel over her. After Daddy died she talked to me about those special prayer times and more than once she said, "I would give anything if I could hear Daddy pray just one more time."

Shortly after Dad and Mom married, Dad felt called to preach. He wanted to move from Colorado to Texas so he could enroll in Bible College to prepare for the ministry. Mother refused to move. She was the only child of elderly parents who were in poor health, and she couldn't imagine moving away and leaving them with no one to care for them. Of course this put my father in a difficult place. How could he force his wife to leave her parents? On the other hand, how could he disobey God?

As he languished on the horns of his dilemma, desperately praying for a way to please both God and his wife, he sensed the Lord speaking to him. "Honor your wife's commitment to care for her elderly parents. I will bless you and use you where you are. And I will fulfill your call to the ministry by giving you two sons who will be ministers." In obedience to that word Dad gave up his plans to enroll in Bible College and immersed himself in his local church, serving in a number of areas including Sunday school superintendent, Sunday school teacher, and deacon. On one occasion he served as the founding pastor of a new church plant until a permanent pastor could be found.

For years he told no one, not even my mother, about God's promise to give him two sons in the ministry. I can only imagine how his heart rejoiced when I became a pastor serving churches in Colorado, Texas, Oklahoma, and Louisiana. The double blessing came when my brother Don graduated valedictorian from the Bible College where my father had wanted to enroll twenty-five years earlier. Years later my mother and father journeyed to Argentina where Don and his wife, Melba, served as missionaries for more than forty years. Truly God was faithful to his promise and my father not only lived to see two of his sons in ministry, but one grandson as well.

Well did the psalmist say: "Blessed is the man who fears the LORD who finds great delight in his commands. His children will be mighty in the land; the generation of the upright will be blessed. Wealth and riches are in his house, and his righteousness endures forever" (Psalm 112:1-3 NIV).

Chapter 29
Telling Daddy Goodbye

Kneeling beside his bed, I took his hand and began to quote John 14:2–3. As I said the familiar words, "In my Father's house are many mansions . . ." he moved his lips, soundlessly mouthing the words along with me. As we sang his favorite hymns, he seemed to draw strength from them. Not strength to live, but the strength to pass from this life to the next without fear.

In November, 2006, my 83-year-old father fell and broke his hip. Subsequently, he underwent surgery and several weeks of rehabilitation before being released to our care. My sister turned the office in her home into a sick room, and all of us children chipped in to purchase a queen-size adjustable bed so Mother could continue to sleep with him.

This was just the latest in a series of health crises that had beset my father. For twenty years he had battled heart disease—undergoing two open-heart surgeries—and fibrosis of the lungs. With a tenacity born of love and desperation, my mother and my sister took Dad from one doctor to another, always hoping for a magical cure. While the doctors were sympathetic, there wasn't really anything they could do except try to make Dad as comfortable as possible. In time he seemed to make peace with his situation, finding joy in reading and playing table games with Mother, but it wasn't much of a life. On more than one occasion he told me that if it wasn't for leaving Mom, he would welcome death. He wasn't being morbid; he was simply tired of suffering and homesick for heaven.

IN LATE JANUARY, THE DOCTORS CONFIRMED WHAT WE COULD NO LONGER DENY, TELLING US THAT OUR FATHER HAD ONLY TWO TO FOUR WEEKS TO LIVE. WHEN MY SISTER BROKE THE NEWS TO DAD, A SMALL SMILE TOUCHED HIS LIPS, AND HE SAID, "WELL, THEY'VE FINALLY GIVEN ME SOME GOOD NEWS."

By the New Year it had become apparent that Dad was dying, although neither my sister nor my mother could bring themselves to admit it. The thought of losing him was simply more than they could bear. In late January, the doctors confirmed what we could no longer deny, telling us that our father had only two to four weeks to live. When my sister broke the news to Dad, a small smile touched his lips, and he said, "Well, they've finally given me some good news."

Soon all the children, grandchildren, and even the great-grandchildren gathered at my sister's home in Friendswood, Texas. On Thursday afternoon, February 8, 2007, my father departed this world. His homegoing was peaceful, although the weeks preceding it were filled with considerable suffering. He bore it all with remarkable grace—the pain and choking, the inability to eat and the humiliation of not being able to care for himself. As the end drew near, he became ever more affectionate, repeatedly kissing and hugging those of us who cared for him.

The last Sunday before his death we all crowded around his bed for worship. For the most part Dad seemed oblivious to what we were doing, but when it came time to receive Communion he opened his eyes and reached for the cup and the bread. Kneeling beside his bed, I took his hand and began to quote John 14:2-3. As I said the familiar words, "In my Father's house are many mansions . . ." he moved his lips, soundlessly mouthing the words along with me. As we sang his favorite hymns, he seemed to draw strength from them. Not strength to live, but the strength to pass from this life to the next without fear.

> AS WE SANG HIS FAVORITE HYMNS, HE SEEMED TO DRAW STRENGTH FROM THEM. NOT STRENGTH TO LIVE, BUT THE STRENGTH TO PASS FROM THIS LIFE TO THE NEXT WITHOUT FEAR.

Two days later he fell into a coma from which he awakened only momentarily at the very end. Mother was lying on the bed beside him, as was my sister. My brothers were at his bedside: Bob was standing at the head of the bed, softly stroking Daddy's hair, while Don was standing beside him, holding Daddy's hand. Standing between them and just a little behind, I had a clear view of my father's face. For days he had lain with his head back and his mouth wide open as he labored to breathe, but as he drew his last breath, he closed his mouth and opened his eyes. Focusing on something only he could see, Daddy smiled and tried to sit up, and then he was gone.

Thinking about it now, I am sure Jesus came for Dad just as He promised He would: "If I go and prepare a place for you, I will come again, and receive you unto myself; that where I am, there ye may be also" (John 14:3 KJV). There was no death angel in that room, just the Lord of life coming to call my father to his eternal reward.

The images of the last days I spent with my father have been forever etched upon my heart. One of the many things I will never forget is the memory of the love and devotion heaped upon him by his family and friends. It was a rare and special thing, and I can only conclude that the man or woman who goes into eternity loved like that is rich indeed.

The funeral service was deeply moving, filled with memories of the past and hope for the future. No one captured the hope of eternal life more powerfully than my brother, Don. Having spent nearly all of his adult life serving as a missionary in Latin America, he understands what it means to be a pilgrim and a stranger in a foreign land. When it was his turn to speak, he said, "For the past thirty years I have been required to carry official documents identifying me as a 'resident alien.' Although I drink *mate* like an Argentine, eat *asado* with the best of them, and speak the language as if it were my mother tongue, I am still a 'resident alien,' and I always will be. I love Argentina and its people, but I will never be an Argentine. I am an American, and America will always be my home."

Pausing to collect himself he continued, "When we went to the mission field in 1976, we were truly cut off from our families and our homeland. There was no satellite television or internet, and it took weeks to arrange an international telephone call, not to mention the prohibitive expense. After four long years we flew home for our first furlough. When we landed at Miami International Airport, I spotted a U.S. Postal Service drop box and begin to weep. I know that must seem silly to you, but it symbolized home to me, and I was overcome with emotion. In the ensuing years we have passed through customs scores of times upon our return to the United States, still each time we do, Melba eagerly waits for the immigration official to stamp her passport and then look up and say, 'Welcome home.'"

> WITH THE EYE OF FAITH I SAW DADDY GETTING HIS PASSPORT STAMPED AT HEAVEN'S GATE. I COULD ALMOST HEAR JESUS SAY, 'WELCOME HOME, DICK EXLEY! WELCOME HOME.'"

Struggling to control his emotions, he said, "When Daddy took his last breath, I knew I had lost an irretrievable part of myself. The man who gave me life was gone, and it felt like I had a hole in my heart. On another level, I rejoiced because I knew Daddy was more alive than he had ever been, and even as I wept with grief, I rejoiced for him. With the eye of faith I saw Daddy getting his passport stamped at heaven's gate. I could almost hear Jesus say, 'Welcome home, Dick Exley! Welcome home.'"

It gives me great joy to recall Don's words, and more especially to know that Dad is no longer a "resident alien" in this world of pain, but a full-fledged citizen of heaven and a member of that great cloud of witnesses (Hebrews 12:1). Of course, this does not eliminate the pain of our loss, but it does put it into perspective. Even as we grieve, we are comforted with the knowledge that one day we will be reunited, never to part.

Goodbye, Daddy. I will always love you. In life you taught me how to live, and in death you have shown me how to die with dignity. Your fingerprints are all over my life, and I will always be in your debt.

Chapter 30
Let Me Tell You a Story

A miracle happens then. Not a miracle of healing, but a miracle of love. My mother's love makes my tragically deformed sister somehow beautiful and I treasure this cameo of mother and child in my heart to this day.

Two ladies approached me as I was leaving the platform at the conclusion of my presentation. Stepping boldly in front of me they blocked my exit. Their body language was aggressive and the tone of their voices hostile. "Abortion is a woman's issue!" they said, glaring at me. "You're a man. You have no right to speak on this issue."

Their antagonism wasn't surprising. They were outspoken activists for abortion on demand and often served as volunteers at the local abortion mill. Just the day before I had led several hundred pro-life advocates in a peaceful prayer vigil at the local abortion "clinic." Both women had been among the two-dozen pro-abortion radicals opposing us. We see women just like them every time we stage a prayer vigil. Sometimes they chanted slogans while we prayed—"'Pro-life,' your name's a lie; you don't care if women die." Or they mocked us by singing "Amazing Choice" to the tune of that great hymn "Amazing Grace." And if that wasn't disgusting enough, they sometimes sang, "It's my baby and I'll abort if I want to," to the tune of the sixties pop song, "It's My Party and I'll Cry if I Want To."

Those images flashed through my mind as they confronted me, tempting me with anger. Breathing a prayer, I reminded myself that regardless of how they acted, these women were not the enemy. They were my mission, the very ones I was sent to reach.

THE REAL ENEMY WAS THE EVIL SPIRIT BEHIND THE IMMORAL AND UNJUST 1973 ROE V. WADE SUPREME COURT DECISION THAT EFFECTIVELY NULLIFIED ALL STATE LAWS OUTLAWING ABORTION.

The real enemy was the evil spirit behind the immoral and unjust 1973 *Roe v. Wade* Supreme Court decision that effectively nullified all state laws outlawing abortion. It gave the United States the dubious distinction of having the most permissive abortion laws in the Western Hemisphere. As a result, in the United States alone, nearly 1.5 million babies are put to death before birth each year. To date more than 58 million babies have been aborted.

"How," they belligerently demanded, "can you possibly oppose abortion for an unmarried teenage girl, when having a baby will ruin her life?"

The last thing I wanted to do was get into an argument so I said, "Let me tell you a story. In 1925 a teenage girl living in Northeastern Colorado became pregnant out of wedlock. Because abortion was illegal and unavailable, she was forced to carry her baby to term. To escape the shame her pregnancy would engender in her rural community, her parents sent her to a home for unwed mothers in Denver. On May 15, 1926, she gave birth to a beautiful baby girl whom she named Jacqueline Rogers. Since she was unwilling, or unable, to care for her baby, she gave her up for adoption.

"Subsequently, Jacqueline was adopted by a childless couple who changed her name to Irene and raised her as their own daughter. Nineteen years later, as World War II was winding down, Irene began exchanging letters with a young man serving in the United States Navy who just happened to be the brother of her best friend. In September, 1945, that young man was transferred from the Hawaiian Islands to Corpus Christi, Texas, and given a two-week furlough. Determined to see if his pen pal was as pretty as her picture, he hitchhiked to Sterling, Colorado.

It was love at first sight and after a whirlwind courtship they were married on November 7, 1945, in a small ceremony at the local Assembly of God church. Thirteen months later Irene gave birth to their first-born child—a dark haired baby boy whom she named Richard Dean.

"I was that dark haired baby boy and I am thankful that my maternal grand-mother—an unmarried teenage girl when she became pregnant—did not abort my mother."

For a few seconds neither woman spoke. Finally one of them said, "That's all well and good, but you have no way of knowing the damage that unfortunate girl suffered. Her life may very well have been ruined."

> "I WAS THAT DARK HAIRED BABY BOY AND I AM THANKFUL THAT MY MATERNAL GRANDMOTHER— AN UNMARRIED TEENAGE GIRL WHEN SHE BECAME PREGNANT— DID NOT ABORT MY MOTHER."

"Perhaps," I said, "but we will never know will we? Maybe she went on to marry and have other children. Maybe her life wasn't ruined at all. One thing we do know—she was never tormented by the guilt that a woman suffers when she aborts her baby."

Ignoring my comments the woman forged ahead. "Surely you can't oppose abortion when medical tests have determined that the fetus will be born severely deformed. To force a woman to give birth under those circumstances would be unspeakably cruel to both the mother and the child."

Once again I said, "Let me tell you a story. When I was nine years old my mother went into labor with her fourth child. Three days later—after the doctors belatedly decided to perform a C-section—she gave birth to our long awaited baby sister. When my grandmother told me the news I ran through our neighborhood, from house to house, telling everyone that I had a baby sister named Carolyn Faye.

"Later Dad came home and instantly I knew something was terribly wrong. His shoulders were bowed with weariness and grief and his face was filled with sorrow. He took my two younger brothers and me into the living room and told us that Carolyn Faye had been born hydrocephalic—at birth her head was larger than the rest of her body. She wasn't expected to live and if she did she would never be normal.

"Dad's words sucked my earlier excitement completely out of me. Bursting off the couch, I ran blindly through the house, choking on my sobs. I ran out the back door and down the steps and into the garage where I flung myself face down on the dirt floor. Great wrenching sobs wracked my body while I pounded my fists into the dirt.

"The doctors suggested that Dad and Mom place Carolyn in an institution in Denver. Although neither Carolyn's quality of life nor her life expectancy would improve, the doctors reasoned that it would be easier on the family. Mom and Dad thanked them for their concern, but they never seriously considered their recommendation. As far they were concerned, Carolyn Faye wasn't an inconvenience to be disposed of in the most humanitarian way possible. She was their child—a gift from God—to be loved and cared for as long as she lived.

"Although Carolyn only lived three months, I have vivid memories from that painful time. In the first, I am sitting in a big green armchair and mother has placed Carolyn in my lap, carefully positioning her huge head on a cushion on the arm of the chair. She watches with a sorrowful love as I feed Carolyn an ounce or two of formula. In the second, Daddy has gathered the whole family around Carolyn's tiny bassinet. We have joined hands and he is praying for a miracle. He is asking God to heal Carolyn. I am supposed to be praying but I can't help opening my eyes just a little to see if anything is happening. To my disappointment nothing has changed. Still I feel better—more secure—with the sound of my father's prayers filling the room.

"In another memory I am sitting at the kitchen table as mother bathes Carolyn on the kitchen counter. When she finishes bathing her she carefully dresses her in a soft gown. Next she takes a cloth tape measure from the pocket of her apron. Tenderly she slips it around Carolyn's huge head, hoping against hope, that God is doing a gradual healing and that Carolyn's head will be smaller than it was the last time she measured it. It never is and mother bites her lip and brushes a tear from her cheek as she folds the tape measure before replacing it in the pocket of her apron.

"Now she cradles Carolyn in her arms and brushes her head with kisses. Her lips are moving but she is not uttering a sound. It doesn't matter. I can read her lips. Or maybe I simply know the words she is mouthing, having heard her sing them to my brothers and me more times than I can count. 'Jesus loves the little children. Red and yellow, black and white, they are precious in His sight. Jesus loves the little children, all the children of the world.'

"A miracle happens then. Not a miracle of healing but a miracle of love. My mother's love makes my tragically deformed sister somehow beautiful and I treasure this cameo of mother and child in my heart to this day."

I pause for a moment to let my words sink in. Looking both of the women in the eye I say, "I do not think it would have been kinder for my parents to have killed Carolyn before birth. Nor do I think aborting a child who may be born deformed or handicapped is ever right. It is never an act of love."

Without another word the two women turned to leave. "Before you go," I said, "let me ask you a question. Have you ever held the mutilated remains of an aborted baby in your hands?"

Gasping in disgust the first woman replied, "Absolutely not!"

"Well I have, and until you do, I don't think you are qualified to speak on this issue."

After they left I placed my notes and my Bible in my briefcase before donning my topcoat. It was late and weariness dogged my steps as I walked across the parking lot toward my car. As I slipped the key into the door lock, the Holy Spirit seemed to speak to me. Gently He said, "Do you see how your life experience has uniquely prepared you to speak to this issue?" Before that moment I had never considered it, I had never connected the dots.

While waiting for the defroster to clear the frost from my windshield, I couldn't help thinking how different things would have been if my mother had been aborted. We tend to think that abortion only takes a single life—the unborn child—but it doesn't end there. Had my mother been aborted, her five children would not have been born. That makes six lives a single abortion would have eliminated. But there's more. My mother's five children have nine children of their own. That makes fifteen lives that would have been eliminated had my maternal grandmother chosen abortion. But there's more. My mother's nine grandchildren have seventeen children of their own. That makes thirty-two lives that would have been eliminated by a single abortion in 1925.

Now let's consider the impact of the lives that would have been lost. Mom had an extraordinary love for children. For many years she ran a daycare in her home, loving and caring for children who desperately needed a stay-at-home mom. Years later those same children—now grown to be adults—often came by the house to see her. They came to tell her how special she was to them and what a difference she had made in their lives. They wanted their children to meet the woman who was like a second mother to them. Consider all the love that one abortion would have wiped out and the children whose lives would have been the poorer because of it.

> CONSIDER ALL THE LOVE THAT ONE ABORTION WOULD HAVE WIPED OUT AND THE CHILDREN WHOSE LIVES WOULD HAVE BEEN THE POORER BECAUSE OF IT.

My brother Don is what missionaries call a "lifer"—a career missionary who spends his entire life serving in a foreign country. Don's love for the unreached is legendary. When he received his missionary call as a teenage boy he asked God to confirm it by giving him such a love for the lost that he couldn't stop weeping. Hours later he was still sobbing over the plight of lost souls. Fifty years later he is still weeping. During his forty-year career in Latin America, he has planted scores of churches and reached tens of thousands of people with the gospel. Who would have reached those lost souls had Don never been born?

Bob, my youngest brother, is the President of Snead State College in Alabama and the recipient of numerous national awards for his exemplary leadership and service. Only God knows how many young people he has touched and influenced and only God knows the void his absence would have left had our mother been aborted.

Sherry, the baby in our family, was an extraordinary woman. She reared three remarkable daughters while serving as the administrative assistant to the president of a large manufacturing company. She loved the Lord passionately and served Him and His church selflessly. Who would have taken her place if she had never been born?

I could continue but I think you get the point. Abortion is a killer—taking not only the life of the unborn child, but also the lives of all the descendants of that child. It is a thief, robbing humanity of the talents and gifts that aborted child and his or her descendants would have brought into the world. In truth, the consequences of abortion reach far beyond anything we can imagine. Its costs are virtually incalculable.

> THE CONSEQUENCES OF ABORTION REACH FAR BEYOND ANYTHING WE CAN IMAGINE. ITS COSTS ARE VIRTUALLY INCALCULABLE.

Which bring us to this question: If abortion is so unspeakably hideous—and it is—how can a civilized nation allow such atrocities?

Several reasons come to mind. 1) Law-abiding citizens have great respect for the law and the Supreme Court has ruled that abortion is legal, therefore many accept it no matter how disgusting they may find it. 2) Abortion masquerades as a medical procedure and it is carried out in a medical clinic under the guise of medical treatment, although it treats no illness and cures no disease. Its only purpose is to kill the unborn child. 3) The victims of abortion are invisible to everyone except those involved in the abortion industry. Their silent screams are never heard. 4) It is cleverly packaged as "Choice"—a woman's right. Well it has been said, "He who frames the question wins the argument." In reality no one has the right to "choose" to end another person's life even if that person is still in the womb. The real question is: Do you believe a mother should have the right to have the baby in her womb put to death before birth? I think not!

I believe it is safe to say that many of us are pro-life by conviction but pro-choice by default. We believe abortion is morally wrong and should be illegal, but we don't do anything about it. Not because we don't care, but because we feel power-less. We don't know what to do.

Let me suggest some things we can do. 1) We can educate ourselves so we can speak knowledgably to the issue. 2) We can wear pro-life jewelry as a conversation starter and prophetic witness. My favorite is a tiny baby's feet lapel pin. The tiny feet accurately represent the size of the baby's feet in the sixth week of pregnancy. When asked why I wear them I explain the stages of fetal development and why I believe abortion is the taking of the baby's life. 3) We can volunteer at a crisis pregnancy center or some other pro-life ministry. 4) We can support the pro-life movement financially. 5) We can vote for pro-life candidates. 6) We can pray without ceasing.

Some may argue that we are wasting our time, that for all our efforts to end abortion on demand it still remains legal and more than one million women seek abortions every year. I beg to differ. Abortions have declined significantly and public opinion is changing. Even if that were not the case, I would still work tirelessly to end abortion. Why? Because if we do nothing in the face of crimes against humanity we betray ourselves. Sometimes the only person we can save is our self, and we can only do that by laying down our life for others.

> IF WE DO NOTHING IN THE FACE OF CRIMES AGAINST HUMANITY WE BETRAY OURSELVES.

Chapter 31
The Beast Within

In our efforts to end the evils so rampant in our society, we must never give into the beast that is within each of us. One act of violence, one fit of temper, one moment of hate, and the beast is loose.

It is an incredibly beautiful morning in Northwest Arkansas. The sky is nearly Colorado blue, the humidity relatively low with temperatures in the mid-seventies. Earlier this morning, I enjoyed a cup of coffee on the porch overlooking Beaver Lake, but in spite of the natural beauty of God's creation my heart was heavy. This peaceful morning belies the reality of our world where violence begets violence and well-meaning people risk becoming monsters in an attempt to destroy a monster. The thing that prompted my melancholy musings this morning was the murder of late-term abortionist George Tiller. He was shot and killed on Sunday morning, May 31, 2009, while serving as an usher at Reformation Lutheran Church in Wichita, Kansas.

The response from both sides has been predictable. Pro-life organizations decry it as a senseless act of violence—an act that is anathema to their pro-life philosophy. Pro-choice groups, like the National Organization for Women, have labeled the murder an act of "politically-motivated domestic terrorism" and have called on the Departments of Justice and Homeland Security to put their full resources behind the effort to "root out and prosecute . . . the criminal enterprise that has organized and funded criminal acts for decades." It doesn't take a prophet to see where this is going.

Everything about this tragedy is grievous. Although I deplore the late-term abortions that George Tiller specialized in I am still grieved that he was murdered and that his wife, children, and grandchildren must suffer this senseless tragedy. To make matters worse, his murder was so pointless. Killing him does nothing to end the tragedy of abortion; in fact it probably hardens the resolve of pro-choice groups and legislatures. Without a doubt it makes it more difficult for pro-life advocates.

> I'M GRIEVED THAT HE APPARENTLY SAW NOTHING INCONGRUOUS ABOUT PROFESSING CHRIST WHILE MAKING HIS LIVING AS A LATE-TERM ABORTIONIST.

I'm grieved that an active churchman like George Tiller could routinely perform late-term abortions. I'm grieved that he apparently saw nothing incongruous about professing Christ while making his living as a late-term abortionist. I'm grieved that the pastor and congregation where he attended did not hold him accountable for his actions.

So how did we get here? How did we get to the place that abortion is considered a woman's right and a reasonable choice? When the National Abortion Rights Action League initially lobbied to have the abortion laws changed in the 1960s and 70s, they positioned themselves very carefully. They focused on a woman's choice and they never talked about the baby. In their strategy sessions they discussed the importance of controlling the debate by carefully framing the question. They made a strategic decision to focus on a woman's choice. It was her body. It was her life. They decided to never talk about the baby. It was a pregnancy. And an abortion was simply the termination of a pregnancy. It was a simple procedure to remove a mass of tissue, a group of undifferentiated cells. That's how they sold it to the public.

Advances in medical science now make it impossible to deny that an abortion takes the life of the unborn child. Nonetheless society continues to justify abortion as a woman's right. In some cases pro-abortion advocates have formed emotional support groups to help mothers make the "difficult decision" to abort and some abortion facilities even provide fetal ashes to the "grieving" parents. And some ministers like the Rev. George Gardner of College Hill United Methodist Church in Wichita, Kansas, even have baptismal services for aborted fetuses if the parents so desire.

Can it get any more bizarre than that? I think not.

We're talking about a deadly descent that threatens our way of life. If we continue to permit abortions on demand in spite of the fact that we now know the unborn are alive, we are jeopardizing our future. To ignore this reality is a denial of the most dangerous kind.

I'm grieved that highest courts in our land do not acknowledge and rectify the inconsistencies in the way the law treats the rights of the unborn child. For instance the United States has a federal statue protecting the life of the unborn child called the Unborn Victims of Violence Act of 2004 (Public Law 108-212). It recognizes a child in utero as a legal victim, if he or she is injured or killed during the commission of any of more than 60 listed federal crimes of violence. The law defines "child in utero" as "a member of the species *Homo sapiens*, at any stage of development, who is carried in the womb." The bill is also known as Laci and Conner's Law after the California mother (Laci Peterson) and her unborn son (Conner Peterson), who were murdered by the husband and father, Scott Peterson. Peterson was convicted of double homicide under California's

DANCING IN THE DARK

fetal homicide law. Thirty-six states have similar laws protecting the child in the womb.

I CAN ONLY CONCLUDE THAT AS A NATION WE ARE SUFFERING FROM LEGAL SCHIZO-PHRENIA.

Comparing the Unborn Victims of Violence Act of 2004 and the 1973 Supreme Court ruling in the infamous *Roe v. Wade* case legalizing abortion on demand, I can only conclude that as a nation we are suffering from legal schizophrenia. Think about it. If the child in the womb is killed without the consent of the mother it is murder according to the Unborn Victims of Violence Act of 2004, but if the mother wants to put her unborn child to death that's called abortion or a woman's right and it is legal according to the *Roe v. Wade* Supreme Court decision. That makes no sense at all. The unborn child is either a human being with all the rights and privileges of a human being or it is not. Whether the mother wants that unborn child or not, does not change the unborn child's inherent right to life.

I'm grieved that so many of us still do not realize who the real enemy is. The woman seeking an abortion is not the enemy, nor is the abortion provider. Of course they must take responsibility for their actions, but in many ways they are victims too. The true enemy is the unjust law that makes it legal to put the child in the womb to death; a law whose unintended consequences we are just beginning to reap. But changing the law is not enough. The only hope we have of ending abortion on demand and stopping society's plunge down this slippery slope is a spiritual awakening, for only the Spirit of God can transform our hearts and minds. Of course this does not mean that we shouldn't do everything we can do legally to end abortion, but our hope must be in Jesus Christ and Him alone.

I'm grieved that the evil that lurked within George Tiller's heart and the heart of the man who murdered him also lurks in mine. Author Phillip Yancey relates an incident from World

War II that illustrates this truth. A friend of Yancey's served in the Army during the closing days of the WWII and participated in the liberation of the infamous Dachau concentration camp. He told Yancey that the most shocking part of the whole experience was not the atrocities that the SS officers had perpetrated upon the helpless Jews, though such cruelty was beyond imagining. The thing that stayed with him was what he discovered about himself.

One afternoon the captain of the liberating forces asked for a volunteer to escort twelve SS prisoners to the interrogation center. The most volatile soldier in the unit volunteered. Grabbing a submachine gun, he herded the captives down the trail where they soon disappeared into some trees in a shallow ravine. Shortly thereafter, a burst of machine gun fire shattered the afternoon stillness. The soldier came swaggering back and announced with a kind of fiendish leer, "They tried to escape."

In that moment, Yancey's friend experienced a nauseating fear that he might be called upon to escort the next group of SS guards to the interrogation center. The thing he feared most was that he too might give in to his unspeakable rage and gun down the guards as that soldier had done.

"The beast that was within those guards," he said, "was also within me."

While most of us will never be involved in the liberation of a Nazi death camp or tempted to gun down a late-term abortionist, we must all contend with the beast that is within. In our efforts to end the evils so rampant in our society, we must always guard our hearts lest we give in to that beast. One act of violence, one fit of temper, one moment of hate, and the beast is loose.

IN OUR EFFORTS TO END THE EVILS SO RAMPANT IN OUR SOCIETY, WE MUST ALWAYS GUARD OUR HEARTS LEST WE GIVE INTO THAT BEAST. ONE ACT OF VIOLENCE, ONE FIT OF TEMPER, ONE MOMENT OF HATE, AND THE BEAST IS LOOSE.

Chapter 32
He Hideth My Soul

The possibility of Leah's death was not diminished; it was no less real. Yet in a way that I cannot explain, we were suddenly at peace. Somehow we were assured that no matter what happened, whether Leah lived or died, God's grace would be sufficient. Somehow life would still be worth living.

It started with a low-grade fever, followed by vomiting that lasted for two days. Since Leah was only eight months old and appeared to be dehydrating, we decided to take her to the doctor. After examining her, the pediatrician gave her an injection. When he did, she suffered a severe seizure—her eyes rolled back in her head and her tiny body went rigid.

Quickly the doctor ordered a second injection, and when that failed to control the convulsions, he ordered a third which also proved futile. By now Brenda and I were nearly beside ourselves. Any illusions we had about the seriousness of the situation were shattered when the doctor scooped Leah's rigid body into his arms and ran for his car. Brenda and his nurse followed and in seconds they were racing for the hospital.

I rushed after them in our car, fear pushing me nearly to the point of panic. It seemed that all I could see was Leah's tiny body, rigid and spastic, her eyes rolled back in her head. Would

I ever see her smile again, hear her giggle contentedly as Brenda pinned a dry diaper on her freshly powdered bottom?

Terrifying thoughts of death . . . Leah's death . . . our baby's death, tried to take control of my mind. With a Herculean effort I dismissed them, only to have them return a minute later and with a vengeance. There were other thoughts too, almost as terrifying—Leah brain-damaged or growing up afflicted with epilepsy.

I skidded to a stop in the hospital parking lot just in time to see the doctor rush Leah into a specially equipped emergency area. For the next two and one-half hours the doctors worked to save her life. Brenda and I clung to each other, hoping against hope that Leah would be all right. In desperation I called our families, begging them to pray. Distinctly I can recall the desolation that washed over me after I hung up the pay telephone. Standing beside the now silent telephone, at the end of the empty hallway, I felt totally alone.

After getting hold of myself, I made my way back to where Brenda was nervously pacing the floor just outside the emergency area. Once more we clung to each other and cried and prayed. Together we faced the harsh reality—Leah might not live, and if she did, she might never be the same again. Never had life seemed so empty of hope, so crowded with pain and fear. Yet even as we came to grips with the terrifying possibility of Leah's death and all that would mean to us, we also began to sense God's presence and His peace.

The possibility of Leah's death was not diminished; it was no less real. Yet in a way that I cannot explain, we were suddenly at peace. Until that moment, I had wondered how anyone survived the death of a child. Now I understood—at least in part, at least as much as anyone who hasn't lost a child can understand. This was what we used to sing about: "He giveth more grace as the burdens grow greater."[30] Somehow we were assured that no matter what happened, whether Leah lived or died, God's grace would be sufficient. Somehow life would still be worth living.

Nearly three hours later the doctor emerged, looking exhausted but relieved. He told us that Leah was out of danger; she would live. She would need to stay in the hospital for a few days. There were a number of tests they wanted to run. The doctor listened patiently as we bombarded him with a host of questions. After answering as best he could, he excused himself and we were left alone once more.

Only we weren't alone—God was with us! We were relieved, yet not nearly to the extent I had expected. The real relief had already come—the peace of God that passes all understanding.

Leah was wheeled out of the emergency area and Brenda gasped. She was clothed only in a diaper, her hands and feet were fastened to the rungs of the crib with strips of cloth, and an IV was flowing into a vein in her head. We followed as the nurse pushed her crib into the nursery. For a long time we simply stood beside her tiny bed watching her sleep, relieved somehow just by the gentle motion of her breathing. The storm wasn't over but the crisis had passed, at least for the moment, and I found myself replaying the entire experience, marveling at the supernatural peace that had sustained us through it all.

A story came to mind. Something I had read somewhere, or maybe heard in a sermon. A group of artists were asked to paint scenes depicting peace. Most of them created the kind of paintings you would expect—a quiet meadow at sunset, a mother holding a sleeping child, an empty sanctuary bathed in the refracted light of stained glass—things like that.

One painting, however, was different, totally different. The artist had painted a stormy scene. The sky was black, rent by jagged flashes of lightning. A lone tree, stubbornly clinging to a rocky cliff, was bent before the fierce wind, and angry breakers crashed on the jutting rocks at the base of the cliff where it met the sea.

"How," someone asked, "can such a violent scene depict peace?"

The artist was standing nearby and overheard the question. Joining the group who were viewing the painting, he encouraged them to re-examine it, to notice not only the obvious, but the detail as well.

Suddenly a lady exclaimed, "I see it! I see it!"

Pointing, she said, "Look, there in the cleft of the rock. There's a bird with its head thrown back singing."

Standing outside the hospital nursery, looking through the window at Leah, I realized that the artist had painted my experience. On this fateful afternoon, I was that tiny bird, sheltered in the cleft of the rock. All around me a storm was raging. Sickness and death threatened my only child, yet I had peace. Now the storm was easing a little and I took comfort in that. Still the true source of my confidence came from a sense of God's presence and the peace it brought.*

---

30 Annie Johnson Flint, "He Giveth More Grace," music by Hubert Mitchell (Lillenas Publishing Co., 1941, 1969).

* To the amazement of the medical professionals, Leah suffered no brain damage from the convulsions that continued for nearly three hours. Although the doctors performed a battery of tests in the ensuing weeks, they were never able to determine what caused her seizures. They prescribed an anti-seizure drug as a precautionary measure but we discontinued it after a short time because of the side effects. Forty-seven years have passed since that fateful day and Leah has never suffered another seizure.

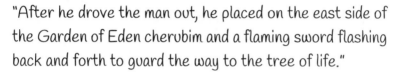

Chapter 33
East of Eden

"After he drove the man out, he placed on the east side of the Garden of Eden cherubim and a flaming sword flashing back and forth to guard the way to the tree of life."

—Genesis 3:24 NIV

Jude and Arg stand shoulder to shoulder, staring into the darkness beyond the chain link fence that is topped by razor wire jutting inward. They are emaciated, their eyes looking huge and empty above their sunken cheeks. In the distance, the crematorium belches its sickly sweet fumes into the night sky, a constant reminder of the atrocities being perpetrated by their fellow men.

Arg, the taller of the two men, speaks, his voice raw with a suffering too deep for words. In another life he was a husband and a father, a college professor, and an author of some renown. Now he is just a prisoner with a number tattooed on his forearm. "How did it come to this?" he asks, his eyes surveying the death camp.

Jude, an ordained minister and an outspoken critic of the government, follows his gaze. Thanks to a full moon, he can see the silhouette of Block 11, the building where the political prisoners are taken to be tortured, and beyond that the "Black Wall" where the executions are carried out in full view of the other prisoners who are forced to watch.

213

"How did it come to this?" Arg asks again. "How did it come to this?"

His troubling question hangs in the darkness for what seems a long time, asked but never answered. Finally he speaks again, his voice tired, stained with incredulity. "We are the most technologically advanced civilization in the history of the world. Medical science has cured a host of diseases once thought incurable. Modern agricultural methods have made it possible to feed the world, ridding it of hunger and starvation . . . so how did it come to this?"

His voice fades into the darkness, disbelief rendering him mute. Finally, Jude takes his arm and guides him to a spot deep within the shadows of the barracks where they can converse without being observed.

"This," he says, with a sweep of his arm taking in the entire concentration camp and the world beyond, "is the culmination of something that began a long time ago. Skeptics dismiss what I am about to tell you as a myth. Scientists claim to have disproved it, but as far as I am concerned, it is the only thing that even comes close to explaining what's happening here."

"Tell me," Arg demands with no little urgency. "Help me make some sense of this madness."

"It's a long story," Jude replies, pursing his lips, "so you will have to be patient. And being an agnostic, you will have to set aside your skepticism regarding God."

"God?" Arg erupts. "Are you telling me this is about God?" Without giving Jude a chance to reply he plunges on. "I don't know how anyone can believe in God given the horrors of this present age. What kind of a God would allow humans to practice genocide and develop weapons of mass destruction?" His anger spent, he stumbles to a stop. After a moment he adds, "If God does exist he must be either cruel of incompetent."

"Are you finished?" Jude asks.

When Arg just stares into the darkness, Jude begins, his voice hardly more than a whisper in the darkness. "On the sixth day of creation, the creator knelt in the garden called Eden. Taking some dirt from the ground, He fashioned it into the form of a man and breathed into his nostrils the breath of life. He called the man Adam.

"God placed him in the Garden to take care of it. In the evening God walked in the Garden with Adam and they conversed as friend with friend. Yet for all of that Adam was lonely. Although he shared a special relationship with all of God's creation, he was still alone in the deepest part of his soul. Even though he walked with God in the Garden, and communed with Him, there remained a part of him that was achingly alone; because "for Adam no suitable helper was found" (Genesis 2:20).

"Where could Adam find his soul mate, that one who would finally end his aloneness? Not in the animal kingdom, for there was none like him; nor in relationship with God, for that was intimacy on an altogether different plane.

"So God caused a deep sleep to fall on Adam and He took a rib from Adam's side and from that rib he created a woman and called her Eve. When He brought her to Adam, Adam was overwhelmed and cried, 'This is now bone of my bone and flesh of my flesh. We will be one. Never again will I be lonely.'

"God told Adam and Eve they could eat from any tree in the Garden, except from the Tree of Knowledge of Good and Evil. 'Don't eat from it,' He said. 'The moment you eat from that tree, you're dead.'

"No one knows how long Adam and Eve lived in the Garden, enjoying their special relationship with God. It may have been just a few weeks or it could have been tens of thousands of years, even millions of years. There was no sickness or death in the Garden. There was no evil or violence, no unspeakable atrocities.

"Then one day God's enemy slipped into the Garden. In eternity past he had been the most beautiful of all of God's angels, but pride filled his heart causing him to rebel and he was cast out of heaven. Now he sees his chance to get even with God. He will deceive the man and the woman who were made in God's image, and in the process he will set in motion a series of events that will totally destroy the world and those who were created by God.

"He waited until Eve was alone and then he approached her. Not only was he dazzling in his beauty, but he was the consummate con man. With a finely honed skill, he convinced Eve that if she ate of the Tree of Knowledge of Good and Evil nothing bad would happen. 'You'll not die!' the serpent hissed. 'God knows very well that the instant you eat it you will become like him, for your eyes will be opened—you will be able to distinguish good from evil!' (Genesis 3:4-5 NLB).

"Having planted his evil seed in Eve's heart and mind he left the Garden. In the days following that encounter, Eve found herself drawn toward the forbidden tree. Day after day she studied it and as she did her desire grew. Finally one day she touched it and when nothing happened, she picked a piece of the fruit. She took it with her but concealed it from Adam. When she was alone she would take it from its hiding place and caress it, savoring its tantalizing aroma. She told herself that she would never eat of it, for that was forbidden by God, but each day her desire grew until it nearly consumed her.

"One bright, sunlit morning she saw Adam approaching. With trembling hands she took the forbidden fruit from its hiding place and as Adam watched she placed it to her mouth. Although she knew what she was doing was wrong she could not stop herself. 'So she ate some of the fruit and gave some to her husband, and he ate it too' (Genesis 3:6).

"They did not die instantly, but something worse than death happened—a kind of living death. They were overwhelmed with emotions that were totally foreign to them; dark emotions, grim emotions for which they had no name. In time they would come to know them well, as would the entire human race—things like shame and fear, anger and hatred, and self-loathing.

"When evening came they heard God walking in the Garden and they were afraid. They hid, unable to bear the thought of facing Him when He discovered what they had done. Of course they couldn't hide for long and when God learned they had eaten of the forbidden fruit He was angry. He was angry because He knew their disobedience had ruined everything. In an instant He saw the centuries of suffering—famine, disease, violence and bloodshed; even this death camp with its unspeakable atrocities.

"He told the Woman: 'I'll multiply your pains in childbirth; you'll give birth to your babies in pain. You'll want to please your husband, but he'll lord it over you.' He told the Man: 'Because you listened to your wife and ate from the tree that I commanded you not to eat from, the very ground is cursed because of you; getting food from the ground will be as painful as having babies is for your wife; you'll be working in pain all your life long. The ground will sprout thorns and weeds, you'll get your food the hard way, Planting and tilling and harvesting, sweating in the fields from dawn to dusk, until you return to that ground yourself, dead and buried; you started out as dirt, you'll end up dirt'" (Genesis 3:16-19 MSG).

217

"Then God banished them from the Garden. They clung to each other, weeping, as they stumbled from Eden. Once they had gone, God placed an angel with a flaming sword at the east entrance to the Garden to make sure they never entered Eden again, lest they eat of the tree of life and live forever.

"Life outside the Garden was hard. Now Adam and Eve experienced things they had never experienced before. Work made them tired and their muscles ached. The ground was cursed and they were able to plant and harvest with only the most determined effort. Sickness racked their bodies with fever and pain. Suffering and death lurked everywhere. Although they tried to comfort one another it was hard. They couldn't stop blaming each other. Adam blamed Eve for eating of the forbidden fruit and she blamed him for not protecting her from the enemy of God.

"Some nights Adam's homesickness of soul was so acute he could not sleep. On those nights Eve would find him sitting on a high hill, alone in the darkness, staring off in the distance toward Eden. She could tell he was remembering life in the Garden before they sinned. Seeing him like that was unbearable. She blamed herself. It was her fault. But she blamed Adam too.

"And then she began to blame God. It was His fault. He should have never put the Tree of Knowledge of Good and Evil in the Garden. And why didn't He protect them from the evil one? How dare He leave them unprotected!

"Once or twice they tried to return to Eden only to be driven away by the angel with the flaming sword. They begged and pleaded but to no avail. They promised that they would never go near the tree of life but the angel remained unmoved. They cried out to God but he did not answer.

"Life outside the Garden was unbearably hard and there was little joy. They longed for the fellowship they once had with God, as He walked with them in the Garden, but God never visited them. Evening after evening came and went, but God remained conspicuously absent and they remained achingly alone.

"Eventually Eve conceived and gave birth to a son. Then she conceived again and gave birth to a second son. Seeing her sons grow into strong young men gave her a measure of joy, but it could not take away the pain of what she had lost—nothing could.

"Then her joy was shattered. The thing God had foreseen manifested itself. Cain, her first-born, murdered his brother Abel. In a single day she lost both her sons—Abel murdered by his brother and Cain driven from their presence by the Lord; punishment for his evil deed. Eve was suffering the consequences of her sin and it was worse than anything she could have imagined and that was only the beginning."

"Hogwash!" Arg muttered. "You're talking nonsense. That's nothing but religious gibberish."

Ignoring him, Jude continued. "Centuries passed and as the human race increased on the earth so did the extent of their evil. The memory of God and the Garden called Eden faded from their collective consciousness. Although the angel with the flaming sword still stood guard at the east entrance into the Garden, no one tried to enter. Human beings had little or no desire to know God and if they had a desire they simply created gods in their own image—idols glorifying their evil passions.

"With each passing century mankind grew more evil. People thought evil, imagined evil—evil, evil, evil from morning to night. They loved only themselves, they were boastful and proud, lovers of money, abusive, disobedient to their parents, ungrateful, unholy, without love, unforgiving, slanderous, without self-control, brutal, treacherous, rash, conceited, lovers of pleasure rather than lovers of God (see 2 Timothy 3:2-4).

"They were filled with every kind of wickedness, evil, greed, and depravity. They were full of envy, murder, strife, deceit, and malice. They were gossips, slanderers, God-haters, insolent, arrogant, and boastful; they invented ways of doing evil; they had no understanding, no fidelity, no love, no mercy (see Romans 1:28-31).

"And so we finally end up here" Jude concludes, gesturing toward the death camp, "with gas chambers disguised as showers, ghouls extracting gold from the teeth of a million corpses before loading them into massive crematoriums. Hundreds of thousands of others machine-gunned down before being buried in mass graves.

> "WHEN EVE PARTOOK OF THAT FORBIDDEN FRUIT AND GAVE IT TO ADAM THEY LOOSED AN EVIL PLAGUE THAT NOW COVERS THE WHOLE EARTH, CORRUPTING EVERY HUMAN BEING."

"When Eve partook of that forbidden fruit and gave it to Adam they loosed an evil plague that now covers the whole earth, corrupting every human being. This evil produces pathological despots who practice genocide on their own citizens, sexual predators who prey upon innocent children, abusing and murdering them. It produces psychopaths who murder without remorse, mass murderers who enter schools gunning down defenseless children, religious fanatics who fly airplanes into public buildings killing thousands. It produces husbands who cheat on their wives and abandon their children. It produces mothers who abort their own babies rather than care for them. It produces pornographers and sex traffickers who enslave and destroy."

He pauses, overwhelmed by the enormity of the tragedy sin has wrought. Before he can resume Arg interrupts, "If what you're telling me is true, there's no hope. I'm not saying I buy it, but if I did I would have to say God has abandoned us. It looks like He has left us to suffer in the hell we created." After a moment he asks almost wistfully, "Is there nothing we can do?"

For what seems a long time the two men sit in the dark without speaking, each locked in his own thoughts, each contemplating the evil they have suffered and the evil they have done. Finally Jude speaks in a voice filled with sadness, "There is nothing we can do to change what has happened. We are powerless to undo what has been done. We cannot change the evil that is in the heart of those who oppress us, nor can we change the evil that is in our own hearts. Hate begets hate, violence begets violence, sin begets sin, and evil begets evil, century after century, and millennium after millennium until finally we end up with this. No wonder God said He was sorry that He had made the human race in the first place (see Genesis 6:6).

"But all is not lost," Jude continues, his voice now taking on a note of hope. "Return with me to the Garden, to the place where it all started, to paradise lost. For centuries the angel with the flaming sword stood guard at the east entrance, lest some sinful man or woman return and partake of the tree of life. One day he saw a man approaching. He was terribly disfigured from the things he had suffered, but his abused countenance evoked no pity from the angelic guard. Brandishing his flaming sword, he commanded in a loud voice, 'Halt! Who goes there?'

"Without a word, the man held out his hands, the nail scars clearly visible. 'These,' he said, 'I received in the house of my friends' (see Zechariah 13:6).

GOD'S HAND OF MERCY HAS REPLACED THE SWORD OF JUDGMENT.

"Trembling the angel lowered his fiery sword before extinguishing its flame and placing it in the nail scarred hands of God's one and only son. On a skull-shaped hill somewhere east of Eden, God did for us what we could never do for ourselves.

He sentenced his own son to suffer the punishment for our sins. God forsook Jesus that we might be reconciled to Him. Jesus died that we might live.

"Today there is no angel with a flaming sword standing between fallen men and the tree of life. God's hand of mercy has replaced the sword of judgment. That which was lost has been restored. Once more the tree of life is available to all who will come through Jesus. He is the way, the truth, and the life and no man comes to the Father except through him (see John 14:6).

"And they are coming—young and old, rich and poor, male and female—from every tribe and tongue, people and nation. They are coming to partake freely of the tree of life (see Revelation 7:9)."

"What you're telling me makes no sense," Arg lamented. "If God made his own Son a curse to free us from the curse of sin why has nothing changed? Evil despots still terrorize ordinary people like you and me. There are killing fields all over this tortured planet—in Africa, in Cambodia, in Syria, in Bosnia, and in Siberia. They still gas our wives and children before cremating them. They torture us. They starve us and work us to death. Sickness and disease ravish the whole human race. Evil abounds. Nothing's changed. Nothing!"

THAT'S HOW GOD WORKS. FIRST HE REDEEMS THE INDIVIDUAL AND THEN HE RESTORES THE PLANET.

"That's where you're wrong!" Jude replied. "Granted, the world remains filled with every kind of injustice and unimaginable evil, but God has changed my heart and there are millions just like me whose hearts have been changed. Where hatred once abounded, now love abounds. Where evil once reigned in my heart, now Christ reigns. That's how God works. First He redeems the individual and then He restores the planet.

"One day soon this polluted planet will be purged by fire. Every evil thing will be consumed (2 Peter 3:7,10). And then God will create a new heaven and a new earth where righteousness reigns (2 Peter 3:13). Once again God will make His home with His human family. He will live with us and we will be his people. God himself will wipe every tear from our eyes, and there will be no more death or sorrow or crying or pain (Revelation 21:4). All these things will be gone forever. The curse of sin will be wiped out. God will totally eradicate all evil!"

"I wish I could believe that," Arg mumbled, "I really do. I can see the hope it gives you and the strength to live with meaning even in this madness, but I can't. I want to believe, but I just can't."

"Believing is a choice," Jude reasoned. "It's not something that just happens. It's something you choose to do."

"What if I choose to believe," Arg asks, "and what you're telling me turns out to be nothing but wishful thinking, just a fantasy?"

"What do you have to lose?"

When Arg doesn't bother to respond Jude answers his own question. "Nothing," he says. "You've got nothing to lose. If what I'm telling you isn't true you've lost nothing. But if it is true and you refuse to believe then you've lost everything. You will have no hope in this world or in the world to come."

For several minutes they sit in silence, each man locked in his own thoughts. Jude prays silently, while Arg struggles to believe. Unfortunately a lifetime of unbelief, not to mention the atrocities he has witnessed and been subject to, makes it virtually impossible. Try as he might he simply cannot allow himself to believe. Finally he pushes himself to his feet, exhausted by his spiritual struggle. Extending a hand toward Jude he says, "You almost convinced me and that's saying a lot. Maybe we can talk again."

Chapter 34

What to Do When Your World Is Falling Apart

When your world is falling apart there is usually not much your friends can do to put it back together. Nonetheless, the emotional support of those you know and trust can be a source of spiritual strength. And their prayers can be a great comfort, enabling you to bear things you never imagined yourself capable of bearing.

Although medical science has made significant advances in recent years, a diagnosis of cancer still has the power to overwhelm most of us. Let the doctor's diagnosis include "stage 3," and the level of fear ratchets up yet again. And should the prognosis include a life expectancy of less than two years, the effect can be absolutely devastating. That's what my sister is facing. In two weeks' time, her world went from safe and secure to one of fearful uncertainty and confusion. Needless to say my heart goes out to her and her family.

So where do they go from here? What do they do now? Of course, they're going to get the best medical advice available before deciding on a course of treatment, but beyond that what can they do? For that matter, what can any of us do when our world is falling apart?

YOUR CRISIS MAY NOT COME AS A DEVASTATING MEDICAL DIAGNOSIS, BUT GIVEN TIME YOU WILL FACE THINGS THAT WILL ROCK YOUR WORLD. SO WHAT CAN YOU DO WHEN YOUR WORLD IS CRASHING DOWN AROUND YOU?

If you haven't been there, you will be. No one goes through this life unscathed. Your crisis may not come as a devastating medical diagnosis, but given time you will face things that will rock your world. So what can you do when your world is crashing down around you?

The first thing you need to do is ask for help. That's what Jesus did in Gethsemane. "He took Peter and the two sons of Zebedee along with him, and he began to be sorrowful and troubled. Then he said to them, 'My soul is overwhelmed with sorrow to the point of death. Stay here and keep watch with me.'" (Matthew 26:37-38).

There was nothing Peter, James, or John could do to change the situation; still Jesus wanted them with Him. He understood the value of their presence, He knew their nearness would sustain Him in a way nothing else could. No one could drink that dreadful cup for Him, but having their spiritual support and physical presence would give Him the strength to do what had to be done.

When your world is falling apart there is usually not much your friends can do to put it back together. Nonetheless, the emotional support of those you know and trust can be a source of spiritual strength. And their prayers can be a great comfort, enabling you to bear things you never imagined yourself capable of bearing; so don't hesitate to ask for their help.

The second thing you need to do is run to the Father. Throw yourself on His mercy. Trust Him with your situation. That's what Jesus did. "Going a little farther, he fell with his face to the ground and prayed, 'My Father, if it is possible, may this cup be taken from me'" (Matthew 26:39).

When your world is crumbling around you, let Father God hold you and comfort you. Meditate on what it means for Him to be your Father. That truth has often given me special comfort, especially during the hard times. Being a father myself, I know the feelings a father has for his children. Nothing pains me more than seeing my daughter or my grandchildren suffer, nor does anything bless me more than their happiness. Whatever touches them touches me. If I, a mere mortal, have these kinds of feelings for my daughter and my grandchildren then I can only imagine how much more Father God cares for us, His children. "As a father pities his children," said the psalmist, "So the Lord pities those who fear Him" (Psalm 103:13).

I am especially sensitive to this truth at the moment, because my daughter is struggling with several serious health issues and has been for several years. No matter what I am doing, Leah's situation is never far from my mind. When I lie in bed at night awaiting sleep, my mind is searching for solutions. My first thought upon waking in the morning is a prayer for her. When I pray, her needs take precedence over almost everything else. I am her father, and I am touched by the feelings of her infirmities. What hurts her hurts me. Her pain is my pain.

Is not my concern for Leah but a dim reflection of Father God's concern for us? Jesus said it like this, "If you then, being evil know how to give good gifts to your children, how much more will your Father who is in heaven give good things to those who ask Him!" (Matthew 7:11).

CHOOSE TO TRUST THE FATHER'S HEART EVEN WHEN YOU DON'T UNDERSTAND HIS WAYS.

Choose to trust the Father's heart even when you don't understand His ways. That's what Jesus did. Even though that foul cup and all it portended repulsed everything within Him, He still trusted the Father. And He prayed, "Yet not as I will, but as you will" (Matthew 26:39).

Trusting God is easy when everything is going well, but let your world come crashing down and the enemy will tempt you to rail at God. When my grandson was just a little guy he was always crashing into things and hurting himself. But instead of running to us for comfort, he would run away. And if we tried to comfort him, he would strike out at us screaming, "Don't touch me. Leave me alone!"

Although we were not in any way responsible for his pain, he blamed us. I cannot help thinking how like him we are. Let life deal us a crushing blow and we are quick to blame God. We are tempted to question His goodness and to rail at Him for the "injustices" we are suffering.

You have a choice. You can respond like my grandson responded to us when he was hurt or you can respond like Jesus did in Gethsemane. You can push God away or you can cling to Him, putting your trust in Him and Him alone. Let me encourage you to trust Father God even when your circumstances don't appear to be changing. That's what Jesus did. ". . . and (Jesus) prayed the third time, saying 'My Father, if it is not possible for this cup to be taken away except I drink it, may your will be done'" (Matthew 26:44).

Ultimately, Jesus suffered unspeakably and died an excruciating death; still He refused to doubt the Father's trustworthiness. Even when it seemed Father God had abandoned Him (Matthew 27:46), Jesus continued to trust Him. And as He was dying, "Jesus called out with a loud voice, 'Father, into your hands I commit my spirit'" (Luke 23:46).

Things looked bleak as Jesus' friends took his mutilated body down from the cross and prepared it for burial. Saturday was gloomy, things looked hopeless, but that wasn't the end of the story. Sunday was coming! And on Sunday Father God turned the tragedy of the cross into the glory of the resurrection. Suddenly it all made sense!

I don't know how God is going to turn your situation around, or how He is going to bring glory out of the tragedy you are living, but I am confident He will! And until His deliverance manifests itself, we have the promise of His presence to sustain us—"Never will I leave you; never will I forsake you" (Hebrews 13:5). We have His miracles and supernatural healings to encourage us. No matter how grim our situation or how hopeless it appears, we know that nothing is impossible for Him. God can turn it around! And ultimately, we have the promise of eternal life. "Jesus said to her, 'I am the resurrection and the life. He who believes in me will live, even though he dies'" (John 11:25).

Chapter 35
The Dark Wood

In the middle of my own journey I unexpectedly found myself in a dark wood. I was blindsided by a devastating loss, people I loved were hurting badly and I couldn't seem to help them or myself. Week after week the darkness deepened and I found myself fearing it would never end.

L eaving the RCA Dome, I turned toward the hotel, depression dogging my steps. I should have felt exhilarated, or at least deeply satisfied, but I didn't. Being one of the speakers at the annual Bill Gaither Praise Gathering was a high honor, one I never expected to have; still, all I felt in the aftermath of my second session was an aching emptiness. The sessions went well enough, with lots of positive affirmation, but I couldn't seem to wring any joy out of the experience.

For the better part of two years I had been living in a fog. Somehow I managed to minister with a measure of proficiency, but nothing I did touched the sadness that was slowing sucking life out of me. Day after day I forced myself to go through the motions, desperately hoping this would be the day some light returned to my gray existence, but it never happened. Instead the gloom seemed to deepen, causing me to doubt if I would ever again know the joy that once defined my life.

In *Dante's Inferno*, the writer takes a walk and suddenly finds himself disoriented, and so begins his journey into the various levels of hell with these words: "In the middle of the journey of our life I found myself in a dark wood."

That best describes what happened to me—in the middle of my own journey I unexpectedly found myself in a dark wood. I was blindsided by a devastating loss, people I loved were hurting badly and I couldn't seem to help them or myself. Week after week the darkness deepened and I feared it would never end.

Reminding myself that I was not the first person to walk this path helped some. I took what courage I could from the knowledge that this dark place, though unfamiliar to me, was not unfamiliar to those who had gone before me. Many who walked this way will remain anonymous, but others are well known. Elijah the prophet found himself in a wood so dark he despaired of life and prayed to die. Even Jesus was tempted to despair and at least on one occasion He confessed that his soul was "exceeding sorrowful unto death." In the classic devotional literature these experiences came to be known as the dark night of the soul and were considered a nearly universal experience. Sometimes, as in my case, the darkness descended as a result of a grievous loss, but at other times it seemed to come for no apparent reason. Whatever the cause it can be debilitating, especially if it continues for any length of time.

The fact that I tried to mask my pain, carefully concealing it beneath a trouble free facade, probably complicated my situation. Still, I didn't know what else to do, not wanting to burden anyone else with my troubles. Thus I found myself walking the streets of Indianapolis in the deepening dusk, a sharp wind tugging at the collar of my jacket, while sorrow gnawed a hole in my heart.

City noise filled my ears—the blaring of car horns, the rumble of a dump truck leaving a nearby construction site, raucous laughter spilling out of a bar as the after work crowd unwound— but I was mostly oblivious to it. I had ears only for the mournful voices within. Self-blame and bitter regret mingled, tempting me to despair. If only I had been a better friend. If only I had been a more faithful intercessor. If only I. . . .

Nearing the hotel I paused, not yet ready to don my game face. Brenda and friends were waiting to go to dinner but I couldn't face them, not yet. Staring, with unseeing eyes, at my reflection in the plate glass window, I felt a stirring deep within; a sense, too subtle to be described, yet too real to be denied. My throat got tight and I teared up.

The sidewalk around me was nearly deserted, yet for the first time in months I didn't feel totally alone. Instead I sensed God's nearness, something I hadn't felt since I got lost in this "dark wood." Yielding myself to His presence, I clung to His nearness as if my life depended upon it, for surely it did. I told Him that I could endure anything as long as He was with me. What I couldn't bear was the thought that He had abandoned me.

> YIELDING MYSELF TO HIS PRESENCE, I CLUNG TO HIS NEARNESS AS IF MY LIFE DEPENDED UPON IT, FOR SURELY IT DID.

The whole experience didn't last more than a minute or two then the darkness closed around me again. Yet, in that unexpected moment of grace, a tiny hope was born. Like the first hint of spring it promised better things to come. In the dark days ahead I would return to it again and again. I knew the tragic things that had rent my life couldn't be undone, but my well-being was no longer dependent upon resolving those issues. God was my hope, the source of my life. He would restore my joy, of that I was sure. Like Elijah I had heard the "still small voice" and it spoke life to me.

My depression didn't miraculously disappear, nor did the things that had caused me so much pain suddenly resolve themselves, but I found my strength somehow renewed. Day after day I put one foot in front of the other, pushing my way through the darkness, always drawing strength from that moment of grace. The promise of His presence sustained me. Like Paul, a man familiar with this dark wood, I learned that the strength of Christ is made perfect in my weakness.

I am no longer wandering in the "dark wood"—thank God— but I have to admit that there are times when I long to relive that moment of grace. That moment when God suddenly felt nearer to me than the breath I breathed and more real than life itself. I pray I never return to that dark place, but I also realize it may be impossible to experience the comfort of God except in times of deepest grief. As I look back over my life, it is the hard times I remember most clearly and it is there that God revealed Himself in truly life changing ways, howbeit His presence was seldom easy to discern.

Chapter 36
With Pen in Hand

Her voice is hauntingly sad, clutching at my heart. At one point it breaks, a sob catching in her throat, and for a moment I'm right there with her; the lyrics invoking stark images—an empty pillow where she once laid her head, a little girl growing up without her mommy, a shaky signature on the divorce decree.

L ike a silver ribbon disappearing into the darkness the highway stretches before me, deserted at this late hour. Beside me Brenda is asleep, her head resting against the window on the passenger side of the car. Driving with one hand on the steering wheel, I fiddle with the radio dial, searching for a station. What I find is mostly static, not an uncommon occurrence in this remote region of Southeastern Colorado. Finally I locate a 50,000-watt clear channel out of New Orleans and I settle back to enjoy the music and the DJ's late night patter.

The highway is straight and I push my 1968 Dodge RT past 90. It's dumb, I know, but I am only twenty-two years old and I feel immortal. Brenda and I have been visiting family and we are returning to Holly, Colorado, where we serve a small congregation. With Sunday less than forty-eight hours away I try to focus on my sermon but my mind keeps wandering. I catch myself humming along when the DJ spins a familiar tune—

Glen Campbell singing "By the Time I Get to Phoenix" or Johnny Cash belting out "Folsom Prison Blues."

Beneath the music I hear the whir of the tires on the black-top and the rush of the wind past the windows. Unconsciously I tap my fingers on the steering wheel, keeping time with the beat. The song ends and the DJ's voice intrudes on my thoughts. After some nonsensical patter and a weather update he says, "Here's a new release from Vikki Carr, recorded live at the Persian Room." Almost as an afterthought he adds, "You might want to get a tissue. This one's a real tearjerker."

I've never heard of Vikki Carr, but after a few bars I'm hooked. The way she sings "With Pen in Hand" is unlike anything I've ever heard. Her voice is hauntingly sad, clutching at my heart. At one point it breaks, a sob catching in her throat, and for a moment I'm right there with her; the lyrics invoking stark images—an empty pillow where she once laid her head, a little girl growing up without her mommy, a shaky signature on the divorce decree.

She's singing about betrayal and regret and not being able to find the love they once knew. These are all things of which I know little or nothing, yet my throat is so tight I can hardly swallow. I glance at Brenda's sleeping profile, silhouetted by the pale moonlight, and try to imagine what unspeakable thing could ever cause us to divorce. We're still newlyweds and madly in love, but I cannot imagine an act so treacherous as to be unforgivable. Or maybe it's that I can't imagine my sweet Brenda capable of such an act.

In the years ahead I will become painfully familiar with the tragedy of divorce. Not my own, thank God, yet neither Brenda nor I will escape unscathed. Dear friends and close kin on both sides of our family will divorce. Some will remarry only to divorce again. Our parents will age before our eyes, dying a little each day as they watch their beloved children struggle to survive the death of their marriages. Worse yet is the suffering of the little ones. Too young to really understand what's going on, they're isolated with emotions they cannot process and suffer for years to come, sometimes for the rest of their lives. They are tangible proof verifying the studies that tell us at least one third of all children whose parents divorce will never fully recover, not even as adults. No wonder God hates divorce![31]

> MOST MARRIAGES DIE SLOWLY, MORE LIKELY FROM IGNORANCE AND NEGLECT THAN FROM ANY OVERT ACTION, LITTLE BY LITTLE, UNTIL THERE'S NOTHING LEFT BUT AN EMPTY SHELL.

Most marriages die slowly, more likely from ignorance and neglect than from any overt action, little by little, until there's nothing left but an empty shell. Often one or the other of the partners has seen it happening, but their pleas and then their warnings fell on deaf ears. Then some little thing most likely, some ordinary thing, signals the end. The youngest child graduates, he plans yet another vacation without consulting her, or she has a sudden vision of growing old together but alone. In desperation the papers are signed and then filed and another marriage ends.

Does this sound familiar? Did you catch a glimpse of your marriage? Have you been secretly contemplating a divorce?

If so, let me invite you to take a late night drive with me. Maybe we can find an all-night radio station that plays nothing but Golden Oldies. Who knows, we might even hear Vikki Carr sing "With Pen in Hand." If you can listen to that poignant song laying bare the tragedy of divorce and not be moved to recommit to your marriage, then all I've got to say is go ahead and sign your name. . . .

[31] As tragic as divorce is I must acknowledge that there are situations where it is the only solution. I am talking about marriages that are characterized by ongoing infidelity and/or abuse, marriages where the abusive spouse has hardened his/her heart, marriages that are a danger to the physical and emotional well-being of the betrayed spouse and/or the children. For this reason God instituted laws through Moses providing for divorce. In such cases divorce is the lesser of two evils, but that does not eliminate the inevitable consequences. There is simply no escaping the emotional fallout from divorce.

Chapter 37

The Gift of Forgiveness

The awful burden of ten long years is lifted. The dark cloud of condemnation is dissipated. That misplaced piece of furniture is gone. There is nothing between us. In the soul of our marriage there is only love, and we are one.

It is December 24, 1988, and for the first time ever, Brenda and I are celebrating Christmas alone. Determining to make the best of it, I build a fire in the fireplace and light the kerosene lamps on the mantle while Brenda prepares eggnog in the kitchen.

After a few minutes, she comes to join me in front of the fire, but instead of sitting beside me on the love seat, she kneels behind me and puts both arms around my neck. "I have something for you," she says, handing me a red envelope.

A Christmas card, I think, *how nice*. Then I see a hand-written note beneath the printed verse. As I begin to read it, my eyes grow misty, and my throat aches, so great is the lump that forms there.

In an instant, I am transported back to a Sunday afternoon in August nearly ten years earlier. We are quarreling as we have done numerous times before during our thirteen-year marriage. I've long since forgotten what started it, some insignificant thing most likely, but it soon turns deadly.

And then Brenda speaks the words that seem to seal my fate. "I hate you," she sobs, "I hate you! Once I loved you with all my heart, but you have killed my love. I can't live this way. I won't. When Leah graduates, I'm going to divorce you."

Stumbling beneath the awful weight of her terrible pain, she flees the room, leaving an unbearable emptiness in her wake. I hear the bathroom door close, then lock. A heavy sadness envelops me. Never have I felt so alone, so helpless.

Descending the stairs toward my study, I fight back my own tears. I try to tell myself that Brenda doesn't really mean what she said. She is just angry. She wouldn't really divorce me. Surely not.

Like a zombie, I go through the motions of preparing a sermon for the evening service. But my mind is grappling with weightier matters. What will I do if Brenda really does leave me when Leah graduates? How will I cope? I truly love her, even if she cannot imagine that I do. And I can change, I will show her.

Yet, even in the aftermath of the revelation of how my anger is destroying her, I am tempted to rationalize, to somehow justify my behavior. I am not a bad man. I compliment Brenda often and express my love to her every day. I am affectionate, appreciative, and I never forget her birthday, or our anniversary. I write her poems and take her out to dinner. Doesn't that count for something?

After a long time I make my way upstairs to dress for church. Leah is at the table eating a sandwich when I pass the dining room, and I pause for a moment in the doorway. Brenda glances my way, but she doesn't say anything. Finally, I ask her

240

if she is ready for church. In a voice that sounds a hundred years old she tells me she isn't going. Nothing more, just that. Sadly, I turn away and continue toward the bedroom. *So this is what it is going to be like*, I remember thinking.

We never speak of that tragic Sunday afternoon again. Never. But for years, nine years and four months to be exact, that painful moment lies like a piece of misplaced furniture in the soul of our marriage. Any time we try to get close to each other, we bump into it.

As the years pass, things seem to improve between us. Many a night I lie on the bed watching Brenda as she prepares to join me and think how blessed we are. Not infrequently I ask her, "Do you think anyone is as happy as we are?" Giving me a quick smile and a hug, before turning out the light, she says, "I'm sure there are others just as happy."

Lying in the darkness I think, "It's going to be all right. She's happier now, I can tell." But oh, how I long to hear her say, "Richard, all is forgiven. I don't hate you anymore. I love you." I can't ask though, lest I awaken her old hurts. I can only wait. And hope.

In May, 1988, Leah graduates from high school and leaves home to begin a life of her own. Now it is just the two of us. June turns into December, and before we hardly know it, it is Christmas Eve . . .

Straining to make out Brenda's words through tear-blurred eyes, I return to the present. Haltingly, I read:

WE NEVER SPEAK OF THAT TRAGIC SUNDAY AFTERNOON AGAIN. NEVER. BUT FOR YEARS, NINE YEARS AND FOUR MONTHS TO BE EXACT, THAT PAINFUL MOMENT LIES LIKE A PIECE OF MISPLACED FURNITURE IN THE SOUL OF OUR MARRIAGE. ANY TIME WE TRY TO GET CLOSE TO EACH OTHER, WE BUMP INTO IT.

"I, Brenda Starr, take thee, Richard Dean, to be my lawfully wedded husband. To have and to hold from this day forward. For richer, for poorer, in sickness and in health, till death do us part. To love, honor, cherish, and obey. Forsaking all others and thereto I plight thee my troth. In the name of the Father, the Son, and the Holy Ghost.

"It looks like you're stuck with me! I'm not going anywhere! Always remember 'I'll never leave thee nor forsake thee.'

> Your Devoted Wife & Lover,
> Brenda Starr"

All at once I am undone, overwhelmed, by such mercy and grace. Turning to Brenda I take her in my arms and hold her close. The awful burden of ten long years is lifted. The dark cloud of condemnation is dissipated. That misplaced piece of furniture is gone. There is nothing between us. In the soul of our marriage there is only love, and we are one.*

---

* On June 10, 2016 we celebrated our 50th anniversary. Between 1979 and 1988 God did a holy work in my life breaking the stronghold of anger. Although I will always have to guard my heart I am not longer the angry man I once was. Brenda no longer fears my temper. We are each other's best friend and more in love than we've ever been.

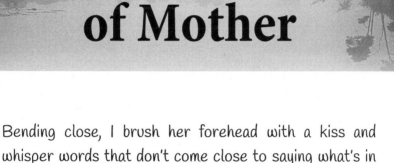

Chapter 38
Memories of Mother

Bending close, I brush her forehead with a kiss and whisper words that don't come close to saying what's in my heart. The love I feel for this remarkable woman is beyond telling.

It is the wee hours of the morning, but sleep won't come, so I stare at the ceiling and listen to my mother's labored breathing. How unnatural she looks, lying motionless in a hospital bed that seems to dwarf her slight body. In life she was a dynamo, constantly in motion, always doing, never one to be still. Now she is comatose. According to the neurologist, the damage caused by the hemorrhage in her brain is irreversible, leaving her partially paralyzed, blind, and unable to speak. Without a miracle her death is imminent; probably sometime in the next few days.

Seeing she had five children, I cannot help wondering how many sleepless nights she spent nursing one or the other of us through a series of childhood illnesses and accidents. I know she sat up with me, in the hospital, after I suffered a brain concussion and a broken arm. All night long I continued to ask the same nonsensical questions. "Where am I? What am I doing here? Why do I have this cast on my arm?" Not once did she grow impatient, although my concussed brain could not long retain the answers she so patiently repeated. In light of that, it seems only fair that I should be sitting with her now. It would be easier if she were conscious so we could talk. Unfortunately, her only response the past five days has been to lightly squeeze our hands. She hasn't responded at all in more than twenty-four hours and the doctors don't think she will.

Maintaining my bedside vigil, I realize I have a choice. I can focus on this tragedy and mother's impending death, or I can revisit the memories of the rich life she so freely shared with those she loved. I choose the latter and thus begins a journey that gives birth to an overwhelming sense of gratitude. As I turn my thoughts toward the past, the harsh realities of this hospital room seem to fade and an earlier, youthful version of my mother comes into focus.

It is a bitterly cold Colorado morning. Although the sun is bright, glistening off the fresh snow, it yields no warmth. I have followed mother into the backyard where she struggles to hang a steaming basket of laundry on the clothesline. Her fingers are red and chapped from the cold, but she works with a practiced skill, fast but not hurried. The socks and underwear, as well as the pants and shirts, freeze almost as soon as she hangs them on the clothesline. Thinking about it now, I can't help but wonder why she didn't wait for a warmer day. Of course the winters are long in Colorado with few warm days; still waiting wasn't mother's way. If something needed doing she wasted no time getting at it, especially if it was something her family had need of—like clean socks and underwear.

WAITING WASN'T MOTHER'S WAY. IF SOMETHING NEEDED DOING SHE WASTED NO TIME GETTING AT IT, ESPECIALLY IF IT WAS SOMETHING HER FAMILY HAD NEED OF—LIKE CLEAN SOCKS AND UNDERWEAR.

My earliest Christmas memory takes place about this same time. I was five, maybe six years old. The folks must have had a lean year for the only presents Don and I received were a Santa Claus coloring book and a box of forty-eight crayons. Knowing how much Mom loved to give, I'm sure that our meager take must have grieved her, but there is no disappointment in my memory, just joy. In later years there were more expensive gifts, but I can't ever remember being happier than I was while coloring at the kitchen table, as Mom busied herself at the counter preparing Christmas dinner. I suppose most folks would have considered us poor but that thought never entered my mind. It's hard to feel poor when your home is filled with love.

Mother hacks a cough, drawing me back to this hospital room and I lean close to make sure she doesn't choke. After a moment the hacking stops and she resumes her labored breathing. Picking up one of her limp hands, I hold it while tracing the purple veins on the back of her hand with my finger. I hate what has happened to her and I hate the thought of living in a world where she is no longer present. I can't help thinking that when Mom dies I will lose the one person who always believed in me, no matter what crazy stunt I might have pulled or how big a mess I might have made. Even when she knew the worst about me she always believed the best!

To make it through these difficult days, I have put my grief in a box and clamped the lid down tight. Unfortunately the lid keeps coming off and this is one of those times. Alone with Mom, in this hospital room, I allow the tears to flow. There are no wrenching sobs—maybe those will come later, maybe not—for now there are just silent tears slipping down my cheeks to lose themselves in my beard.

With a determined effort I turn my thoughts to an earlier, happier time. Mom and Dad have stopped for the night at a no-name motel somewhere between Friendswood, Texas, and our cabin on Beaver Lake in northwest Arkansas. She has telephoned to let me know that they are safely situated for the night. On the phone, Mom is gushing with childlike enthusiasm. Their room has a small table where she and Daddy can play Dominoes, and an in-room coffee maker. And the people at the front desk are so nice!

After Mom bids me goodbye, I sit for a moment, holding the now silent telephone in my hand. I can't help smiling at her childlike enthusiasm. I've stayed at enough no-name motels to know that the best of them leave much to be desired. And the people in the office are seldom friendly, except in the most cursory way. Yet, Mom is as excited as a child on Christmas morning and that's one of the things I love most about her. The simplest things could bring her such joy.

> MOM IS AS EXCITED AS A CHILD ON CHRISTMAS MORNING AND THAT'S ONE OF THE THINGS I LOVE MOST ABOUT HER. THE SIMPLEST THINGS COULD BRING HER SUCH JOY.

Brenda and I have been married for forty-two years and she cannot recall ever having a cross word with Mom. She has only the fondest memories of her; a scrapbook filled with the good times they shared. One of her favorite memories comes from 1967. We were serving our first church in Holly, Colorado, and the folks came for Christmas. Mom took one look around Brenda's sparsely furnished kitchen and then went to town and came back with a set of mixing bowls, telling Brenda, "You can't be a cook without mixing bowls."

When Brenda was rushed into emergency surgery, after suffering a life-threatening hemorrhage following Leah's birth, Mom sat with me while the surgeons worked to save Brenda's life. She didn't say much, at least nothing I can remember after all these years, but I'll never forget the strength her presence provided. Holding her limp hand now, I pray she senses my presence and is comforted by it. It seems such a small gesture, futile almost, but as she taught me nearly forty years ago, there is a remarkable power in presence. Bending close, I brush her forehead with a kiss and whisper words that don't come close to saying what's in my heart. The love I feel for this remarkable woman is beyond telling.

Concentrating on an image from Mom's last visit to our cabin, I bring it into focus. I see myself opening the door to the small guest apartment just a crack. Mother is on her knees, her Bible open on the bed before her. It isn't the first time I have found her in prayer, and in those private and unguarded moments her face is full of feeling, as she pours out her heart to the Lord she so dearly loves and so devotedly serves. The intensity of her intercession always humbles me, and I listen in a kind of awe as she bombards heaven on behalf of her children, grandchildren, and great-grandchildren. Who, I wonder, will take her place? Who will pray for us when she is gone?

Mom loved the work of the Lord and she supported it, not only with her prayers, but also with her finances. Each month she sent a check to the Division of World Missions in Springfield, Missouri, to help support her second son, my brother Don, who serves with his wife, Melba, as life-long missionaries in Argentina. In a second envelope she mailed a check to Richard Exley Ministries. After Dad died, I encouraged her to consider cutting back on her giving since her income had been significantly reduced, but she wouldn't hear of it. As far as she was concerned nothing was more important than the work of the Lord. What was any earthly thing compared to that?

During the past three or four years we have had some financial challenges in the ministry. I've had knee surgery and a debilitating back injury and both caused me to cancel several meetings. Of course, when an itinerate minister is not preaching, most of his income stops. I never mentioned any of this to Mom, but she seemed to know. On more than one occasion she called and asked me if I needed money. She had so little and yet she was offering it to me. Thankfully I never had to take her up on her offer, but it did my heart good to know how much she cared. And I have no doubt that she would have done the same thing for any of her children. Knowing Mom, she probably made the same offer to each of us.

The long night finally ends and to my surprise mother is still with us. For four more nights my two brothers, my sister, and I take turns spending the night at the hospital. Like me, they each have their own special moments. Finally, on Friday morning, December 19, all four of us are in mother's hospital room at the same time. We gather around her bed and talk quietly. The hospice doctor comes and goes, telling us that Mom will probably linger a couple more days, maybe as long as a week. After she leaves, I notice that the pulse in mother's neck is beating erratically. Don places his finger on her pulse trying to get a count, but gives up when it becomes apparent that Mom is leaving us.

For another minute, maybe two, she lingers, her breathing becoming shallower with each breath, and then she is gone. We had prayed that her home going would be easy and it was. There was absolutely no crisis. She simply stopped breathing. One moment she was trapped in a body paralyzed by a severe stroke and the next she was in the glorious presence of our Lord and Savior Jesus Christ! For more than fifty years she could only hear with the aid of the most powerful hearing aid and even then she was severely hard of hearing. Now she is not only free from all sickness and suffering but she can hear! Praise the Lord!

Mother's passing has left a huge hole in our lives and we are grieving deeply, but our grief is richly seasoned with hope—the hope of eternal life!

Chapter 39
No Easy Answers

Truthfully there doesn't seem to be any rhyme or reason to healing. Faith is a factor to be sure, but not the only factor and not necessarily the deciding factor. There are other forces at work here, things veiled in mystery, things like the sovereignty of God. More and more I am forced to concede that we only know in part, that "we see through a glass, darkly" (1 Corinthians 13:12 KJV).

While preaching in the Tulsa area some weeks ago, I bumped into an old friend. Well, actually she is the widow of one of my dearest friends. He went to be with the Lord just over a year ago and she is learning to live alone again after more than forty years of marriage, and that's no easy task. She's a remarkable lady with a gritty faith and an incredible sense of humor. Still the months since her husband's death have taken their toll and I could see the pain and loneliness in her eyes.

As we talked she asked me if her husband would have been healed if she had had more faith or prayed harder. I responded with a question of my own, "Why do you ask?"

Although she was careful not to speak critically, she told me that both her pastor and a guest speaker had said as much in recent sermons. She hastened to add that she might have misunderstood but I could tell that she was bothered by the implications. She couldn't help thinking that maybe it was her fault that her husband wasn't healed. She didn't say it but I could hear the concern in her words.

That conversation triggered a hodgepodge of memories—a young woman instantly healed of an incurable bone disease, another woman received a regenerative miracle when her dead thyroid was fully restored, a six-year-old boy healed of cancer, a pastor's blocked arteries instantly opened making heart surgery unnecessary. Then there were the other memories, the desperate prayers when there was no healing, the relentless illness, the terrible suffering, and finally death. The same person prayed, the same faith was exercised—I know because I was the one praying—but sometimes it resulted in a healing and sometimes it ended in death.

Was it my fault? Was my faith insufficient, my prayers inadequate, as some would suggest?

While I don't think I'm to blame, I will admit that my faith is never what I would like it to be and my prayers are often fumbling at best. Yet that didn't seem to hinder God when it came to the aforementioned healings, so why should it have been a deciding factor when those I prayed for weren't healed? Truthfully there doesn't seem to be any rhyme or reason to healing. Faith is a factor to be sure, but not the only factor and not necessarily the deciding factor. There are other forces at work here, things veiled in mystery, things like the sovereignty of God. More and more I am forced to concede that we only know in part, that "we see through a glass, darkly" (1 Corinthians 13:12 KJV).

FAITH IS A FACTOR TO BE SURE, BUT NOT THE ONLY FACTOR AND NOT NECESSARILY THE DECIDING FACTOR.

I'm thinking of a couple who came to me for prayer. They were childless and in their late 30s or early 40s. When they

250

approached me, the woman was weeping and when she spoke it was with great emotion. "I don't want you to pray for me," she sobbed, "but you must!" Then she proceeded to tell me that neither prayer nor medicine had been helpful. After nearly twenty years of trying they had lost all hope of ever having children of their own.

Having finally made peace with their situation they decided to make the best of things. If she couldn't have children of her own she would simply love the children God had placed in her life—her nieces and nephews as well as the boys and girls in her Sunday school class. She told me she could live without children, but what she couldn't bear was to get her hopes up only to be disappointed yet again. "That's why I don't want you to pray for me," but she quickly added, "You must!"

Grasping her hands I prayed a hasty prayer not expecting much of anything. Then the Holy Spirit came upon me and I heard myself saying, "About this time next year, the Lord will give you a son."

Once I had uttered those words I was dumbfounded. What was I thinking? How dare I speak so presumptuously? How dare I give them false hope?

But I hadn't given them false hope, for twelve months later she gave birth to a healthy baby boy!

How do I explain that? I can't. They had been prayed for scores of times across the years and nothing happened. What was different this time? Who knows? She didn't appear to have much faith—a desperate hope maybe and a fearful obedience, but not much faith. My faith certainly wasn't anything to write home about, but still God intervened and gave them a son.

I can only conclude that when it comes to healing there are no easy answers. I have been witness to enough supernatural healings to never lose hope no matter how desperate the situation. I know God is able! Yet, I've preached enough funerals that I dare not be presumptuous. Christ has defeated death but He has not yet destroyed it (1 Corinthians 15:26) and until He does we will have to contend with both disease and death.

"Faith," as Winn Collier says, "is a call to hope. It enables us to believe again, to stare our disillusionment in the face and grab on for another round."[32] With that in mind, I'm going to continue to pray for miracles, but I'm going to put my hope only in Jesus.

---

[32] Winn Collier, *Restless Faith,* (Colorado Springs: NavPress, 2005) p. 45.

Chapter 40

Putting Humpty Dumpty Back Together Again

As we received communion that night, a miracle happened in that old farmhouse, a miracle of grace and forgiveness, a miracle that continues to this very day. What all the king's horses and all the king's men couldn't do, the King's Son did. He put this broken man back together again.

A t the age of twenty-three I was called to be the pastor of First Assembly of God in Florence, Colorado, at that time one of the better churches in the Rocky Mountain District. It was heady stuff for a novice pastor and I soon fell prey to the deadliest of all ministerial temptations—pride. Almost without realizing it I began to think more highly of myself than I should have. From a child I had been taught that "Pride goes before destruction and a haughty spirit before a fall" (Proverbs 16:18), but I never thought it could happen to me. Unfortunately, like Humpty Dumpty, I had a great fall and not all the king's horses or all the king's men could put this broken man back together again.

Here's what happened. I began to think that with a ministry gift like mine it was a shame to limit my ministry to one congregation. I was convinced that the Holy Spirit wanted me to share my gift with the world and after fifteen months in Florence, I resigned the pastorate and launched into evangelistic ministry.

Had I been older and wiser I would have known that my reasoning was flawed. The only gift the Holy Spirit wants to share with the world is Jesus.

THE ONLY GIFT THE HOLY SPIRIT WANTS TO SHARE WITH THE WORLD IS JESUS.

Initially things went very well. Several significant churches invited me to preach crusades and the Lord moved in remarkable ways, which only served to exacerbate my haughty spirit. Of course "God opposes the proud" (James 4:6), so it was just a matter of time before things began to fall apart. There is nothing to be gained by rehashing the messy details, so let me just say that I experienced some painful disappointments, not to mention devastating rejection, and soon found myself without a place to preach.

In order to provide for my wife and infant daughter I worked in the hay fields of southeastern Colorado. When that work ran out we returned to Houston, Texas, where we moved in with Brenda's parents. Once again I found temporary work loading 100-pound bags of rice into the belly of ships at the Port of Houston. It was back-breaking work, especially given that it was July with both the temperature and the humidity climbing to nearly 100. After that I spent some days roofing houses in Idaho and by October I had a bit part in a Hollywood movie called *Brothers O'Toole*. It was being filmed at Buckskin Joe's, a restored western town located on the Royal Gorge near Canon City, Colorado.

We were nearly destitute and managed to hang on only because some friends took pity on us and invited us to live with them for a while. Brenda cleaned the house and babysat their infant son to help pay part of the rent. I was mostly gone, leaving the house early in the morning to go to the movie set and returning home late at night after the Belvedere Bar and Grill finally closed.

Night after night I sat in the bar feeling sorry for myself. I still felt called to the ministry, but there didn't seem to be anyplace for me in the church. I loved God, but I no longer trusted Him. To my way of thinking He had let me down. Proverbs 19:3 says, "A man's own folly ruins his life, yet his heart rages against the Lord" and that's exactly what I was doing. My own pride and foolishness had destroyed my ministry and yet I was blaming God. Of course, I couldn't see it at the time.

PROVERBS 19:3 SAYS, "A MAN'S OWN FOLLY RUINS HIS LIFE, YET HIS HEART RAGES AGAINST THE LORD."

As the weeks passed I grew more and more depressed. Day after day I would sit on the movie set comparing the illusion of movie making with the reality of ministry, especially the reality of the ministry we had experienced in our first pastorate in Holly, Colorado. During our three-year tenure, several people had been gloriously saved, among them Bob and Diane. Following their conversion God restored their marriage and Brenda and I were privileged to spend the next two years mentoring them in the ways of the Lord. Holy Communion was especially important to Bob and almost every week Brenda and I shared the Lord's Supper with them in their home.

In my deepening depression I hungered to experience something like that again and one day I simply walked off the movie set and never went back. In town I started throwing our things into suitcases, informing Brenda that we were going to Bob and Diane's. "But we don't know where they live," she protested. "They've moved and we haven't talked to them in more than two years."

Undeterred, I continued to pack our suitcases. "We'll find them," I said, "we have to."

After making a half-dozen phone calls and driving for more than eight hours, we finally located them. They were living in a farmhouse in southwestern Kansas and when they saw us it was like we had never been apart. Two days later, on the last Saturday in November, 1972, Diane baked bread and I bought a bottle of grape juice. After putting the children to bed, the four of us went into the living room where we gathered around the scarred coffee table that loomed so large in my memory.

The old farmhouse creaked and groaned in the cold as the wind howled, whipping up a high plain's blizzard. Inside, the floor furnace wheezed as it fought to hold its own against the freezing November night, but I hardly noticed so intent was I on the task at hand. Carefully, I filled the Melmac cups with grape juice before picking up the bread, still warm from the oven.

GONE WAS MY FOOL-
ISHNESS AND PRIDE.
GONE WAS
MY HURT AND
DISAPPOINTMENT.
ALL WASHED AWAY
IN THE MEMORY
OF AN EARLIER TIME,
A TIME WHEN
LOVE AND GRACE
HAD MADE ALL
THINGS NEW.

Kneeling there, a wave of memories washed over me. In an instant, I was back in Holly, Colorado, in Bob and Diane's doublewide trailer house. Gone was the craziness of the last two years. Gone was my foolishness and pride. Gone was my hurt and disappointment. All washed away in the memory of an earlier time, a time when love and grace had made all things new.

Always before when we shared communion I heard their confession, but on this night the three of them heard mine and when I finished we were all crying— tears of remorse and tears of joy. Although the Lord would have been well justified in washing His hands of me, He did not. Instead of rejecting me, God restored me.

As far as the east is from the west so far did He remove my sins from me (Psalm 103:12).

With trembling hands I finally broke the bread, realizing as never before that it truly was my sins, my disobedience, and my rebellion that had broken His body. The Sanhedrin may have unjustly condemned Him and delivered Him to Pontius Pilate (Matthew 27:1-2); His own countrymen may have screamed for His blood (Matthew 27:25); Roman soldiers may have driven the nails (Matthew 27:31-37); but it was my sins that crucified Him!

After the bread I took the cup and said, "In the same manner Jesus gave them the cup saying, 'This is my blood of the covenant, which is poured out for many for the forgiveness of sins'" (Matthew 26:28).

As we received communion that night a miracle happened in that old farmhouse, a miracle of grace and forgiveness, a miracle that continues to this very day. What all the king's horses and all the king's men couldn't do, the King's Son did. He put this broken man back together again!

> WHAT ALL THE KING'S HORSES AND ALL THE KING'S MEN COULDN'T DO, THE KING'S SON DID. HE PUT THIS BROKEN MAN BACK TOGETHER AGAIN!

Have you lost your way; have you made some bad decisions; have you hurt those you love most? Are you trapped in a secret life, living a lie? Are you a stranger to your spouse and estranged from your children? Don't despair. All is not lost. What Jesus did for me in a farmhouse in Kansas more than forty-five years ago, He will do for you!

I had to stop blaming others and take responsibility for my sinful choices and you will have to do the same. There are no extenuating circumstances, no self-justifying rationale that can excuse your sins. It is your fault! You are to blame and your only hope of deliverance is to throw yourself on the mercies of God.

The good news is that God's mercies are always greater than our sins (Romans 5:20). "He does not treat us as our sins deserve or repay us according to our iniquities" (Psalm 103:10) and there is nothing, absolutely nothing that can separate us from His love (Romans 8:35-39). If you will call upon the Lord, He will deliver you. He will forgive your sins and heal your hurts. He will do for you what He did for me. The King's Son will put your broken life back together again.

Why not pray this prayer with me right now. "Lord Jesus, I have sinned and made a mess of my life. I have hurt those I love most. I cannot save myself. You are my only hope. Forgive my sins, heal my heart, and give me another chance. In Your holy name I pray. Amen."

If you prayed that prayer by faith, I declare on the authority of God's Word that your sins are forgiven. Romans 10:9, 10, and 13 says, "That if you confess with your mouth, 'Jesus is Lord,' and believe in your heart that God raised him from the dead, you will be saved. For it is with your heart that you believe and are justified, and it is with your mouth that you confess and are saved . . . for, 'Everyone who calls on the name of the Lord will be saved.'"

Chapter 41

Don't Let Your Resources Determine Your Destiny

Little did I know that God was about to give me a lesson in how resources follow vision! Here's how it works. First God gives you the vision, then you step out in obedient faith, and God provides. If you wait until you have the resources before you act, you will likely miss God's best!

Some years ago the Lord spoke to me in a dream. In my dream, one of the elders was showing me through the church facilities. The last area he took me through was a huge unfinished basement. It was clean and well lighted but totally unfinished and much larger than the footprint of the sanctuary above it. I was impressed and heard myself saying, "This is awesome. The potential is unlimited! There's so much we can do with this."

Shaking his head sadly, the elder replied, "We don't have the resources to develop it."

In my dream I heard God speak in an audible voice: *"Don't let your resources determine your destiny!"*

IN MY DREAM I HEARD GOD SPEAK IN AN AUDIBLE VOICE: *"DON'T LET YOUR RESOURCES DETERMINE YOUR DESTINY!"*

As I think about that dream, two things come to mind. First, those things that are unseen are much larger than the things that are seen. The unfinished basement was much larger than the footprint of the sanctuary above it. Second, we seldom have the resources to fulfill our destiny, but we can't let that stop us. Pursue your God-given destiny and the resources will follow. That's how God works!

Let me illustrate. When my brother, Don, returned from his first four-year term as a missionary in Argentina he said, "Richard, I believe the Lord wants Christian Chapel (the church where I was serving as senior pastor) to make missions its highest priority. One way to do that is to establish a missionary-in-residence program that will become a prototype for other missionary churches."

"What," I asked, interrupting him, "is a missionary-in-residence program?"

Nonplussed, he continued, "As you know, missionaries usually serve a four-year term and then return home for a year-long furlough. When they return to the States they bring only what they can carry in their suitcases. Shortly after they arrive in the States they have to find a place to live, furnish it, buy a car, and enroll their children in school. It's extremely stressful and we do it every five years.

"During the year that we are in the states we preach 100 to 150 missionary services in supporting churches. To book those services we have to make approximately 1000 telephone calls. About 50% of our calls are ignored. The pastor simply does not take our call or fails to return it. Another 375 calls produce no results. Only about one in ten calls bears fruit. Once we book services we drive upwards of 100,000 miles getting to and from the churches where we are scheduled to minister. Most missionaries need 150 to 180 supporting churches to raise their budget making this demanding ministry schedule absolutely mandatory.

"If you adopt this plan, Christian Chapel would select five missionaries whose furloughs fall on consecutive years. They would provide a fully furnished house for the missionary and his family to live in while they are in the States, at no cost to the missionary. Christian Chapel would also pledge up to 25 percent of the missionary's budget reducing the number of supporting churches he would need.

"The benefits to the missionary are obvious—a significant reduction in stress as he no longer has to find a house to rent or purchase furniture. Less wear and tear on his body as he would not have to schedule as many services. He and his family would also have the benefit of being part of Christian Chapel, enabling them to build emotionally supportive relationships. The congregation would also benefit. They would be able to develop close relationships with each missionary family, giving them a greater appreciation for the missionary's life and ministry."

We were a small congregation at the time with a Sunday morning attendance of just over 100. We had no building of our own. We were meeting in a Jr. High building on Sundays, which meant that we had to spend hours every Sunday loading and unloading equipment, setting up the auditorium and nurseries. To complicate matters, we were in default on a mortgage of nearly $500,000 on forty acres of undeveloped land.

FIRST GOD GIVES YOU THE VISION, THEN YOU STEP OUT IN OBEDIENT FAITH, AND GOD PROVIDES. IF YOU WAIT UNTIL YOU HAVE THE RESOURCES BEFORE YOU ACT, YOU WILL LIKELY MISS GOD'S BEST!

We also owed more than $150,000 to other lenders and the IRS. Shaking my head I replied, "Don, it sounds like a great idea, but you have the wrong church!"

Little did I know that God was about to give me a lesson in how resources follow vision! Here's how it works. First God gives you the vision, then you step out in obedient faith, and God provides. If you wait until you have the resources before you act, you will likely miss God's best!

In the weeks ahead I tried to dismiss the idea of a mission-ary-in-residence program, but God would not let me. I found myself thinking about it almost continually. Like a cocklebur caught in my sock, I couldn't get it out of my mind. Still, try as I might, I couldn't imagine a way we could make it work—not given the size of our congregation, our indebtedness, and the fact that we had no church building of our own.

I HAVE A VERY SUCCESSFUL FRIEND WHO SAYS THE KEY TO SUCCESS IS TO DREAM BIG, START SMALL, AND WORK HARD.

I have a very successful friend who says the key to success is to dream big, start small, and work hard. Starting small and working hard has always been easy for me but when it comes to dreaming big I falter. I'm a practical person by nature, not a dreamer; more a detail person rather than a visionary. The missionary-in-residence program was simply too big for me. I couldn't wrap my mind around it so God decided to give me some help.

While I was still wrestling with the idea, a real estate agent stopped by the church office, which was located in southeast Tulsa near St. Francis hospital—a yuppie part of town. At first glance he seemed out of place. He was wearing out-of-style, too-short, double-knit slacks over scuffed cowboy boots. He had a potbelly and a cowboy hat. Needless to say I was not impressed.

After introducing himself he asked, "Do you own the forty acres of undeveloped land on 91st Street?"

"That depends," I replied with something of a grimace, "on what you mean by own? Technically we own it but we have defaulted on our mortgage and the mortgage holder is in the process of foreclosing."

"Good," he said. "I have a client who wants to buy it."

"Unless he has deep pockets you're wasting your time. Once we defaulted on our payment the mortgage holder exercised his right to demand payment of the full balance plus interest."

After considerable discussion, the real estate agent convinced me to sign a one-time showing agreement. I told him we would have to have $720,000 cash in order to sell. He seemed unfazed by that information and returned about thirty minutes later with a signed contract. I was stunned but my amazement soon turned to disgust as I read the contract. The buyer was agreeable to the $720,000 purchase price, but he only wanted to put 10 per cent down. He was asking Christian Chapel to carry the balance.

Of course that wasn't going to work. We had to have a cash sale in order to pay the balance of our mortgage and the timing was critical. We had to close the deal before the foreclosure became final. Although I had already explained this to the real estate agent once I went over it all again. He insisted on going through the figures with me. After considerable calculation we concluded that Christian Chapel needed $640,000 cash to make the deal work—$50,000 plus interest to repay the Bank of Oklahoma, another $50,000 plus interest to repay the Oklahoma District Council of the Assemblies of God and the balance to pay off the original mortgage and interest, plus the real estate agent's commission. Nonetheless I told him we wouldn't sell for anything less than $720,000.

I am not an astute businessman or a gifted negotiator, but on that occasion I was being hardnosed. I think it was because I didn't truly believe the deal was real. Imagine my surprise when the real estate agent returned with a signed contract for $720,000—$640,000 down and an $80,000 promissory note for one year at 10% interest. I was ecstatic! Once we closed on the sale of that forty acres, Christian Chapel would be completely debt free.

That remarkable turn of events convinced me that with God all things are possible, so I decided to share the missionary-in-residence vision with the official board. I acknowledged that we had absolutely no way to buy a mission house or to provide 25 percent of the budgets for five missionaries. Nonetheless I felt God was asking us to simply say "Yes" to the impossible. God would do the rest. To my amazement the official board unanimously adopted the missionary-in-residence vision.

Almost immediately God began to provide. The very first Sunday following the official board's decision, a new family visited our congregation. The first week they worshipped with us they put a thousand dollars in the offering and they continued to do so each week thereafter. At that time our weekly offerings were about $2,500. That meant that our weekly income increased by 40% overnight! On October 3, 1981, we closed on the sale of the forty acres and Christian Chapel was debt free. One Sunday morning a few weeks later, a man handed me a $30,000 check at the close of service. "I didn't have my tithe check ready when the offering plates were passed" he explained, "so I couldn't put it in. Please take care of it for me."

In light of the remarkable financial provision that had followed the Official Board's commitment to the missionary-in-residence vision, I decided it was time to share the story with the entire congregation. They responded with unabashed enthusiasm. Although we had no church building of our own, and no plans for one in the foreseeable future, they were still excited about buying a house for missionaries to live in.

Early the next week, a new member of our congregation invited me to lunch. He informed me that he wanted to buy the MIR house and donate it to the church. I told him that we would need a four-bedroom house with approximately 2,200 square feet. Without blinking an eye, he said, "Up to $100,000, I'll buy it." (Remember, this was 1981.) Ninety days later we closed on the MIR house. Truly God's resources were following our obedience, but He wasn't finished yet!

A man in our congregation was a junior partner in an independent oil company. The company was highly leveraged and with escalating interest rates they were on the verge of bankruptcy. My friend said if that happened he would lose everything. Taking his hand I prayed with him, asking God to supernaturally intervene. When we finished praying, I asked him to have his secretary type up of a list of the specific things that needed to happen in order to ward off bankruptcy, so I could pray specifically.

A few days later I received his letter and this is where my story takes its most embarrassing turn. For whatever reason I never opened that letter and I never prayed about his situation again. I'm ashamed to admit my prayerlessness, but I feel I must be completely transparent. I want you to know that the amazing things the Lord did for Christian Chapel was the result of His faithfulness and not because of my great faith. If the absolute truth be told, I failed the Lord and I let my friend down, but God remained faithful. 2 Timothy 2:13 declares, "If we are unfaithful, he remains faithful, for he cannot deny who he is."

A few weeks later the Kuwaiti government made an offer to buy Andover Oil that was considerably more than the amount my friend hoped to receive in his best-case scenario. There was one fly in the ointment however—at that time it was against the law for a foreign government to purchase a United States oil company. Andover Oil petitioned Congress and was granted a special exemption allowing the sale of Andover Oil to the Kuwaiti government.

A few days before the scheduled closing my friend took me to lunch. "What are you doing next Thursday?" he asked.

"Nothing in particular. Why?"

"We're closing the sale of Andover on Thursday. I'm selling a portion of my stock in Christian Chapel's name and I think you should be there to pick up the church's check. I'm telling you now so you can meet with the Official Board and decide where you want to deposit the money so you won't lose the interest over the weekend."

I wasn't into high finance but even I knew that if he was concerned about losing the interest over the weekend we weren't talking about $500. Clearing my throat I said, "Do you mind telling me how much Christian Chapel will receive?"

A small smile touched the corners of his mouth as he extracted a scrap of paper from his shirt pocket and handed it to me. When I unfolded it I was dumbfounded. He was selling $429,444.79 worth of Andover stock in Christian Chapel's name!

When the Lord directed us to make world missions our highest priority and commit to the missionary-in-residence vision we were more than $600,000 in debt and in default on our mortgage. Seventeen months later we were debt free, we owned a 2,200 square foot missions house, we had nearly a half-million dollars on deposit and an $80,000 promissory note coming due in sixty days. A coincidence? Hardly! When we said, "Yes" to the Lord's direction and stepped out in obedience, He opened the windows of heaven (Malachi 3:10).

A few days after Christian Chapel received the $429,444.79 check, the Official Board and I met to discuss where to give a tithe on that gift to missions. We decided to use $21,000 to furnish the MIR house and just in time, too, as our first missionary-in-residence family was arriving in a few days. That left us with $22,000 to invest in another missions project. While we were trying to decide what to do with that money the telephone rang. The caller was Loren Triplett, the field director for the Assemblies of God missionary work in Latin America. He informed me that the exchange rate between the Argentine peso and the US dollar had shifted dramatically that very day. A property in Argentina that had cost $100,000 US the day before was now selling for $17,000 US.

That was the good news. Here was the kicker. My brother, Don, had written a $17,000 faith check on his missions account to purchase the property for a new church plant. Unfortunately he did not have funds in his account to cover the check so he called Loren and asked the missions department to cover the check. Loren was calling to see if I could help him raise $17,000 in the next forty-eight hours. Consider the timing. On the very day the exchange rate flip-flopped, we were meeting to decide where to give $43,000. Only God could have orchestrated that series of events!

Of course we sent the foreign missions department the entire $17,000 to cover Don's faith check. Later that year I was privileged to preach the first service in the building on that property in Argentina. In the ensuing thirty years that church plant has become the greatest missionary church in Argentina, sending out scores of missionaries to the ends of the earth.

While I served as the senior pastor of Christian Chapel I preached a sermon titled "The Miracle of Missions" every year in which I reiterated this story. Hundreds of new people were joining our congregation and I wanted them to hear the Christian Chapel story. Only then could they fully understand our commitment to missions. Assembly of God missionaries heard about "The Miracle of Missions" and begin ordering cassette tapes of the sermon. With our permission, they duplicated those tapes and began giving them to pastors wherever they went. Soon hundreds of pastors heard the Christian Chapel story. Many of them were inspired to begin a missionary-in-residence program in their own church.

Of course as the story spread, I began receiving invitations to preach missions conferences around the country. Everyone it seemed wanted to hear "The Miracle of Missions." When I shared the Christian Chapel story with Gateway Church in Shreveport they were inspired to buy a missions house and start their own missionary-in-residence program. Several years later the church suffered a tragic split with all of the accompanying fallout—painful misunderstandings, the loss of longtime friends, dwindling attendance, and financial pressure.

When they were still without a pastor months later, they decided to contact me to see if I would be interested in becoming their pastor. Although their telephone call came out of the blue I wasn't totally unprepared. For nearly two years I had been dreaming the same dream month after month; sometimes two or three times in a single month. In my dream I was called to serve a church in crisis. The church never had a name and I never had any idea where it was located, but it was always in crisis. As a result of that dream I began to prepare my heart for a major change in our ministry.

When the pulpit committee called I told them I would pray about becoming their pastor but I didn't see how we could make it work financially. Brenda and I owned a home and small acreage on Beaver Lake in northwest Arkansas. We planned on retiring there and unless God spoke in an unmistakable way we had no intention of selling it. Since Gateway Church was in a financial crisis I couldn't imagine that the salary package would be large enough to enable us to pay our mortgage in Arkansas and get a house in Shreveport.

When I explained my situation to the pulpit committee, they informed me that Gateway Church owned a fully-furnished missions house that Brenda and I could live in rent-free if we became their pastors. All we would have to do was bring our clothes and move in. When they elected us to be their pastors that is exactly what we did. I couldn't help but marvel that the Christian Chapel story lived on in Gateway Church and that missions house made it possible for us become their pastors. Once again God had provided an answer years before we had a problem!

Is there a lesson for us in the Christian Chapel story? So it seems to me. Both Scripture and experience teach us that God seldom intervenes on our behalf until we step out in obedient faith. The servants at the wedding in Cana of Galilee had to put plain water into empty barrels before Jesus turned it into wine (John 2:1-11). The boy had to give Jesus his lunch before the Lord blessed it and multiplied it to feed five thousand people (John 6:8-13). The disciples had to cast their nets on the other side of the boat before they caught a boatload of fish (Luke 5:4-8). The man born blind had to go and wash in the Pool of Siloam before he received his sight (John 9:6-7).

Is God asking you to dream a big dream? Is He asking you to attempt something that looks absolutely impossible? Don't let your resources determine your destiny. Sometimes you have to say yes to the impossible before God intervenes on your behalf.

> I COULDN'T HELP BUT MARVEL THAT THE CHRISTIAN CHAPEL STORY LIVED ON IN GATEWAY CHURCH AND THAT MISSIONS HOUSE MADE IT POSSIBLE FOR US BECOME THEIR PASTORS. ONCE AGAIN GOD HAD PROVIDED AN ANSWER YEARS BEFORE WE HAD A PROBLEM!

You have to be willing to risk failure by stepping out in faith before you will receive your miracle. At least that's the way the Lord has worked in my life and ministry.

Chapter 42
One Big Family Reunion

Not only will we be united with Jesus our Lord and savior, but with our loved ones as well. One huge family reunion—parents and grandparents, brothers and sisters, children and grandchildren, aunts and uncles, nieces and nephews. As wonderful as my memories of Sherry are, they pale in comparison with what is to come. What God has prepared for us is beyond imagining!

The ringing of my cell phone jerks me out of an uneasy sleep. It is Tom, my brother-in-law. "You better hurry," he says. "It looks like she's leaving us."

Brenda is already getting dressed as I hastily pull on my jeans and a pullover shirt. Although we have been expecting this call—hoping for it even, as my sister has suffered terribly—I am not prepared for it. Sherry is only fifty-six years old. To my way of thinking she is far too young to die. Besides she has a husband who needs her, and three daughters, not to mention four grandchildren, with another one on the way.

For nearly five years she has fought a heroic battle against a rare and insidious form of cancer identified as an internal melanoma. According to the doctors there are less than five hundred known cases and no one has survived. When Sherry received her original diagnosis the oncologist told her to go home and prepare to die.

A lesser woman would have probably done exactly that, but not my sister. She is a fighter and she determined she would use everything at her disposal—including prayer—to defeat this evil thing. She knew that a faith-filled mind and a positive attitude was a must so she established a daily routine designed to that end. She read and memorized Scripture, listened to praise music continually, and adhered to a healthy diet. She refused to say she "had" cancer. She didn't "have" cancer. She was "battling" cancer and she was going to defeat it.

TAKING CHEMOTHERAPY IS REALLY A DANCE WITH DEATH. THE ONCOLOGIST TRIES TO GIVE THE PATIENT ENOUGH CHEMICAL DRUGS (POISON) TO KILL THE CANCER WITHOUT KILLING THE PATIENT.

Medically speaking, chemotherapy was her first line of defense. Although it offered her best hope, it was a dangerous choice. Taking chemotherapy is really a dance with death. The oncologist tries to give the patient enough chemical drugs (poison) to kill the cancer without killing the patient. Sherry willingly subjected herself to a variety of chemotherapies—some FDA approved and some experimental—in hopes of killing the cancer. The drugs ravished her body, burning her skin and causing her hair to fall out. She developed huge sores in her mouth and down her throat. She vomited incessantly and suffered terrible diarrhea. She was so weak she could hardly walk across the room.

During chemo treatments she was in the hospital for seven days at a time. The first five days she received chemo and then she remained in the hospital for another one to two days until she recovered enough to go home. She had her blood checked each week during her two-week recovery period at home. When her blood count indicated that she had recovered sufficiently from the last treatment, she would return to the hospital for another round of chemo.

During her recovery period at home she required constant care, which her two older daughters provided. Once I flew in from Arkansas so I could be with her. She was too weak to do much, so I read to her while she laid on the couch. Crystal (Sherry's second daughter) was there from San Antonio with her baby daughter. Of course caring for her mother and her newborn had worn Crystal completely out. Since Sherry was asleep on the couch, I volunteered to hold the baby. I placed Tempe on my chest and covered her with a blanket before reclining my chair. In just a few seconds she stopped crying and fell asleep, giving Crystal a chance to rest. Holding her, I prayed for Sherry. This tiny baby was going to need her Mimi. Surely God knew that.

Another day Sherry wanted to go for a car ride so I helped her into the luxurious BMW that Tom had purchased for her. It was a beautiful spring day in South Texas and once she was situated in the car she seemed to perk up. As I drove she told me about taking Mom to the Farmer's Market and then to the cemetery to put flowers on Daddy's grave. Now Mom was buried beside him and Sherry wished she were strong enough to take flowers for both their graves. Her voice was growing weak and I could tell she was tiring. When I asked if she was ready to go home she nodded her head, too exhausted to speak.

For a time it looked like she was going to beat it. She was finished with the chemo. Her hair was growing back and she was regaining her strength. Every two months she went for a scan and while fear lurked around the edges of her mind she never gave into it. Once she received the "all clear" report from the doctor she cast aside her fear and embraced life with a holy enthusiasm.

In September 2010 Tom and Sherry drove to Shreveport so they could spend the weekend with Brenda and me. At the time we were serving as the lead pastors of Gateway Church and I invited Sherry to share her story with our congregation. She truly believed the Lord had healed her and her testimony encouraged many others to believe God for a miracle in their own lives.

DURING THOSE GLORIOUS CANCER-FREE DAYS, HOPE WAS AS BRIGHT AS THE FIRST BAREFOOT DAYS OF SPRING.

During those glorious cancer-free days, hope was as bright as the first barefoot days of spring. Tom was starting a new business with his son-in-law and it was going amazingly well. Sherry was enrolled in Global University studying for ministry. She had two new grandbabies and life was wonderful, so full of possibilities. The only "fly in the ointment" was the nerve-wracking bi-monthly scans. No matter how hard we tried, we could not escape the every present reminder that there was a possibility of a reoccurrence.

Then early in 2013, the thing we most feared reared its ugly head. The cancer had returned and with a vengeance. Hard decisions had to be made. Radical surgery seemed the best option at this point, although there were no guarantees. With the kind of faith and courage we had come to expect from her, Sherry looked the situation in the eye and told the surgeon to schedule the surgery.

The day of the surgery arrived and we gathered around Sherry's hospital bed for prayer. Her immediate family was there as well as Brenda and me. The room filled up with love and faith as we prayed, placing Sherry in the Lord's hands. The orderlies arrived and with practiced care they wheeled her out of the room and down the long hallway toward the operating room. Tom and Kami (her oldest daughter) walked beside her, holding her hands until they reached the entrance to the operating room. Tom hugged her and kissed her goodbye and then she was wheeled out of sight.

We returned to the family waiting area where we tried to settle in for our twelve-hour vigil. Tom's pastor came and stayed for a while, as did several other friends. Their presence was an encouragement, but the hours dragged. We couldn't help wondering how things were progressing in the operating room. Periodically someone would give us an update, but it told us almost nothing other than the fact the surgery was on schedule. Late that evening, the surgeon arrived looking absolutely exhausted. He was positive. The surgery had gone just as they expected. Sherry was in recovery and from there she would be moved to intensive care. He assured us that they had "got" all of the cancer. When Brenda pressed him, he acknowledged that there was no guarantee that it would not return.

Sherry's recovery was long and arduous. For the first six weeks she was unable to sit down. She either had to lay flat or stand up. The pain was unrelenting, but I never heard her complain. Not one time! Neighbors and friends from the church rallied around Tom and Sherry, bringing them meals and running errands. Sometimes they just sat with Sherry, keeping her company even though she was too exhausted to converse. Slowly, ever so slowly, she began to recover.

Then the cancer returned again. This time it had spread to her liver. MD Anderson Cancer Treatment Center had exhausted all treatment options, so they helped Sherry get into a special protocol in Florida. Tom chartered a private jet to fly them to Tampa, as Sherry was too weak to travel any other way. Once again the protocol was ineffective and the cancer continued to metastasize.

Having run out of medical options, Tom and Sherry returned to their home in Friendswood, Texas. Brenda and I drove in from Shreveport to lend our support. Her brothers—Don from Argentina and Bob

THROUGH IT ALL SHERRY REMAINED POSITIVE AND FAITH-FILLED AND MY HEART SWELLED WITH PRIDE TO SEE HOW GREATLY SHE WAS LOVED.

from Alabama—arrived to shower her with love. Carolyn, her closest high school friend, flew in from Florida to see her one last time. Through it all Sherry remained positive and faith-filled and my heart swelled with pride to see how greatly she was loved.

She rallied one last time and on a Thursday evening, just six days before she went to be with the Lord, she sat at the table playing games with her family. The next day was Good Friday and she asked Brenda to prepare a special meal—fried chicken, Mom's potato salad (without onions), and baked beans. To our amazement she stayed up most of the day and enjoyed her "made to order" dinner. Although she was completely exhausted on Saturday, she still insisted on getting a shower and shampoo-ing her hair in hopes of attending Easter services the next day.

Unfortunately, when Easter morning dawned Sherry was too weak to get out of bed. I was sitting beside her bed holding her hand and for the first time ever she acknowledged her impending death. In a voice that was hardly more than a whisper she said, "I'm not going to make it, am I?"

QUICK AS A FLASH DON SPOKE UP, "IF HEAVEN IS YOUR FINAL GOAL, YOU'RE GOING TO MAKE IT."

I was tempted to tell her otherwise, but I loved her too much to give her false assur-ance. Leaning close I put her hand next to my cheek. Finally I said, "No sweetheart, you're not going to make it."

Quick as a flash Don spoke up, "If heaven is your final goal, you're going to make it."

Sherry seemed to be encouraged by his words and I couldn't help wishing I had said that.

Later that afternoon Pastors Greg and Deana came by and we all gathered in Tom and Sherry's master bedroom to receive Holy Communion. As we were passing the communion emblems,

Travis (Sherry's son-in-law), who has been known to be some-thing of a klutz on occasion, dropped an empty communion cup. Instantly Sherry said, "You better be glad that was empty. I don't think you can afford to replace my Persian rug." We all laughed and Travis turned red. That incident, maybe more than any other single thing, typified her indomitable spirit. No matter how bad things got, she never lost her sense of humor.

These and a host of other memories jostled for my attention as I followed Brenda down the wide staircase and across the foyer into Tom and Sherry's bedroom. Don and Melba were already there as were Sherry's two oldest girls. Tom was kneel-ing beside Sherry's bed while the hospice nurse stood nearby, ready to assist if needed. I found a place in the corner of the bedroom and breathed a prayer, asking the Lord to let Sherry's homegoing be peaceful.

A few minutes later she simply stopped breathing and I was seized with conflicting emotions. A part of me was thankful her terrible suffering was finally over. Never again would she writhe in pain or cry out for Daddy in her sleep. Never again would she worry about her children and grandchildren—who would pray for them when she was gone, who would plan their birthday parties, who would cook Thanksgiving dinner and where would they celebrate Christmas? Never again would she be troubled with the inevitable cares of this life. Never again. . . .

Yet another part of me ached with an ache I suspected would never completely go away. During the past five years Sherry and I had grown especially close. When she told me of her diagnosis I promised to be there for her and I believe I was. We prayed together several times a week by telephone. We talked often. When the end drew near I took a leave of absence from my church so I could be with her.

I couldn't help wondering why it had taken this terrible ordeal to make me realize how much I loved my only sister? Why

DANCING IN THE DARK

had I wasted all those years having only a token relationship with her when we could have enjoyed life together? Sure we were separated by hundreds of miles and the demands of ministry were unrelenting, not to mention how busy she was, still I should have made time for us to be together. Now it was too late.

The hospice nurse noted the time of death but no one moved. We just sat there, each of us immersed in our own thoughts. With an effort I pushed all thoughts of Sherry's death out of my mind. Instead I remembered the day she was born and how much joy she brought to our lives. An earlier daughter (Carolyn Faye) had died at three months leaving Mom and Dad bereft. For more than a year and a half our house was a gloomy place. Every joyous moment was tainted by the memory of Carolyn's death. All of that changed one Sunday afternoon in March, 1958. Following lunch mother went into her bedroom and shut the door. A few minutes later she emerged wearing a blue and white maternity smock. Although I was only eleven years old I knew what that meant—she was pregnant. To celebrate we spent the afternoon driving the back roads of the South Platte River bottom while trying to pick out names for the baby. We just knew it would be a baby girl, and it was.

NOW THEIR GRIEF WAS RICHLY SEASONED WITH HOPE AND WHEN SHERRY WAS BORN ON SEPTEMBER 20 THAT HOPE WAS REALIZED.

I'm sure Mom and Dad continued to grieve Carolyn's passing, but not like before. Now their grief was richly seasoned with hope and when Sherry was born on September 20 that hope was realized. Being the youngest child, and the only girl, Sherry always had a special place in our family. She was a beautiful child with gorgeous blond hair, which made her stand out in a family where everyone else was dark-headed.

Of course she wasn't perfect, no child is. In fact she was a strong-willed child before that term was in vogue. One time she

278

dumped all of her crayons on the floor and refused to pick them up. Dad spanked her, if you can call the sorry little swats he gave her a spanking, but she still refused to pick up her crayons. To my father's credit he did not give in to her but neither did he continue spanking her. Instead he got down on the floor beside her and took her tiny hand in his own and "helped" her pick up each and every crayon.

After three rowdy boys Mom was thrilled to have a little girl. She dressed Sherry like a doll and she always curled her hair. After shampooing Sherry's hair Mom would rinse it with lemon juice to keep it the white blond color she was born with. Then she rolled it in a jillion tiny pen curls. Sherry sat patiently through it all, never complaining. Looking back I think she enjoyed being the center of attention, a role she monopolized at the Exley house.

As beautiful as she was, her beauty was marred by a small scar high on her forehead, a souvenir of a camping trip our family took to Vaughn Lake high in the Colorado Rockies. Don hit her in the head with an axe. Not on purpose. He was chopping firewood for the campfire and she walked up behind him and he hit her on the backswing. Thankfully it wasn't too serious, but it gave us all a good scare.

Like Don and Bob, Sherry suffered from asthma as a child. Some nights it was so bad she would literally gasp for breath. That was before inhalers and other asthma treatments. The only relief she could get was when Daddy sat on the edge of her bed rubbing her back. I don't know if that helped her breath or if it just made her feel better—loved and safe—but it remained a special memory her whole life long.

When Brenda and I were dating it was against our "religion" to go to movie theaters, nor did Brenda's parents own a television, but that did not keep Brenda from loving movies. Apparently my parents were more "worldly" because we had a black and white television set in our living room. One of Brenda's favorite "dates" was to watch the Late Show with me at the Exley house. As far as I was concerned that was fine as long as Sherry didn't join us. If Sherry wasn't sitting on the couch with us it was easy for me to tune the movie out and focus on Brenda. Unfortunately Brenda was single-minded. She had absolutely no interest in anything but the movie. Growing weary of rebuffing my romantic advances, she decided to recruit Sherry and they became loyal comrades, much to my chagrin.

Brenda became the big sister Sherry never had. When Sherry was ten years old, she spent the summer with us in Holly, Colorado, and again a couple of years later in Florence, Colorado. She idolized Brenda and hung on every word Brenda said and followed her everywhere she went. Brenda showed her how to do her nails and fix her hair. The two of them were inseparable and became lifelong sisters. I don't think they ever exchanged a cross word.

Years later, when I was awarded an honorary Doctor of Divinity degree, Sherry celebrated with me as if the honor was her own. Not only did she fly to Washington D.C. to attend the ceremony, but she surprised me by flying Mom and Dad in as well and at her own expense. It was one of the nicest things anyone has ever done for me and when I think of her, it is gestures like that I remember.

"How long has it been?" Kami asked, drawing me back to the present. Looking around I thought, *Why are we all sitting here? Isn't there someone we need to call? Shouldn't we contact the rest of the family and let them know that Sherry has passed?*

Looking at her watch Crystal replied, "It's been thirty minutes."

For several seconds no one moved then Kami took a deep breath and said, "Well, I guess she really likes it there! She's not coming back. We can call the mortician now."

Later I asked Brenda what was going on. Looking puzzled she replied, "Don't you know?"

"Obviously not or I wouldn't be asking."

Quickly she filled me in. "The last thing Sherry said to Kami was, 'After I die I want you to wait thirty minutes before you call the mortician. As soon as I get to heaven I'm going to try to get God to change His mind and let me come back.'"

Why, you may be wondering, did Sherry fight so hard to live? Why would she even think of asking God to let her come back?

Not for herself, I can assure you. The thing that gave her the will to live, and the strength to endure such unspeakable suffering, was her love for her family. She would gladly bear any amount of suffering for them. Tom had already buried one wife and Sherry would do everything in her power to spare him from going through that again. Then there were her girls. Their biological father had abandoned them and if they lost her they would have no one. Tom was there for them, to be sure, and no one could ask for a better father, but he wasn't their flesh and blood. And those grandbabies needed their Mimi.

She subjected herself to any and all medical treatments and endured unimaginable suffering, all in an attempt to survive, and she did it for her family. But it was not to be. On Wednesday morning, April 23, 2014, she breathed her last and left this world for a better place. A better place where there is no more sickness or death, no more sorrow or crying (Revelation 21:4).

Nearly three years have passed since Sherry left us and not a day goes by but what I think of her. Several times I've reached for my cell phone to call her, only to remember she is no longer with us. How I wish I could sit at her kitchen table and study the scriptures with her one more time. How I wish I could take her for one more car ride through Friendswood in the spring or sit with her and her children and grandchildren around her huge dining room table at Thanksgiving. How I wish we could sit on the cedar swing on the porch at Emerald Pointe and relive our childhood. How I wish . . . but all the wishing in the world will not bring her back. Now all I have are the memories and the promise of eternal life together.

> SHERRY IS NOT REALLY DEAD; SHE IS JUST GONE. SHE HASN'T CEASED TO EXIST SHE HAS JUST CHANGED ADDRESSES. NOW SHE LIVES WITH JESUS.

Sometimes my grief is so fresh I am tempted to wallow in it, to live only in the past, but I dare not. Instead I focus on the promises of God. In John 11, Jesus says, "I am the resurrection and the life. The one who believes in me will live, even though they die" (John 11:25 NIV). If I understand that verse correctly, Sherry is not really dead; she is just gone. She hasn't ceased to exist she has just changed addresses. Now she lives with Jesus. I love the way the Message Bible puts it. "Don't let this throw you. You trust God, don't you? Trust me. There is plenty of room for you in my Father's home. If that weren't so, would I have told you that I'm on my way to get a room ready for you? And if I'm on my way to get your room ready, I'll come back and get you so you can live where I live" (John 14:1-4 MSG).

One day soon we will join Sherry. Jesus will come for us just like He came for her. Some of us may go by the way of death as Sherry did, but others of us will go by way of the rapture. Here's how the Apostle Paul explains it: "let me reveal to you a wonderful secret. We will not all die, but we will all be transformed! It will happen in a moment, in the blink of an eye, when the last trumpet is blown. For when the trumpet sounds, those who have died will be raised to live forever. And we who are living will also be transformed. For our dying bodies must be transformed into bodies that will never die; our mortal bodies must be transformed into immortal bodies" (1 Corinthians 15:51-53 NLT).

"We can tell you with complete confidence—we have the Master's word on it—that when the Master comes again to get us, those of us who are still alive will not get a jump on the dead and leave them behind. In actual fact, they'll be ahead of us. The Master himself will give the command. Archangel thunder! God's trumpet blast! He'll come down from heaven and the dead in Christ will rise—they'll go first. Then the rest of us who are still alive at the time will be caught up with them into the clouds to meet the Master. Oh, we'll be walking on air! And then there will be one huge family reunion with the Master. So reassure one another with these words" (1 Thessalonians 4:13-18 MSG).

"One huge family reunion!"

Think about it. Not only will we be united with Jesus our Lord and savior, but with our loved ones as well. One huge family reunion—parents and grandparents, brothers and sisters, children and grandchildren, aunts and uncles, nieces and nephews. As wonderful as my memories of Sherry are, they pale in comparison with what is to come. What God has prepared for us is beyond imagining! "No eye has seen, no ear has heard, and no mind has imagined what God has prepared for those who love him" (1 Corinthians 1:9 NLT).

Chapter 43

Thoughts on Turning Seventy

I hate hard times, but in looking back over my life I can see that the hard times have been used by God to make me who I am today. Without them I wouldn't be the man God has called me to be.

A few days ago I celebrated my seventieth birthday. After reflecting on that momentous event for a few minutes I decided to share some of my thoughts. Unfortunately, by the time I made it to my computer I couldn't remember what I was going to share. I'm just kidding . . . but I do have to admit that, like a lot of other things, my memory isn't what it once was. In all seriousness, here are some of my thoughts on turning seventy.

Wow! I got here a lot faster than I would have ever imagined possible (James 4:14). It seems only yesterday I was a twelve-year-old boy roaming the South Platte River bottom in northeastern Colorado, living my own version of Huck Finn. Then we moved to Houston, Texas, and I had my first date—with Brenda Starr of course. We went to my ninth grade football banquet where I received my Letter. At seventeen I bought my first car—a 1960 Ford Starliner. Mom and Dad never paid a penny on it. I covered all expenses while making $1.25 an hour cutting donuts after school and on Saturdays. On June 10, 1966, I married Brenda; Leah was born four years later; and now I'm seventy years old and I have two wonderful grandchildren. Like I said, I got here a lot faster than I would have ever imagined possible

Along the way I've learned some things: No one goes through life unscathed (Job 5:7). Sooner or later someone you trust will betray you, a business deal will go south leaving you in a financial crisis, illness strikes, or someone you love dies. You will be tempted to define your life by that painful experience. Don't! Refuse to define your life by any single event, whatever it may be. It is a real part of your life but that is all—just a part.

Make peace with your pain. When you have been wounded it is important to turn your pain into an ally. Embrace it and learn from it. Remember God has a long history of turning life's tragedies into opportunities for personal growth and development. Storms produce strength and character (Romans 5:3-4). I hate hard times, but in looking back over my life I can see that the hard times have been used by God to make me who I am today. Without them I wouldn't be the man God has called me to be.

LIFE IS TOO SHORT TO HOLD A GRUDGE. LET IT GO AND GET ON WITH THE BUSINESS OF LIVING. YOU CAN'T EMBRACE LIFE IF YOUR FISTS ARE CLENCHED, READY TO TAKE REVENGE.

God always uses imperfect people (1 Corinthians 1:26-29) because that's the only kind of people there are.

I am a flawed man. If I deny this painful truth I condemn myself to a life of secrecy and deception. If I acknowledge it I am free from the need to pretend to be something I am not and, freed from pretending, I can honestly embrace the grace of God that makes me a new man.

Life is too short to hold a grudge. Let it go and get on with the business of living. You can't embrace life if your fists are clenched, ready to take revenge.

Life is often a mystery. When tragedies strike we are often tempted to ask why. While this is natural, it is an exercise in futility. Even if we could figure out "why" something happened it wouldn't change a thing. At seventy, I am finally learning to replace the "why" questions with "how" questions. Instead of asking, "Why did this happen?" I am learning to ask, "How is God going to use this for my good and His glory?"

In every situation I can be part of the problem or I can be part of the solution. The choice is mine.

I never have to let anyone make me into something I am not.

We cannot escape life's difficulties but we can prepare for them.

God never gives us wisdom for imaginary problems or strength for imaginary challenges. He gives us grace only for real ones and His grace is always sufficient. Nor does He give us grace in advance. It always comes "just" when we need it. That's why people often say, "I could never bear something like that." Yet when it comes, they not only bear it but they do so with remarkable grace. Truly God's grace is sufficient (2 Corinthians 12:9), but it doesn't make things easy—just possible.

And the most important thing I have learned is that the security of my salvation does not rest on what I do for Jesus, but on what He has done for me!

Do I have any regrets? A few. I wish I had been less full of myself. I wish I had invited people to receive Jesus every time I preached. I wish I had prayed for my family more faithfully. I wish I had been a better friend. I wish I had been a more godly man.

> THE MOST IMPORTANT THING I HAVE LEARNED IS THAT THE SECURITY OF MY SALVATION DOES NOT REST ON WHAT I DO FOR JESUS, BUT ON WHAT HE HAS DONE FOR ME!

I'm no longer driven by the need to prove myself, or to serve as the pastor of a large church, or to write a bestselling book. Such things never concerned Brenda so she is glad I have finally given them up. Now I simply want to please the Lord, be a good friend, love my family, and make Brenda laugh every day. If I can do that I will die a satisfied man.

So where do I go from here? Wherever God leads! I am in good health and I plan to keep writing and preaching as long as God gives me open doors and the strength to walk through them. I intend to live life fully until I die and I truly believe the last years of my life can be the most fruitful.

Chapter 44

The Author and Finisher of Our Faith

Don't look at your circumstances or you may despair. You may feel that you simply do not have the wherewithal to see your God-given dreams become reality or you may feel that your willful disobedience has disqualified you, either way you will be tempted to discard your dreams. Instead, look to God, for He is the author and finisher of our faith (Hebrews 12:2) and He who has begun this good work in you is faithful to bring it to completion (Philippians 1:6).

Outside my office window the sun is sparkling off the crystal clear waters of Beaver Lake on this, the last day of the year. Earlier this morning the lake was shrouded in fog but the sun has burned it away and I can see clearly now. As I scan the lake I can't help reflecting, not only on the past year, but also on the past fifty years. Given our humble beginnings I would never have imagined that we could have ended up here; that is until I remember the dreams God placed in my heart when I was just a young man—dreams that He has been faithful to fulfill.

When Brenda and I were newlyweds and just starting out in the ministry, we spent nearly a year and a half preaching revival meetings in country churches from Cuero, Texas, to Post Falls, Idaho, and a half a hundred places in between. We spent hours in the car together, driving from one small church to the next. Sometimes Brenda read to me—alternating between sermons by Charles Spurgeon and western novels by Louis L'Amour—but more often than not we just talked. That is, I talked while Brenda mostly listened, being a person given to few words.

Mile after mile, I regaled her with dreams about our future together. Someday, I told her, we are going to live in a cabin, on the side of a mountain, overlooking a lake. I will write books and preach in churches large and small all over the world. Someday I will have a national radio broadcast and be invited to preach at District Councils and camp meetings. Someday. . . .

She would smile and listen politely, but I could tell she didn't really believe me and who could blame her, given our limited circumstances. In the course of time my dreams were put on the back burner as we immersed ourselves in the ministry, serving churches in Colorado, Texas, Oklahoma, and Louisiana. I began writing and published my first two books while serving the Church of the Comforter in Craig, Colorado. In 1980, we became senior pastors of Christian Chapel in Tulsa, Oklahoma, and the Lord impressed me to give up writing for a season and concentrate on serving the church. For nearly seven years I did not write a thing for publication and I sometimes wondered if I would ever write another book.

During those seven years, God did many remarkable things at Christian Chapel and our congregation grew from barely one hundred people to more than a thousand. We purchased property and built our first facility. God granted me favor with the seminary at Oral Roberts University and I was frequently invited to lecture there. I also served as a group leader in the

Field Education program at the seminary. Through a truly remarkable series of events, God brought me into contact with a radio executive whose vision helped me launch a nationwide via satellite call-in radio program called *Straight from the Heart*. Because Christian Chapel was an exceptionally strong missionary church, I began receiving invitations from missionaries to minister in a number of foreign countries. Almost without me realizing it, the Lord was fulfilling the dreams He had put in my heart when I was just a young man starting out in ministry.

In the spring of 1987, Honor Books approached me about writing four books for them. They had heard my radio broadcasts and felt that I would be a good fit for their publishing house. Of course, I was excited but I wanted to pray about it. In 1980 the Lord had told me not to write until He released me and I did not want to be disobedient. After three weeks I felt released to write again and I signed a contract with Honor Books. Over the next five years I published seven books with them including *The Making of a Man*, which was a finalist in the Devotional category for the Gold Medallion Book of the year in 1993.

In 1991 Brenda and I bought a small acreage on Beaver Lake as a twenty-fifth wedding anniversary gift to ourselves. We resigned from Christian Chapel a year later and with the help of Brenda's parents we built a small cabin overlooking the lake. I planned to write each morning and when I completed my day's work, I would cut firewood or go fishing. Brenda would prepare healthy home-cooked meals, catch up on her reading, and indulge her penchant for crafts.

At that time the nearest paved road was nine miles away and the closest town three times that far. Carroll Electric Cooperative brought power to the property, but we had to provide our own water and sewer system. Subsequently we drilled a well and put in a septic system. The first two years were nearly idyllic. Without telephone service or television it was almost like going back in time. On long winter evenings we read by the wood burning stove, played table games, or just talked. Sometimes we chose to chat with only a kerosene lamp for light in memory of my Grandma Miller.

By the second year we had telephone service, if you can call a four-party line telephone service. We had a private telephone line and satellite television by the third year and shortly thereafter the internet. Now we are much better informed, but not nearly as content. Although we live in the country, the internet and satellite television have brought the world right to our door.

Twenty-five years ago, when I left the pastorate and moved to the lake, I thought my ministry would be primarily writing. Boy was I wrong. Although I've written more than 25 books in the last 24 years, I've also traveled almost one million miles and preached more than 2,500 times.

I'M NO ONE SPECIAL AND NEITHER IS BRENDA, EXCEPT TO ME. WHAT GOD HAS DONE FOR US, HE WILL DO FOR YOU.

Why do I tell you all of this? Because I want you to see how God's faithfulness manifests itself in an ordinary life. I'm no one special and neither is Brenda, except to me. What God has done for us, He will do for you. The Lord would have been well justified had He given up on me any number of times during the last fifty years, especially during the early years, but He refused. Even though my faith failed on occasion, He has always remained faithful, for He cannot deny Himself (2 Timothy 2:13).

Take a moment now and examine your own life. What dreams has the Lord placed in your heart? I'm not talking about personal ambitions but dreams birthed by the Spirit. Dr. Jim Horvath, a personal friend of mine, carried a God given dream of ministering in the Philippines in his heart for nearly twenty years before the Lord brought it to fruition. Now he has one of the most effective evangelistic ministries to the islands. What God has done for Jim, He will do for you!

Don't look at your circumstances or you may despair. You may feel that you simply do not have the wherewithal to see your God-given dreams become reality or you may feel that your willful disobedience has disqualified you, either way you will be tempted to discard your dreams. Instead, look to God for He is the author and finisher of our faith (Hebrews 12:2) and He who has begun this good work in you is faithful to bring it to completion (Philippians 1:6).

Nearly thirty years ago I was facing some unusual challenges. It seemed I had reached a stalemate in my life and ministry. After several years of remarkable growth the church I was serving had reached a plateau. No matter what I did, we seemed stuck. To complicate matters, a small, but vocal group was critical of my leadership. On top of everything else, my latest book was not selling nearly as well as anticipated. As a result I was experiencing some doubts regarding the effectiveness of my ministry.

One morning, during my devotional time, I was reading in the Psalms when I came across Psalm 138:7-8. I had read that passage numerous times before but that particular morning the words seemed to leap off the page. "Though I walk in the midst of trouble, you preserve my life; you stretch out your hand against the anger of my foes, with your right hand you save me. **The Lord will fulfill his purpose for me;** your love, O Lord, endures forever—do not abandon the works of your hands" (emphasis added).

Although my situation did not immediately change I was at peace. God had spoken to me through His Word. No matter what others did, He would fulfill His purpose in my life! Not necessarily my goals and ambitions, but His purpose, those God-given dreams He had placed in my heart—and that was enough.

As you think about your own God-given dreams, remember His faithfulness and take heart. "This is what the Lord says: '...For I know the plans I have for you,' declares the Lord, 'plans to prosper you and not to harm you, plans to give you hope and a future'" (Jeremiah 29:11).

Brenda and I are living God's dream for our life, not because of our faith but because of His faithfulness, and so can you. "Trust in the Lord with all your heart and lean not on your own understanding; in all your ways acknowledge him and he will make your paths straight" (Proverbs 3:5-6). That is, He will fulfill your God-given dreams!

Author Bio

Richard Exley is a man with a rich diversity of experiences. He has been a pastor, conference and retreat speaker, as well as a radio broadcaster. In addition he has written more than 30 books including *Authentic Living, The Rhythm of Life, Man of Valor, When You Lose Someone You Love,* and *The Alabaster Cross. The Making of a Man* was one of five finalists for the Gold Medallion Devotional Book of the Year. The Methodist Episcopal Church USA and the National Clergy Council Board of Scholars awarded him the Doctorate of Divinity honoris causa for his life's work in ministry and writing.

As a boy, Richard lived part-time with his widowed grand-mother. Her home had electricity but she didn't trust it, so she only used it to power her refrigerator. When darkness fell she lit the kerosene lamps, casting the tiny living room with its braided rag rugs and coal oil stove in its ambient light. During those long winter evenings she spun out the story of her life. It was there Richard learned the art of storytelling, a craft that enables him to touch the heart through both his writing and speaking.

He loves spending time with his wife, Brenda Starr, in their secluded cabin overlooking picturesque Beaver Lake. He enjoys quiet talks with old friends, kerosene lamps, good books, a warm fire when it's cold, and a good cup of coffee anytime. He's an avid Denver Broncos fan, an aspiring bass fisherman, and an amateur photographer. And he hopes to become one of your favorite authors.

www.RichardExleyBooks.com

www.RichardExleyMinistries.org